*L*IVING WISELY

WITH THE

CHURCH

FATHERS

CHRISTOPHER

A. HALL

IVP Academic

An imprint of InterVarsity Press
Downers Grove, Illinois

InterVarsity Press
P.O. Box 1400, Downers Grove, IL 60515-1426
ivpress.com
email@ivpress.com

InterVarsity Press® is the book-publishing division of InterVarsity Christian Fellowship/USA®, a movement of students and faculty active on campus at hundreds of universities, colleges, and schools of nursing in the United States of America, and a member movement of the International Fellowship of Evangelical Students. For information about local and regional activities, visit intervarsity.org.

Scripture quotations, unless otherwise noted, are from the New Revised Standard Version of the Bible, copyright 1989 by the Division of Christian Education of the National Council of the Churches of Christ in the USA. Used by permission. All rights reserved.

Excerpts from Abortion in the Early Church by Michael J. Gorman: Used by permission of Wipf and Stock Publishers. www.wipfandstock.com.

Excerpts from The Body and Society by Peter Brown: Copyright © 1988 Columbia University Press. Reprinted with permission of the publisher.

Excerpts from The Early Fathers on War and Military Service by Louis J. Swift: © Louis J. Swift. Used with permission.

Excerpts from Social Thought by Peter C. Phan: © Peter C. Phan. Used with permission.

Excerpts from Women in the Early Church by Elizabeth Clark: © 1983 by Order of Saint Benedict. Published by Liturgical Press, Collegeville, Minnesota. Used with permission.

Cover design: Cindy Kiple
Interior design: Daniel van Loon
Images: Central panels depicting three kings, Ezekiel, Solomon, and David, German School at Church of St. Michael, Hildesheim, Germany / Hirmer Fotoarchiv / Bridgeman Images

ISBN 978-0-8308-5188-1 (print)
ISBN 978-0-8308-8918-1 (digital)

Printed in the United States of America ∞

 green press INITIATIVE

As a member of the Green Press Initiative, InterVarsity Press is committed to protecting the environment and to the responsible use of natural resources. To learn more, visit greenpressinitiative.org.

Library of Congress Cataloging-in-Publication Data

A catalog record for this book is available from the Library of Congress.

P 25 24 23 22 21 20 19 18 17 16 15 14 13 12 11 10 9 8 7 6 5 4 3 2 1

Y 36 35 34 33 32 31 30 29 28 27 26 25 24 23 22 21 20 19 18 17

This book is dedicated to the memory of Tom Oden,
my friend, colleague, and mentor.
It was Tom who introduced me to the church fathers.
May he rest in peace.

CONTENTS

Acknowledgments

So many people have helped me across the years in my research and writing of *Living Wisely with the Church Fathers* and with the first three volumes in this church fathers series: *Reading Scripture with the Church Fathers*, *Learning Theology with the Church Fathers*, and *Worshiping with the Church Fathers*. I think particularly of Tom Oden, my dear mentor and friend, who recently passed away in December 2016. It was Tom who first introduced me to the church fathers and encouraged me to study assiduously their thought. I miss him very much.

I think also of Mike Glerup and Joel Elowsky. Tom, Mike, Joel, and I have worked together on many patristic projects across the years, and their friendship has meant all the world to me. I also give deep thanks to Howard and Roberta Ahmanson, close, valued friends and avid students of the Fathers. Thanks too to Steve Ferguson and Lamin Sanneh. I always felt I could bounce ideas off you.

At IVP, thanks to Dan Reid for editorial help on all four volumes. Dan has been an excellent editor and friend. I also think of Bob Fryling, Andy Le Peau, Jim Hoover, and Cindy Bunch. You gave me my first opportunity to write, and I'm deeply grateful.

At Eastern University—my academic home for many years—I'm grateful for the constant encouragement and friendship offered to me by David Black, Joe Modica, Duffy Robbins, Kent Sparks, Bob Duffett, John Pauley, David King, Dwight and Margaret Kim Peterson, Steve Boyer, and the entire Christian Studies Department.

I've had the opportunity to read parts of *Living Wisely with the Church Fathers* to members of the Renovaré community, and I thank them for their feedback and friendship. Thanks also to Joshua Cunningham for careful indexing work.

Finally, where would I be without the love and support of my family? A big hug to Debbie, Nathan, Nathalie, Sean, and Joshua.

I have set you an example, that you should do as I have done to you. Very truly, I tell you, servants are not greater than their master, nor are messengers greater than the one who sent them. If you know these things, you are blessed if you do them.

JOHN 13:15-17

Everyone then who hears these words of mine and acts on them will be like a wise man who built his house on rock. The rain fell, the floods came, and the winds blew and beat on that house, but it did not fall, because it had been founded on rock.

MATTHEW 7:24-25

Brothers and sisters, join in imitating me, and observe those who live according to the example you have in us.

PHILIPPIANS 3:17

For, while physical training is of some value, godliness is valuable in every way, holding promise for both the present life and the life to come.

1 TIMOTHY 4:8

Perhaps, then, the memory of anyone distinguished in life would be enough to fill our need for a beacon light and to show us how we can bring our soul to the sheltered harbor of virtue where it no longer has to pass the winter amid the storms of life or be shipwrecked in the deep water of evil by the successive billows of passion. It may be for this very reason that the daily life of those sublime individuals is recorded in detail, that by imitating those earlier examples of right action those who follow them may conduct their lives to the good.

GREGORY OF NYSSA, THE LIFE OF MOSES[1]

INTRODUCTION

Living Wisely with the Church Fathers

With the publication of *Living Wisely with the Church Fathers*, my series on the exegesis, theology, prayer, and ethics of the church fathers draws to a close. The first volume of the series, *Reading Scripture with the Church Fathers*, appeared in 1998. This book was a basic introduction to the church fathers, with a special emphasis on how they read and interpreted the Bible. My goal was "to present as clearly, simply and accurately as possible the methodology and content of patristic interpretation. Why should we bother reading the church fathers? What is a church father? How do the fathers read the Bible? What methodologies and techniques do they employ? . . . How can the fathers help us to read the Bible well today?"[2]

When I wrote *Reading Scripture with the Church Fathers*, I did not foresee writing a series of four volumes. I originally planned to write one book that hopefully would serve well as a handbook for readers of the Ancient Christian Commentary on Scripture series, and that would be that. Indeed, though other volumes have followed, my vision for the project has remained the same: relatively short, accessible handbooks on the church fathers' lives and work, written for a popular audience. I have written all four books for folks who, perchance late one evening while enjoying a cup of hot chocolate—or perhaps something stronger— might find themselves asking: "I wonder what ancient Christians thought about . . ." or "I've heard the name Augustine and I really must learn something about him. His name keeps popping up. There must be a reason why his books are still in print."

What did these ancient Christians—whose thoughts and practices continue to be read, pondered, discussed, debated, and embraced to-day—think about the Bible, God, worship, and prayer? More importantly for this book, how did the fathers answer a very specific question: How can God's image bearer learn to live a good life, a life nourished by the values of the kingdom of God, a life of deep and lasting human flourishing, a life filled with love for God and neighbor? If, as Athanasius puts it, transgression has "taken hold" of human beings, and "natural corruption" now characterizes the human condition, how can we as God's image bearers be made right again—made right not only in our relationship to God but in relationship to one another and to the entire created order?[3]

More questions and concerns quickly follow. How is living a good life specifically related to the teachings of Jesus, the life Jesus lived, and the spiritual disciplines he practiced? And what of the teaching and lives of the apostles? What aspects of Paul, Peter, James, and John's teaching caught the eye of the church fathers and informed their choices and actions as they sought to love God and neighbor well? For loving God and neighbor was for the fathers the heart of the matter.

As Augustine considers the love Jesus expressed in healing the paralytic in John 5, his thoughts are drawn to a more general principle, one based on Jesus' concrete action in reaching out to this very ill man: "Consider it at all times your absolute duty to love God and neighbor. . . . This at all times you must consider, must think on, must keep in mind, must perform, must fulfill. Love of God is first in the order of instruction, but in the order of performance love of neighbor is first. . . . You, however, since you do not see God, deserve to see him by loving your neighbor."[4]

WHAT CHARACTERIZES A GOOD LIFE
LIVED WELL BEFORE GOD?

What characterizes a good life, a life Jesus would recognize and applaud as a life lived well before God and in relationship with God? How is a good life developed and nurtured? What must be received, learned and practiced, unlearned and rejected? What habits, dispositions, and virtues are necessary to acquire and cultivate if we are to love God and neighbor well through the power of the Holy Spirit? The church fathers were intensely interested in questions such as these, for—as we have seen in Augustine's exegesis of John 5—they viewed the telos or goal of Christian living as love. In addition, they did not believe that love inevitably or automatically appeared in believers' lives once they came to know God through Christ, an idea we will need to explore more fully as this chapter develops.

So, as this book progresses we will examine closely the church fathers' words and actions—their habitual thoughts and practices—as they sought to learn to live and love in the power of the Holy Spirit *coram deo*, "before God."

We will also take a penetrating look at ourselves and the lives we have lived thus far. What are the life experiences that have deeply shaped us? Who has taught us about God? Were the words spoken to us about God helpful or harmful, life giving or death dealing? Who are the exemplars we admire and purposely imitate as we seek to live well before God? Do we have any? Have we become disillusioned about the possibility of living well, perhaps because those we chose to imitate and admire have let us down, or because our own moral failures and repeated sins have discouraged us so profoundly we doubt the possibility of actually changing?

In a manner of speaking, our goal in this book is a lengthening of ethical memory, knowledge, perspective, and practice by entering the world of Christians who lived before us, who remain alive in the communion of the saints, and who are cheering us on in our attempt to run our life's race well through the power of the Spirit (cf. 1 Cor 9:24-27; Heb 12:1-3).

ANCIENT AND MODERN INFLUENCES

I will occasionally refer to the influence of culture on God's image bearers, whether ancient or modern.

Ancient Christians were surely impacted by their culture—for good and for ill. This shaping will become increasingly clear as we listen to ancient perspectives on the good life. Among these influences are swaths of historical, cultural, linguistic, ecclesial, and theological factors that affected the church fathers as they related to one another in their ancient setting and sought to live well in that context.

We will also have to explore how our own culture—or cultures—have shaped our perspective on what a good life looks like. The culture with which I am most familiar is that of the United States; my religious beliefs have been influenced by evangelicalism, as is probably true for many readers of this book. I have had other cultural experiences outside a North American context—I lived in France for five years and have traveled in Asia, Africa, and Latin America—but my deepest cultural shaping has been that of an American living most of his life in the United States. Similarly, my earliest years as a Christian were spent in the theological, ecclesial, and cultural context of evangelicalism, though over the past thirty years I have had a deep immersion in the Anglican Church and become much more familiar with Roman Catholic and Orthodox thinking and practice.

Of course, my family experiences across the years have also affected me. I think of my earliest years in my family circle, my first eighteen years—in the 1950s and '60s—and how these early life experiences deeply shaped me, in some ways helping me spiritually and in other ways confusing me. At home we had occasional family devotions and often attended church—in both a conservative and liberal context. In my conservative church experiences as a very young boy, it's fair to say I heard quite a bit about how to get saved but relatively little about how to live once I had "asked Jesus into my heart." During my teenage years, my family attended a more liberal church in southern New Jersey, and I experienced the dulling effect of theological, spiritual, and ethical drift. By the time I turned eighteen I was wondering whether anyone actually believed the Bible to be true and relevant for living. I was increasingly confused and disillusioned, both with Christians and with myself. I deeply desired to know God and to know how to live, but my own skewed perspectives, desires, and appetites—along with the profound cultural confusion of the late '60s—blurred my vision and crippled my behavior. I didn't always realize it, but I was walking with an ethical limp. Perhaps you have had similar experiences.

And so I ask you, what have been your familial, cultural, and religious learning spaces, especially as you have sought to live a life in line with Jesus' own teaching and actions? Our modern learning spaces are in some ways vastly different from those of the church fathers and in other ways strikingly similar.[5] We will explore these continuities and differences in this chapter and in future ones as well.

The Learning Space of the Roman Empire

Consider one of the cultural environments the Christian community occupied for hundreds of years, that of the Roman Empire. At first glance the Roman world seems a highly unlikely and unpromising environment for the spread of the gospel and the health of the tiny Christian church. Among other things, Rome was a sexual hotbox, in love with war and conquest, obsessed with power, seemingly tolerant toward other cultures while ruthlessly eliminating anyone who challenged its cultural and political supremacy, religiously diverse yet apt to persecute those who refused to acknowledge the Roman deities, generous to its citizens while maintaining its economy and government on the backs of its slaves. Rome was courageous yet cruel, licentious yet loyal, pragmatic yet wildly superstitious, religiously devout yet theologically confused.

How were the reborn, renewed, re-created image bearers of Christ to learn to live a good life from Jesus' perspective—a perspective on living that was Jewish and formed within the context of Israel's relationship with God—while simultaneously inhabiting the broader cultural learning space of the Roman world? Other learning spaces would have to be created if the Roman world was not to squeeze God's image bearers and church into a foreign mold.

My thought is drawn to a very popular bumper sticker from the 1990s. "He who dies with the most toys wins." The slogan represents a not uncommon assumption in American culture: the more stuff I have the greater the pleasure I'll experience and the happier I'll be, an idea that surely some Greeks and Romans would attest as true, and others would hotly dispute. The bumper sticker would have been a sign of cultural foolishness to Aristotle, who refers to "persons of low tastes (always in the majority)" who "hold that it is pleasure" that is the highest good. "Accordingly they ask for nothing better than the sort of life which consists in having a good time," a life that Aristotle identifies "with the sort of existence a cow leads."[6]

QUESTIONS TO PONDER

As we begin to ponder together the question of what a good life looks like, you might consider these questions: How has my culture shaped me? What have been my significant learning spaces? How have my family, my church, my work environment, my entertainment choices, my political affiliations, my favorite authors, influenced my perspective, choices, and habits as I live my life from day to day? How have I come to be the person I actually am, characterized by certain specific traits that those who know me well could readily identify? How have I come to believe that certain thoughts and actions are morally right and others morally wrong? Why am I behaving the way I am? If Jesus and I had the opportunity to spend the afternoon together to talk about how things have been going in my life, how might he feel about the way I've been thinking and acting over the past week, month, and year? What would please him? What might disappoint him? Where might he be apt to comment, "It looks like we need to work on this"? Or "What were you thinking?"

Let's focus more thoroughly for a moment on the way culture shapes us all, for good and for ill. The apostle Paul understood the dynamic of cultural pressure well. He warns Roman Christians of the dangers of cultural accommodation and conformity.

> Therefore, I urge you brothers and sisters, in view of God's mercy, to offer your bodies as a living sacrifice, holy and pleasing to God—this is your true and proper worship. *Do not conform to the pattern of this world*, but be transformed by the renewing of your mind. Then you will be able to test and approve what God's will is—his good, pleasing and perfect will. (Rom 12:1-2 NIV)

Paul warns that certain attitudes and behaviors, sometimes ones readily accepted in the Greco-Roman world, must not characterize the lives of Christians. They have entered a new kingdom under the leadership of a new king. A new life in Christ should be marked by new values.

> Do you not know that wrongdoers will not inherit the kingdom of God? Do not be deceived! Fornicators, idolaters, adulterers, male prostitutes, sodomites, thieves, the greedy, drunkards, revilers, robbers—none of these will inherit the kingdom of God. And this is what some of you used to be. But you were washed, you were sanctified, you were justified in the name of the Lord Jesus Christ and in the Spirit of our God. (1 Cor 6:9-11)

The church fathers took Paul's apostolic teaching as foundational for learning to live a good life. Gregory of Nyssa asks, "How can the person who is conformed to this age, who is not transformed in the newness of his mind and who does not walk in the newness of this life but instead follows the life of the old man, obey Paul, who commanded you to present your body as a sacrifice living, holy and pleasing to God?"[7]

Likewise, Ambrosiaster comments, "It is for this purpose that we are cleansed from our sins by God's gift, that henceforth we should lead a pure life and stir up the love of God that is in us, not making his work of grace to no effect."[8] Chrysostom inquires, "How is the body to become a sacrifice?" and immediately answers his question:

Let the eye look on no evil thing, and it has already become a sacrifice. Let the tongue say nothing filthy, and it has become an offering. Let your hand do nothing evil, and it has become a whole burnt offering. But even this is not enough, for we must have good works also. The hand must do alms, the mouth must bless those who curse it, and the ears must find time to listen to the reading of Scripture.[9]

KEY THEMES

Key themes emerge from Gregory, Ambrosiaster, and Chrysostom's comments:

+ the danger of unthinking conformity to the moral patterns of this present evil age;
+ the necessity of the mind's transformation;
+ the call to walk in newness of life;
+ the promise of grace for living a new life of love; and
+ specific ethical exhortations concerning what God's image bearers are watching, saying, and doing.

Origen makes some of the same points, but develops them more concisely. "By this Paul shows that there is one form of this world and another of the world to come. If there are those who love this present life and the things which are in the world, they are taken up with the form of the present age and pay no attention to what is not seen."[10] Origen believes that living well always involves love and attentiveness. Similarly, living poorly results from loving the wrong things, not paying attention to what really matters, and paying too much attention to things that are not all that important.

The question for Origen and indeed for all the church fathers is, How does one become the kind of person who is naturally and habitually attentive to the right things? How can the disciple of Christ learn to live a good life, one habitually characterized by the attentiveness and care that love naturally manifests? Origen suggests that "the apostle's words urge us to cast" wickedness "off and to be reformed in the likeness of the individual virtues, so that once the face of our heart is revealed we may be transformed by God's image and contemplate his glory."

Origen recommends practicing a specific spiritual discipline to aid us in the development of Christian character: *reading and meditating on Scripture*. "Our mind is renewed by the practice of wisdom and reflection on the Word of God. . . . The more one reads the Scriptures daily and the greater one's understanding is, the more one is renewed always and every day. I doubt whether a mind which is lazy toward the Holy Scriptures and the exercise of spiritual knowledge can be renewed at all."[11]

Origen is insistent. If we are to know what the will of God is—how we are to live good lives, holy lives, loving lives—*our minds must be renewed*. "*It is not every mind but only one which is renewed and conformed* (as I say) to the image of God which can tell whether what we think, say and do in particular instances is the will of God or not."[12]

GREEK *PAIDEIA* AND CHRISTIAN SPIRITUAL FORMATION

Origen's thoughts on a particular spiritual discipline—studying and meditating on Scripture—introduce us to an important principle and practice that the church fathers believed was fundamental for living a good life: *askesis*, a word we can translate "exercise," "regimen," or "workout program."

Before we discuss the church fathers' understanding of *askesis* and its relationship to the development of a good life, though, a brief look at Greek education in general will help us comprehend aspects of the fathers' thoughts and practices on ethics and how we become a good person. Consider a comment a friend made to me as she considered the difference between the church fathers' Christian approach to the pursuit of a good life and that of leading Greek minds such as Aristotle. "Chris," she said, "Christian spiritual formation is not Greek *paideia*." She got me thinking. Here's why.

Greek *paideia* or education, the Greek curriculum and method designed to teach children how to live well as members of Greek society, was familiar to many of the church fathers.[13] Many of them—I think of Basil the Great, Gregory of Nazianzus, and Gregory of Nyssa—had received a solid Greek education. They would have been familiar, for instance, with Aristotle's teaching on the good life and how to live well. So it will be profitable for us to spend a few moments with perhaps the greatest Greek philosopher, Aristotle, whose ideas on moral development were well known to the church fathers.

ARISTOTLE ON THE GOOD LIFE

Aristotle taught that a good life is acquired through the acquisition of moral knowledge and the practice of virtue. For example, ignorance has to be overcome. "To be sure every bad man is ignorant of what he ought to do and refrain from doing, and it is just this ignorance that makes people unjust and otherwise wicked."[14] So, if I am to acquire the virtue of acting justly, I must clearly understand what justice is. More generally, if I remain ignorant of what the virtues are and what their cultivation entails, Aristotle would brand me a fool and have no doubt that my life will never attain genuine flourishing and fulfillment. I would think most Christian readers would readily agree with Aristotle at this point.

Aristotle believed, though, that mere knowledge of the virtues will not produce a virtuous person. Rather, I become a just person *not simply by learning what justice is, but by practicing the habits that will develop the disposition of justice in me*, so that I habitually act in a just fashion day in and day out. "Moral goodness," Aristotle writes, "is the child of habit, from which it has got its very name, ethics being derived from *ethos*, 'habit.'"[15] And, Aristotle teaches, the only way to develop a habit is to choose to do so. If justice is to mark my character, if I am to become a person with a just disposition, choosing to act justly must become a habituated response in me toward those around me.

Habit and the Formation of Moral Character

So, how does justice become habituated in me so that my disposition disposes me to act justly? Through my choosing to act repeatedly in a just manner. Knowledge (*understanding* the nature of justice) combines with practice (*acting* in a just manner) to form a just person, one who is disposed to act habitually in a just manner. I act justly because I have been *trained* to do so; I have learned what justice is and practiced acting justly. Of course, the dynamic Aristotle is describing assumes that moral knowledge concerning justice is identifiable and available to all those searching for it.

From Aristotle's perspective, human transformation occurs as I know the good and practice the good. Good habits, wise habits formed on the basis of knowledge of the good and practice of the good, form a good person. Similarly, the ignorant person is one who doesn't know the good and inevitably leads a foolish life driven by foolish desires, a life that harms himself and others. He thinks and acts falsely and fails to think and do those things that should be done, things that, in a manner of speaking, embody the truth. The unhappy result is moral disaster, for the ignorant person and for the broader society in which he lives.

More positively, Aristotle is convinced that if I learn the good and practice the good my character will be transformed. I will become a good person, and in turn the society in which I live will prosper. Indeed, Aristotle argues that it is the responsibility of a good legislator to teach human beings what good behavior is and to train them in it. "We find legislators seeking to make good men of their fellows by making good behavior habitual with them. That is the aim of every law-giver, and when he is unable to carry it out effectively, he is a failure; nay, success or failure is what makes the difference between a good constitution and a bad."[16] Hence, for Aristotle, "it is a matter of real importance whether our early education confirms us in one set of habits or another. It would be nearer the truth to say that it makes a very great difference indeed, in fact all the difference in the world."[17]

Most Christian readers could hardly disagree with Aristotle's main emphases in his discussion of moral awareness and behavior. As I will discuss in some detail as this book progresses, Paul frequently employs the language of training and purposeful, habitual exertion when discussing Christian formation into the image of Christ. "For, while physical training is of some value," Paul comments to Timothy, "godliness is valuable in every way, holding promise for both the present life and the life to come" (1 Tim 4:8). "This saying is sure and worthy of full acceptance. For to this end *we toil and struggle*" (1 Tim 4:9-10). Clearly for Paul, training in godliness trumps training to keep in shape physically. My point here is simply that *the idea of Christian moral formation as requiring training, exertion, and habit formation would not have been foreign or surprising to Paul, the great apostle of grace.*

Aristotle quite clearly believes that to know the good and to practice the good are possible for all human beings, *with the right coaching and example from a virtuous mentor.* Yet he does not perceive the need for God to act on a human being's behalf to empower her transformation into a good human being. We find nothing in Aristotle concerning the absolute necessity of God's grace to empower moral development in an image bearer's life, no expectation that human beings might experience a personal relationship with a personal God, and no awareness of the need for human beings to be saved from the ravaging effects of sin on human nature itself.

THE IMPORTANCE OF IMITATION

Let's pause for a moment and consider the importance of imitation in ancient thinking on the cultivation of a good life, and how early Christians adapted this insight and shaped it into a Christian pattern for learning to live well before God. Both Greeks and Latins emphasized that a virtuous life and its accompanying good deeds flow from identifying and imitating good examples. Plutarch, for example, writes, "Virtuous deeds implant in those who search them out [with] a zeal and yearning that leads to *imitation*. . . . The good creates a stir of activity towards itself and implants at once *in the spectator* an impulse toward good action."[18] We see "the good" in another human life, it stirs us "towards itself and implants" in us "an impulse toward" doing what's right and good.

From the perspective of the church fathers, the pattern is similar for Christians. We need to identify wise and skillful physicians of the soul, tutors of the good life who can guide, discipline, model, and encourage us to live good lives, with Jesus as our chief teacher and example. Jesus himself taught that he had given his life to his disciples—and to us—as an example to be imitated. "I have set you an example, that you also should do as I have done" (Jn 13:15).[19]

We learn to live a good life as we receive and pattern our lives on the insights and practices of those wiser than us, people who can teach and model for us what a good life looks like and how it can be developed and nurtured.

Let's develop this principle more thoroughly. Rabbis in Israel gathered disciples or apprentices around them and expected their disciples to memorize their teaching and to practice it. Jesus illustrates the teacher-student dynamic during his last meal with his disciples. He washes the disciples' feet—a shocking example of humility and service—and then promises the disciples that blessing will come *if they follow his example.* "Do you know what I have done to you? You call me Teacher and Lord— and you are right, for that is what I am. So if I, your Lord and Teacher, have washed your feet, you also ought to wash one another's feet. For I have set you an example, that you also should do as I have done to you. . . . If you *know* these things, you are blessed *if you do them*" (Jn 13:12-15, 17). Paul also emphasizes the importance of imitation. "Brothers and sisters, *join in imitating me*, and *observe* those who live according to the example you have in us," he exhorts the Philippians (Phil 3:17).

The church fathers are convinced that observation and imitation deeply form our disposition toward good or toward evil. Robert Wilken turns our attention to the relationship of mentor to student between Origen and Gregory the Wonderworker and its fruitful result. In his panegyric on Origen's life, Gregory comments that Origen urged him to live a philosophical life; Gregory then carefully defines what Origen meant by the term *philosophy*: "only those who *practice* a life genuinely befitting reasonable creatures and seek to live virtuously, who seek to know first who they are, and to strive for those things that are truly good and to shun those which are truly evil . . . are lovers of philosophy."[20]

John Chrysostom says much the same thing in a treatise he wrote at the very end of his life on the providence of God. After a series of conflicts with the Roman empress Eudoxia, not infrequently over ethical issues, John found himself exiled by her to a small, isolated town in the Armenian mountains named Cucusus. How was John to respond to this unforeseen, tragic turn of events in his own life? How was he as an apprentice of Christ to act in the midst of these unexpected circumstances? How was he to exercise his will in such a way that the choices he made in response to his circumstances—he would never return to Constantinople as bishop, and his life was soon to end—*reflected his life spent in training as a disciple or apprentice of Jesus?*

Circumstances had gone bad, strikingly awful, yet God still existed, Christ continued to reign at the right hand of the Father, and the Holy Spirit still filled John's mind, heart, and body. It was as though John had trained all his life for this moment; now the opportunity—unexpected, sudden, and difficult though it was—offered itself to him to think and act like a Christian as his life drew to a close.

John's circumstances and his response to them illustrate what living a good life before God looks like. An opportunity was given to John by God to allow the Holy Spirit to manifest his presence in John's life, with the fruit of the Spirit—kindness, gentleness, faithfulness, perseverance, and self-control—naturally appearing in the midst of John's painful and perplexing difficulties (cf. Gal 5:22). These fruits had slowly developed and matured in John through a lifetime of training in the virtuous life, through the *askesis* John had engaged in on a daily basis:

+ constant memorization of Scripture,

+ practicing simplicity in the midst of the extravagance that surrounded him as a bishop of the church,

- ✦ consistent fasting,
- ✦ service to the poor on a daily basis, and
- ✦ daily worship that nourished John's life and heart.

Note that John did not engage in any of these spiritual disciplines to earn anything from God; he practiced them because Jesus himself did and had given them to Chrysostom as concrete means of grace. The result of Jesus' mentoring in John's life is encouraging and enlightening; when John's circumstances suddenly changed—as they drastically did at the end of his life—he was not swept off his feet. Instead, Chrysostom responded faithfully and courageously as he replicated the pattern of Jesus. He had trained himself to live—and die—as a faithful apprentice of Christ. Or, to use John's own language—and earlier that of Origen— John lived and died like a Christian "philosopher."

The Good, the Bad, and the Indifferent

John's perspective and life exemplify that of a mature Christian, one who has trained himself to distinguish wisely between good things, bad things, and indifferent things. Chrysostom teaches that genuinely good things are fundamental virtues such as temperance and generosity. He categorizes bad things (*kaka*) as any sinful attitudes or acts such as luxury or lust. Indifferent things (*adiaphora*) *become good or bad according to how one uses them or responds to them.* For example, possessing wealth may lead to avarice or generosity, depending on the character of the person experiencing it.

Good things (the virtues, i.e., the fruit of the Holy Spirit, to use Paul's language) possess as a primary characteristic that they can never become bad. Truly bad things (evil and sin) can never become good. Other things, such as sickness, death, insults, riches, dishonor, freedom, and servitude, *become good or bad according to how they are understood and responded to by the human being experiencing them.* In turn, our ability to respond to evil and indifferent things in a Christian fashion is determined by our reliance on the Holy Spirit and the training we have undergone to prepare for living life well in Christ's kingdom.

If we have engaged in robust, consistent, demanding training under the guidance of a wise mentor, we will form correct judgments for how to respond to our circumstances and will act accordingly. One's ability to live life well, John believes, is an art that has been honed through *training* oneself to think and act like a disciple of Jesus Christ. And to reiterate, for Chrysostom a disciple of Christ is by definition an apprentice of Jesus; disciples have willingly attached themselves to a master whose teachings and actions they must *learn* thoroughly and *imitate* faithfully.

Living a good life before God always entails disciplined Christian thinking and living in the midst of our surrounding culture, one whose values may more or less align with those of Jesus. Christian "philosophy" as defined by the church fathers is a matter of living in line with the truth given to us in Christ. Genuine moral knowledge and practice is possible.

The Christian philosopher—by definition one who is living a good life—has become a living incarnation of the Christian faith, a little Christ, modeling or imitating the life of Christ itself. Christian philosophers in this sense—Christian lovers of wisdom—may be relatively unlettered but deeply learned. A stay-at-home mother, for instance, occupied for most of her day with raising her children, is a Christian philosopher in Chrysostom's eyes if she is living her life and her vocation as a mother as an apprentice of Jesus.

Wise Christians are those who have chosen to apprentice themselves to Christ by imitating key patterns in Jesus' life or the lives of others who knew Jesus well and who patterned their thinking and acting after his (Paul, Peter, Mary, great Christians in the history of the church, and so on). As we imitate Jesus as students imitate their master, our ability to live life well expands. We increasingly discern good from evil, right from wrong, important things from indifferent things, and live life as God designed it to be lived. *We walk with the grain of the universe rather than against it.*

Recall that Chrysostom believed indifferent things (*adiaphora*) become good or bad according to the disposition of the individual. Has our disposition, our character, the way we habitually respond to what life offers day in and day out, been prepared through the power of the Spirit to live well in the world God has created?

THE KEY ROLE OF MORAL DISPOSITION OR CHARACTER

Our disposition significantly determines how we exercise our will in response to the moral choices we face daily. Those who through the power of the Holy Spirit *and* rigorous training (*askesis*) learn to behave in a Christian manner make the right choices because their disposition and will have been molded by the specific instruction and examples found in the gospel of the kingdom; they have learned to imitate other believers who are living the gospel well. They interpret and respond to life wisely because their mind, heart, and body have been habituated to respond faithfully to the realities of Christ's kingdom and Christ's teaching. How so? By adopting the very practices Christ himself engaged in to stay spiritually healthy. Luke tells us, for instance, that in the midst of his busy ministry Jesus would often withdraw to lonely places and pray (Lk 5:16). His wise apprentices observe this pattern and imitate it in their own lives. Jesus' practices—his spiritual disciplines—become key aspects of his apprentices' own spiritual training program.

THE PROBLEM OF THE PASSIONS

The church fathers frequently refer to *the passions* in their diagnosis of what's gone wrong with human beings. What did the fathers mean when they spoke of the passions? The church fathers refer to the passions as *vices that cripple our ability to pray and to live life well.*[21]

Let me take a moment to explain what ancient Christian writers did not mean when they spoke of the passions. For instance, modern people often connect *passion* or *passions* with "any very strong emotion, positive or negative. 'She has a passionate desire to serve the poor.' 'He was in a real passion when he killed the man.' 'She is a passionate lover.' 'He has a passion for chocolates.'"[22]

For early Christians a passion may have a strong emotional element or tone, but can just as often refer to a "state of mind, or even a habitual action. Anger is usually a passion, but sometimes forgetfulness is called a passion. Gossip and talking too much are also regularly called passions. . . . Depression, the very opposite of a passion as we usually use that term in our modern world, is one of the most painful of the passions."[23] In a nutshell, the passions are a "conglomerate of obsessive emotions, attitudes, desires, and ways of acting. . . . It is these passions that blind us in our dealings with ourselves, each other, and the world, and so pervert perfectly good and useful impulses which take away our freedom to love."[24]

The Greek word *logismoi* was occasionally used by ancient writers to describe the evil thoughts, impulses, motives, and actions that an unredeemed mind naturally births, like the maggot eggs that soon appear on rotten meat left in the sun. John Ortberg describes the "seeds of the 'passions'" as "those suggestions or impulses that emerge from the subconscious and soon become obsessive."[25] From the perspective of the church fathers, as Olivier Clément explains, the passions "are blockages, usurpations, deviations. . . . They are forms of idolatry, of that 'self-idolatry' that deflects towards nothingness our capacity for transcendence."[26]

Cleansing from the passions, the church fathers argue, is an indispensable aspect of developing a good life. "And once the tottering and dead rubbish of the passions has been dug out, the firm foundations of simplicity and humility can be placed in what may be called the living and solid ground of our heart, on the gospel rock."[27] This preliminary weeding of the passions through the practice of key spiritual disciplines such as prayer, silence, solitude, and simplicity ensures the stability and strength that leading a good life before God demands.

Consider, for instance, the materialism that characterizes North American culture, and compare it to that of the Roman world. Gregory of Nyssa, in his analysis of Roman materialism, links the desire for more and more stuff to the dulling effect of the passions on the human mind and especially on our memory. Too quickly we forget, Gregory believes, that everything begins with God's grace, the grace that richly offers human fulfillment to God's image bearers. Forgetfulness of God's grace and gifts foments a decline into materialism, where the pursuit of more and more stuff becomes the end all of life. As Gregory puts it, a sinful image bearer left to himself "is almost completely involved in the pursuit of material things."[28] We will return to these issues more thoroughly in chapter two.

THE EFFECTIVE ANTIDOTE

As Chrysostom's life was nearing its end in his cramped, smoky room in Cucusus, his thoughts were drawn continually to the gospel as the effective antidote for the disease of the passions. John pictured himself as a physician preparing a remedy for "all who are appalled by the events occurring in the world."[29] How? "By preparing the medicine of the word. . . . For this remedy nourishes more than bread, restores more effectively than a drug and cauterizes more powerfully than fire, without causing any pain. At the same time it checks the foul-smelling tides of perverse reasonings."[30]

John's goal was to release his ancient readers—and us—from the influence of passions that cripple our ability to think and live in line with life as God has designed it to work. All too frequently we attempt to live against the grain of the universe; we continually ram our heads into reality, and it hurts!

In a sermon from a series John delivered on the book of Acts he writes:

It is not possible to be master of one's self, being in a passion. Like a sea rolling mountains high, it is all hurly-burly: or even as a pure fountain, when mire is cast into it, becomes muddied, and all is in turmoil. . . . It is your own soul that you have cut open; it is there that you have inflicted a wound: you have flung your own charioteer from his horses, you have got him dragging along the ground upon his back.[31]

The passions, then, throw the faculty of reason, the *logismos*, off balance. They blind the eyes of the mind and cripple the mind's ability to form a realistic and fitting opinion or judgment regarding a specific ethical question or dilemma. In turn, our ability to live well and accept, appreciate, and praise God's providence in our life and in the world is undercut.

Chrysostom's lifelong project as a Christian, priest, and bishop was to help Christians live well as Christ's disciples—his apprentices—and to release them from the influence of passions that prevented them from thinking and living in a manner congruent with the values of Christ's kingdom. John teaches that if we allow ourselves to be governed by our passions, our reasoning about and response to life will inevitably be distorted and twisted; we will lack the eyes to discern truly what God is up to in the world.

Not only will we fail to recognize God at work, but we will end up living in a shallow, surface fashion, on the basis of appearances alone. We will identify genuinely good things as evil, evil things as good, and unwisely judge indifferent things as either good or evil. The result will be a life that doesn't make sense. Indeed, a life gripped by the passions will often look like one long horror show.

The next chapter of this book will concern the early Christian martyrs, folks who freely and sacrificially died for their faith rather than succumb to the Roman demand to worship the emperor as god or to sacrifice to Roman deities. No psychiatrically healthy human being desires to die; we will investigate closely why the early Christian martyrs acted in such a counterintuitive way. Might the death of a martyr actually illustrate what a good life looks like, a life freed from the passions, a life that sees reality clearly and is acting accordingly? Chrysostom thought a lot about death and dying in his cramped, smoky quarters in Cucusus; his thinking can help us understand why the martyrs were acting as they were and has profound implications for our lives today.

A GOOD LIFE AND A GOOD DEATH

At first glance death appears to be an evil one must avoid at all costs. Yet, John writes, death benefits both the one who has died and those who are left behind.[32] How so? Imagine those who have witnessed the execution of a Christian martyr. Would they not learn a powerful lesson on the transitory nature of life and on the danger of acting and living as though life would never end? One is "humbled," Chrysostom writes, "learns to act in a more level-headed fashion, is taught to think in a more spiritual manner, and introduces into his mind the mother of all goods, humility."[33]

Those who have died are in no way wronged, for the dead "will receive this same body pure and incorruptible." In the light of the gospel, death can be viewed as "a teacher of the spiritual life, instructing the understanding, bridling the passions of the soul, quelling its billows and creating calm."[34] If we judge simply on the basis of appearances, how can we not view death as an evil to be feared? Death's meaning, however, is dramatically changed when we view it through the lens of the gospel. In fact, Chrysostom argues, death can serve as a genuine good, as the lives of the martyrs clearly demonstrate; they die, but their dying generates encouragement, insight, courage, and perseverance in others.

Chrysostom teaches that key virtues such as humility arise in the human heart as God's image bearers contemplate how quickly life passes. When a Christian says goodbye to a loved one whose life has drawn to a close, she naturally feels grief. Yet, if she is willing to interpret the death of her loved one through the meaning the cross and resurrection of Christ offers, she can learn valuable lessons. Among others, we will notice how brief life is and perceive the danger of thinking and living as though life in this present world will never end.

Chrysostom warns that if we live life only on the basis of appearances, death will remain a terror. If we faithfully discern more deeply, though, thinking and praying to the heart of the matter through the light of the gospel, our understanding of death can be transformed. The pain of parting from our loved ones will remain—saying goodbye will be terribly difficult—but what looked like eternal loss now can be seen to be only a temporary separation.

THE EXAMPLE OF JOSEPH

Chrysostom illustrates his key points through the lives of biblical characters such as Abraham, Sarah, John the Baptist, and Joseph. All are examples of persons who loved God, learned to see below the surface of things to perceive God at work, and led good and fruitful lives as a result.

Consider the life of Joseph. Joseph's life and relationship with his brothers and father illustrate well the danger of the passions running wild in image bearers' lives. Joseph plainly represents the ideal of the true Christian philosopher, i.e., the wise and genuine Christian who bridles his passions, refuses to judge by appearances, and waits for the final outcome of events as God's providential love unfolds in his life. Other characters in the story line, such as Joseph's brothers and Potiphar's wife, serve as prime examples of the folly and ruin that occur when the passions run wildly out of control.

Consider for a moment the reaction of Joseph's brothers to his dream that one day he would rule over them (Gen 37:1-28). Their response, individually and as a group, is a veritable litany of disordered passions. Rather than acting as brothers, they react like wild animals and seek Joseph's life. They are "more savage than wolves toward their brother."[35] "The father of this war," Chrysostom writes, "was *irrational envy and unjust malice. Seething with anger . . . envy kindling this furnace and stirring up the fire.*"[36] When Reuben prevents the brothers from actually killing Joseph, "their anger boiled anew, their wrath reached its zenith, and *their passions raged out of control like a storm at sea.*"[37] Consumed by the "madness" of their passions, they sell Joseph into slavery.

Joseph's trials, however, are only beginning. In a sense he leaves one insane asylum—a family circle consumed by raging passions—only to enter another, the passionate world of Potiphar's wife (Gen 39:1-20). Once Potiphar's wife lays eyes on Joseph, her passions erupt in heated desire. She is "beside herself over the beauty of the young man."[38] Each day, like a wild lioness, she goes out in search of her prey, "*incited by her passion and unbridled love.*"[39] Still, despite "her appearance and frenzied passion," Joseph withstands her temptations. When Joseph refuses her advances and flees the scene naked, with Potiphar's wife clutching his robe, another passion—anger—overwhelms her. As

Chrysostom puts it, *"another even more grievous passion* joined in with extreme savagery."[40]

Compare Joseph's response to his difficulties to the passions running wild in his brothers and Potiphar's wife. Chrysostom's point is that in the midst of his life's difficulties—all allowed by God's sovereign providence—Joseph continues to lead a good life, a wise life, a discerning life, a courageous life, marked by his deep trust in God's promises. *Joseph refuses to judge by appearances.* He discerns God at work in his circumstances despite how things look on the surface. When Joseph's brothers plot against him, he exhibits "the *disposition* of a brother."[41] When he is sold into slavery he maintains an even keel.

Joseph is not overwhelmed by these difficult, indeed horrific, events. He resists faithfully and effectively the allurements of Potiphar's wife because his *disposition* in the midst of his difficult circumstances is one of habitual trust in God's providential care. Joseph recognizes "full well the resourcefulness of God and the ingenuity of his wisdom."[42] God has *trained* Joseph to trust; Joseph's habitual responses to life arise out of a mature personality, a wise personality, one tested in the fire and strengthened in the very testing. From an early age Joseph had been learning to trust God's promises. The result of this training process, an apprenticeship under God's guidance, was a good life, a life characterized by wisdom, discernment, perseverance, courage, and love.

JESUS AS THE PERFECT MODEL OF THE GOOD LIFE

The church fathers believed the perfect model of the good life is Jesus himself. Jesus' teaching and Jesus' practices captivated them. Their deepest desire was to become ever more like Jesus, to act as his mind, eyes, mouth, ears, hands, and feet in the world. For the fathers, the good life was Jesus' life lived through them; they desired to become "little Christs" in the time and space God had given them to live.

How does one become increasingly like Jesus? How can Christ's mind, Christ's thinking, Christ's perspectives, Christ's power, and Christ's love increasingly embed themselves in his image bearer's heart, mind, and concrete bodily behaviors? Is it possible to learn to live like Christ in a natural, Spirit-empowered, deeply habituated fashion, so that sin, rather than virtue, is the exception rather than the rule? The church fathers clearly believed the answer is *yes*.

The fathers insist that Jesus both taught and modeled how to live well in God's kingdom. Palladius puts it this way: "Words and syllables do not constitute teaching. . . . Teaching consists of virtuous acts of conduct. . . . This is how Jesus taught. . . . His aim was the formation of character."[43]

The church fathers were deeply aware—in a way similar to Aristotle and surely to Jesus—that simply thinking well about a specific ethical issue is not enough. The fathers knew it is possible for an image bearer to *think correctly* on an issue of ethical significance, say the importance of living a sexually pure life, while simultaneously *behaving* in a rampantly promiscuous fashion. What one knows must be consciously practiced if obedience and love for the long haul are to be attained.

The question is plain: *How are the thoughts of the mind and the actions of the body to be brought into ever greater congruence with the values of the kingdom of God?* How is the behavioral dissonance that too often characterizes disciples' lives—the disjunction between faith and practice, thought and behavior—to be increasingly overcome? Congruity between the currency of our thoughts and words and the gold of our lives—a life that rings true to the broader watching world—is the goal. If the goal is to be reached, the race run well, the church fathers argue that a specific training program for the development of goodness and love is absolutely essential, a workout routine based on Jesus' own thinking and practice. In chapter eight we will examine this proposal carefully.

HOW SHOULD WE THEN LIVE?[44]

As we move into our discussion of martyrdom in the ancient church, keep in mind key questions and issues we have introduced in this introductory chapter. They will come up again and again in the pages to come.

+ What characterizes a good life lived well before God?
+ How is a good life developed and nurtured?
+ What habits, dispositions, and virtues must we develop through the power of the Holy Spirit?
+ How has culture influenced God's image bearers in their desire to live a good life, whether ancient image bearers or modern?
+ How have our family, our church, our work environment, our entertainment choices, our political affiliations, our educational setting, our favorite authors, and other key factors influenced the formation of our disposition, choices, and daily habits?
+ How have we become the persons we actually are, characterized by certain specific traits that those who know us well could readily identify?
+ How have we come to believe that certain thoughts and actions are morally right and others morally wrong?
+ Why are we behaving the way we are?
+ What is the relationship between Greek *paideia* and Christian spiritual formation? How are they similar? How are they different?
+ For the church fathers, what role does imitation play in leading a good life?
+ Why is it important to distinguish between good things, bad things, and indifferent things in learning to live well as a Christian?
+ From the church fathers' perspective, what is the problem of the passions?
+ What is the antidote to the poison of the passions?

ABBREVIATIONS

ACCS	Ancient Christian Commentary on Scripture
ACD	Ancient Christian Doctrine
ACW	Ancient Christian Writers
ANF	*Ante-Nicene Fathers*
CSEL	Corpus Scriptorum Ecclesiasticorum Latinorum
EAC	*Encyclopedia of Ancient Christianity.* Edited by Angelo Di Berardino. Downers Grove, IL: IVP Academic, 2014
NPNF¹	*Nicene and Post-Nicene Fathers,* Series 1
NPNF²	*Nicene and Post-Nicene Fathers,* Series 2
PG	Patrologia Cursus Completus: Series Graeca. Edited by Jacques-Paul Migne. 162 vols. Paris, 1857–1886
SC	Sources chrétiennes

Look! For you, there are threats, punishments, tortures, and crosses. . . . Where is that God who is able to help you when you come to life again, if he cannot help you while you are in this life?

PAGAN ANTAGONIST, IN MARCUS MINUCIUS FELIX, *THE OCTAVIUS OF MINUCIUS FELIX* [1]

It is evident that no one can terrify or subdue us. For, throughout all the world, we have believed in Jesus! It is clear that, although beheaded, and crucified, and thrown to wild beasts . . . and fire, and all other kinds of torture, we do not give up our confession. But the more such things happen, the more do other persons and in larger numbers become faithful believers and worshippers of God through the name of Jesus.

JUSTIN MARTYR, *DIALOGUE WITH TRYPHO* [2]

"THEY LOOKED LIKE FLAMING ANGELS"

Martyrdom

THE EARLY CHRISTIAN MARTYRS

Dietrich Bonhoeffer, while imprisoned at Tegel Prison, commented in one of his letters on the reading program he was following in prison: "I'm now reading Tertullian, Cyprian, and others of the church fathers with great interest. In some ways they are more relevant to our time than the Reformers."[3] Eric Metaxas, author of a recent bestselling biography of Bonhoeffer, believes that Bonhoeffer's interest in the church fathers during his imprisonment

> wasn't so much theological as it was practical. Cyprian was beheaded by the Roman government. Bonhoeffer was soon to be hanged by the Nazis. To be a serious believer in the early days of Christianity was to be a marked man, and I think Bonhoeffer saw in Cyprian and the others a passion and a commitment that seems only to come from religious persecution—something that he personally knew and experienced.[4]

While I disagree with the distinction Metaxas draws between the theology and practice of the church fathers—their willingness to suffer on behalf of Christ is derived directly from the cruciform shape of their theological reflections—his main point is well taken. The church fathers would not be surprised at the suffering the church in the twentieth and twenty-first centuries has experienced. In all likelihood they would be more surprised and concerned if the church were not suffering. "Are they preaching and living the gospel?" the church fathers might well ask, if they looked at the church and all appeared well with the world.

INCREASED PERSECUTION IN AN INCREASINGLY RELIGIOUS WORLD

Although the world today is increasingly religious, it is simultaneously less and less tolerant of Christians and their distinctive beliefs. "In two-thirds of the world's countries . . . persecution has worsened in recent years. The Vatican has reported the same conclusion. Why," Metaxas asks, "aren't the media talking about this?"[5] Good question. Surely, then, the thoughts and practices of the ancient Christian community in response to the threat of persecution and martyrdom, from the second into the early fourth century, can inform Christian perspectives today—particularly in the West—toward the suffering church, the church inhabited by the majority of Christians living today.

Andrew Walls, who holds an Oxford PhD in patristics and is one of the great missiologists of the twentieth century, experienced a significant shift in perspective with his move to Sierra Leone in West Africa when he was thirty years old. In his new African home it dawned on Walls that he was actually working in a second-century church environment. Walls writes:

I arrived in West Africa in my thirtieth year, with an assignment to teach those in training for the ministry in Sierra Leone, and in particular to be responsible for teaching them church history. I had received, as I thought, a pretty good theological education; and my graduate work had been in patristics at Oxford. . . . I still remember the force with which one day the realization hit me that

I, while happily pontificating on the patchwork quilt of diverse fragments that constitutes second-century Christian literature, I was actually living in a second-century church. The life, worship and understanding of a community in its second century of Christian allegiance was going on all around me. Why did I not stop pontificating and observe what was going on?[6]

So, as Walls encourages us, we will be observing what the ancient church experienced as it followed Christ while living on foreign turf.

We will not be studying the church fathers' views on martyrdom, though, simply as an abstract exercise in historical theology and church history. Rather, we must have two questions constantly in the back of our minds:

1. What are the implications of the ancient church's suffering for Christ's suffering church today?

2. What are the implications of the ancient church's suffering for Christians living in the West or in other largely persecution-free zones? How might the church's suffering—ancient and modern—speak to those who are encountering a time of relative peace and prosperity, one with its own blessings and temptations?

Origen clearly believed the gospel addresses both these questions. "We have learned from the Gospel *neither to relax our efforts in times of peace and to give ourselves up to leisure, nor, when the world makes war upon us,* to become cowards and apostatize from the love of the God of all things, which is in Jesus Christ."[7] We will return to Origen's thoughts later in this chapter.

SOME GENERAL OBSERVATIONS

"We don't easily fathom why God does not seem to protect good people from the violence of evil people. Mysteriously, he seems to have a preference for martyrdom."[8] So poignantly comments Bert Ghezzi, echoing the sentiments of Christians across the years. Whether it is Origen dying in prison in the third century, Edith Stein in the gas chambers of

Auschwitz in 1942, or Jim Elliot and Nate Saint in the jungles of Ecuador in the 1950s, God extravagantly spends the lives of his saints. Yet as the ancient martyrs spent the currency of their lives on behalf of Christ, Christ within them often manifested his grace, glory, and deep fellowship with his dying disciples. Consider the following passage from the Martyrdom of Polycarp.

> Blessed and noble, therefore, are all the martyrdoms that have taken place in accordance with the will of God (for we must reverently assign to God the power over all things). For who could fail to admire their nobility and patient endurance and loyalty to the Master? . . . But they themselves reached such a level of bravery that not one of them uttered a cry or a groan, thus showing to us all that at the very hour when they were being tortured the martyrs of Christ were absent from the flesh, or rather that the Lord was standing by and conversing with them. And turning their thoughts to the grace of Christ they despised the tortures of this world. . . . The fire of their inhuman torturers felt cold to them, for they set before their eyes the escape from that eternal fire which is never extinguished, while with the eyes of their heart they gazed upon the good things that are reserved for those who endure patiently, things that neither ear has heard nor eye has seen, nor has it entered into the human heart, but that were shown to them by the Lord, for they were no longer humans but already angels.[9]

We do well to note a number of emphases in this passage as we begin to explore the early church's understanding of martyrdom.

The ancient church understood martyrdom to be the primary, quintessential example of devotion to Christ. Genuine martyrdom is Christ centered; in union with Christ the martyr imitates, though on a vastly reduced scale, important aspects of Christ's own suffering for his fallen creation. As martyrs suffer, Christ suffers with them. Surprisingly, through the martyr's intimate union with Christ, the physical suffering of martyrdom is sometimes dramatically reduced. Boniface Ramsey comments:

At the root of the physical and psychological transformation attributed to the martyrs was the firm conviction that they were not suffering alone. They were following Christ as closely as possible and experiencing his presence in their sufferings. . . . This union with Christ is understood to be so overwhelming that it obliterates any sense of pain: in the very act of martyrdom the sufferers are already out of the flesh.[10]

Hence, the comment in the Martyrdom of Polycarp that martyrs "were no longer human beings but already angels" makes sense from an ancient Christian perspective. Martyrdom, as Ramsey points out, models a specific theology of the body, particularly of "the imitation of Christ and the glory of the cross, which are Pauline and Johannine themes. . . . Everything that the martyrs do is characterized by an austere single-mindedness that is typical of the Gospels themselves: as Jesus' life is directed toward Jerusalem and there fulfilled, so that of the martyrs is directed toward the supreme moment of their own death."[11]

Accounts of early Christian martyrdom often accentuate the martyr's ability to see beyond the horror of present events. Frequently the martyr is enveloped in deep, poignant, loving fellowship with Christ in the midst of horrendous suffering; this fellowship and intimacy provides sustenance in the transition from the life of this present age to that of the age to come. Christ is often vividly present and ministering to the mind, soul, and body of the martyr.

ROMAN PERSECUTION

For the first three centuries of the church's history, persecution tended to be sporadic and localized; years might pass without the church experiencing significant suffering at the hands of Rome. Ramsey observes, "There were comparatively large spaces of time—between the death of the emperor Septimius Severus in 211 and the accession of Decius in 249, for example—when there was no general persecution and when the Church experienced a considerable amount of freedom."[12]

When persecution did occur, it was sometimes related to misunderstanding and fear. The situation facing the Roman governor Pliny in the province of Bithynia-Pontus is a case in point.[13] Roman governors such as Pliny had difficulty in discerning the difference between early Christian communities and other political, religious, and social groups, associations that could undermine the stability and order of the Roman world. For instance, the Roman emperor Trajan, under whom Pliny served as provincial governor of Bithynia-Pontus, was extremely sensitive to the threat posed by political associations, even when an association seemed as harmless as people joining together to form a company of firemen. In a very interesting letter, Pliny asks Trajan whether a "company of firemen" should be limited to 150 members. Trajan's response is strict, cautious, and worth quoting at some length.

> I have received your suggestion that it should be possible to form a company of firemen at Nicomedia on the model of those existing elsewhere, but we must remember that it is societies like these which have been responsible for political disturbances in your province, particularly in its cities. If people assemble for a common purpose, whatever name we give them and for whatever reason, they soon turn into a political club (*hetaeria*). It is a better policy then to provide the equipment necessary for dealing with fires, and to instruct property owners to make use of it, calling on the help of the crowds which collect if they find it necessary.[14]

Trajan's response to Pliny vividly illustrates the prevailing Roman suspicion of individuals or groups that threatened to subvert fundamental loyalty to Rome. Better to have an inefficient fire department than to allow people to gather in groups that could soon become seditious. Robert Wilken observes that the word Trajan employs to describe a political club, *hetaeria*, "is the same word Pliny was to use later when he wrote to Trajan about the Christians."[15] When Pliny encountered Christians, he thought "sedition" and acted accordingly.

Pliny himself had only a limited knowledge of Christianity. He writes to Trajan:

> I have never been present at an examination of Christians. Consequently, I do not know the nature or the extent of the punishments usually meted out to them, nor the grounds for starting an investigation and how far it should be pressed. Nor am I at all sure whether any distinction should be made between them on the grounds of age, or if young people and adults should be treated alike; whether a pardon ought to be granted to anyone retracting his beliefs, or if he has once professed Christianity, he shall gain nothing by renouncing it; and whether it is the mere name of Christian which is punishable, even if innocent of crime, or rather the crimes (*flagitia*) associated with the name.[16]

Pliny proceeded to investigate the Christian community and found little cause for concern in common Christian rites such as the Eucharist.

> They declared that the sum total of their guilt or error amounted to no more than this; they had met regularly before dawn on a fixed day to chant verses alternately among themselves in honor of Christ as if to a god, and also to bind themselves by oath, not for any criminal purpose, but to abstain from theft, robbery, and adultery, to commit no breach of trust and not to deny a deposit when called upon to restore it. After this ceremony it had been their custom to disperse and reassemble later to take food of an ordinary harmless kind.[17]

The early Christians, as Pliny judged matters, were "a *superstition*, a foreign cult." As such, Pliny determined that they were disturbing the public peace, especially by refusing to purchase meat used in Roman religious rites. In Pliny's mind, the Christians were an economic and political threat; he found little in their religious beliefs to keep him up at night.

Pliny took action against the Christian community by employing "a trial procedure known as *cognitio extra ordinem*," a legal process that allowed Pliny to avoid the need for judges, lawyers, or jury. Pliny simply ordered "the party or parties to appear before the governor." He would then "hear the evidence and adjudicate the matter on his own authority."[18]

Imagine the scenario. Pliny asks each person brought before him whether he is a Christian, simultaneously warning each person that "if he answered yes he would be executed. After asking him the first time he put the same question a second time, and then a third time. When he had received a definite yes from some members of the group, Pliny sent them off to be executed."[19] What is striking, indeed horrifying from a Christian perspective, is that Pliny felt that membership in the Christian sect was a capital offense.

OBSTINACY

The Christian community, Pliny believed, was not only a threat to Roman social order and economic stability. The Christians were also guilty of the crime of *contumacia*, or "obstinacy." "Whatever the nature of their admission," Pliny writes to Trajan, "I am convinced that their *stubbornness and unshakeable obstinacy* ought not to go unpunished." The charge of obstinacy also appears in other narratives regarding Christian martyrs. "'Since they remained unbending, obstinate, I have condemned them,' said another Roman magistrate."[20]

Many Romans could not comprehend why any social or religious group should attempt to distinguish itself from the broader Roman community and obstinately refuse to engage in common Roman practices and perspectives, whether these were religious, political, or economic. The key problem that led to the shedding of Christian blood was the thorough intertwining of politics, social life, and religion in the Roman world. Sacrificing a pinch of incense on a pagan altar to the Roman emperor as a god, for example, was a political as well as religious act. And it was just such an act that Christians refused to perform, casting the long shadow of doubt on their loyalty to the Roman Empire.

It was their stubborn exclusivity that endangered others. If only they would show tolerance and appropriate respect to the gods, they might well be able to keep their distinctive faith without persecution. Not only, however, did Christians cause offence by failing to sacrifice, they also openly broke with society, provocatively repudiating previous religious obligations in their baptismal pledge to renounce Satan and his pomp and his angels. Christians were therefore to blame when the world went wrong.[21]

The demonization of the church did not always lead to violence, but the danger of violent aggression from suspicious Romans constantly simmered. Occasionally Christians were branded as atheists for their refusal to worship the Roman gods, the gods who protected the Roman world and provided good weather, fertile lands, health for families, and so on. Tertullian comments, "They think the Christians the cause of every public disaster, of every affliction with which the people are visited. If the Tiber rises as high as the city walls, if the Nile does not send its waters up over the fields, if the heavens give no rain, if there is an earthquake, if there is famine or pestilence, straightway the cry is, 'Away with the Christians to the lion!'"[22]

Years could pass without the shedding of blood. Yet when persecution against the church broke out, as it did during the reign of emperors such as Nero, Domitian, Decius, and Diocletian, it was harsh and vicious. In a well-known passage, Roman historian Tacitus describes the horrors of the Neronian persecution:

Mockery of every sort was added to their deaths. Covered with the skins of beasts, they were torn by dogs and perished, or were nailed to crosses, or were doomed to the flames. These served to illuminate the night when daylight failed. Nero had thrown open his gardens for the spectacle, and was exhibiting a show in the circus, while he mingled with the people in the dress of a charioteer or drove about in a chariot. Hence, even for criminals who deserved extreme and exemplary punishment, there arose a feeling of compassion; for it was not, as it seemed, for the public good, but to glut one man's cruelty, that they were being destroyed.[23]

Bryan Litfin comments that the

Christians' repudiation of their [Roman] culture's values therefore constituted a real and present danger. . . . . Such individuals were like cancer cells on the face of a steadfastly religious society. Christianity was a *superstitio* in the true Roman sense of the term: not just something to mock as ignorant, but a set of beliefs so antisocial it could only lead to deadly repercussions from the heavens.[24]

In AD 301, the Roman emperor Diocletian issued an empire-wide declaration that all persons—apart from Jews—were to declare their religious and political allegiance to Rome by sacrificing to Diocletian as a god. Lactantius, who had converted to Christ in the midst of a distinguished career as a scholar and public speaker, knew Diocletian personally. He describes Diocletian as possessing a "nervous disposition" and "devoted to investigating the future through divination."[25]

On one occasion, Lactantius relates, while Diocletian was "conducting business in the eastern regions, he was sacrificing cattle and examining their livers to predict what was about to happen." As Diocletian was doing so, "some of his attendants who knew the Lord were standing nearby, and they made the everlasting sign on their foreheads [the sign of the cross]. At this the demons fled away, which disrupted the sacred rite." Further sacrifices were offered by Diocletian's soothsayers, but with "the usual signs in the entrails" disrupted. Finally, the chief priest in charge of the rites realized what was going on: "the sacrifices were not providing an answer" because "sacrilegious men were present at the holy ceremonies." In Lactantius's words, Diocletian "flew into a rage."

Who were the sacrilegious men that were defiling the sacrifice? Diocletian determined a clear and direct strategy to surface the religious conspirators. "He ordered not only those who were ministering at the sacrifice but everyone who lived in the palace to make an offering.

Anyone who refused was to be severely flogged." Not only so, but Diocletian "sent letters to the military officers directing that every soldier be forced to make the impious sacrifice or be dismissed from the army." For the present, Lactantius comments, "this was as far as Diocletian's furious anger went."[26]

How Would We Respond?

I ask myself how I might have responded during the Diocletian persecution. Roman troops arrive in my town, perhaps a small village in North Africa, to guarantee that Diocletian's edict to sacrifice to the emperor is faithfully observed. The soldiers set up a small, portable altar, on which they quickly light coals. Sacrificial meat is prepared for cooking and consumption. Every person living in my village, including small children holding their fathers' hands and mothers holding babies in their arms, lines up; local commissioners tasked with overseeing the sacrifice are watching all the villagers closely, including me. These Roman officials know the name of every person living in the village; each name has been recorded in a local registry—in all likelihood a scroll or book—including the names of recently born babies.

One by one each villager reaches the head of the line, identifies him- or herself, is asked to sacrifice, tosses a pinch of incense on to the altar's coals, and consumes a bit of sacrificial meat—an unexpected treat for some. In turn, all those who have sacrificed receive a *libellus*, an official certificate attesting that one has sacrificed to the emperor. I suddenly find myself at the head of the line. I hesitate and catch the interest of the Roman troops and commissioners. What would I do as a disciple of Christ?[27]

A Case Study: Origen on Martyrdom

A close look at Origen's thoughts on martyrdom may well prove helpful at this point. Origen witnessed his own father's death as a martyr and desired to imitate his father's martyrdom in faithfulness to Christ. At the end of Origen's life he suffered dearly at the hands of the Roman government. Eusebius relates how many and of what nature were the sufferings which the man [Origen] endured for the word of Christ, bonds and tortures of the body, and torments under iron and in the recesses of a prison, and how for a great many days, with his feet stretched four spaces in that instrument of torture, the stocks, he steadfastly bore threats of fire, and all the other things inflicted by his enemies.[28]

Though Origen suffered horrendous torture at the hands of the Roman government, he survived for a short time and continued to encourage the persecuted church. Soon, though, he died of his sufferings, pains willingly endured for the sake of the God he loved. Henri Crouzel comments that the Roman judge in charge of Origen's case "was in no hurry to put him to death, hoping to obtain from this most celebrated of Christians an apostasy that would have had a widespread effect." This Roman's wish was never fulfilled, for after his release Origen continued to write letters to the imprisoned and tortured, "words full of value for those needed to be strengthened."[29]

Origen fully expected Christians to suffer for their faith. In his treatise on martyrdom, a work that is challenging and daunting in its content, Origen encourages his readers to move beyond milk to meat, beyond the elementary teachings of the faith to a more hearty diet. He, like the apostle Paul, employs athletic imagery to portray the training program necessary for Christ's athlete to succeed when the great test of faith finally arrives.

The athletes of the church. God promises his grace to the church's spiritual athletes, contestants who clearly see the hope and glory held out to those who suffer on behalf of Christ and his kingdom. Origen realizes that some will try to discourage Christ's followers from the path of faithful witness to the gospel. He exhorts his readers to pay no heed to those who would discourage them from competing well in the arena; instead, Origen writes, pay close attention to "the good which will accrue to us from endurance of them [troubles and present evils] and is reserved for them that by the grace of God have struggled lawfully in

Christ." God is not "parsimonious," reluctant to award those who willingly suffer on Christ's behalf. No, God "is a generous giver towards those who through their contempt of this earthen vessel show with all their might that they love Him with their whole soul."[30]

An unexpected opportunity. Origen teaches that faithful witness to Christ is closely linked to our understanding of suffering, death, and the human body itself. Perhaps too strongly, Origen's Greek background may be manifesting itself—Origen writes that we love God with our "whole soul" when we "separate and cut off" our soul, "not only from the earthly body but from every kind of body." Origen rightly sees, though, that death is an "opportunity" to put "away the body of this death" (cf. Rom 7:24). Would we "not give thanks to God" to at last be delivered from this "corruptible body"? Through "communion with" Christ this deliverance is indeed possible, and martyrdom provides just such an opportunity.[31]

Christ and the martyrs. For Ambrose and Protoctetus, two men who faced imminent persecution during the time of Maximin Thrax, Origen's words were indeed relevant. Origen reminded them that they, like other martyrs, can expect to be "persecuted and mocked for justice's sake and the Son of man."

Origen's point must be grasped; martyrdom is at its heart the mark of devotion to Jesus. As martyrs suffer they bear testimony to Christ; in their faithful witness martyrs find hope and deliverance. "O that our soul might not be troubled, but that even before the judgment seats, before the swords ready to behead us, may our soul be preserved by the peace of God which surpasses all understanding, and be tranquil in the thought that they that leave the body live with the Lord of all things."[32]

Martyrdom and God's providence and justice. Origen's firm faith in God's providence and justice supports his insight and advice on martyrdom. Nothing, Origen strongly believes, occurs apart from God's providential ordering of events. Consider the rhythms of the natural world; their wonderful consistency and intricacy point to God's overarching providence. "God manifestly watches over the movement of the heavens and the stars and over all the animals and plants of all kinds that are on the earth and in the sea. Through His divine art they are brought to perfection in birth, development, nourishment, and increase."

If God so carefully governs creation, we can be assured God will surely act justly on behalf of his saints. The martyrs of the church need not fear their suffering and deaths are in vain. It would be "absurd for us to close our eyes to this and not to look to God, and to have regard rather for men and to fear them—men who will soon die and be delivered up to the punishment which they deserve,"[33] a theme Origen will return to in his discussion of Antiochus Epiphanes and the Maccabean martyrs.

Dispositions and virtues for the athlete and the pilgrim. Origen describes the martyr as both an athlete and a pilgrim, a voyager heading home and traveling light. The Christian athlete and pilgrim must develop specific dispositions and virtues that the rigors of the arena and the voyage home require. Some virtues Origen discusses, such as fortitude, temperance, prudence, and justice, would have been familiar to a wide audience in the ancient world, both Christians and non-Christians.

Citizens of Christ's kingdom, though, must also plant and water the seeds of specifically Christian virtues. The Christian pilgrim, for instance, must develop a piety that is monotheistic and Christlike in character, unlike the piety praised and practiced in the Roman world. Sooner or later those who follow the incarnate Christ will be asked to witness publicly to their king, a public confession that distinguishes true believer from mere pretender. "[Martyrs] realize that they cannot be justified except they believe in God in this way and their heart be so disposed, and that they will not be saved unless their speech correspond to such disposition."[34]

Two principal dangers. Two principal dangers face those who would be faithful martyrs: the temptation to *idolatry* and to *apostasy*. Idolatry was a heated temptation in times of persecution, largely because Roman authorities often demanded that Christians show homage to Roman deities as a sign of loyalty to Rome. Simply dropping a pinch of incense on the coals of an altar could save one's life or deliver one or one's loved ones from the horror of the mines. The temptation to acquiesce to Roman pressure would have been well-nigh overwhelming. It seemed so easy to avoid persecution by pretending to worship common idols or the emperor as god, while simultaneously maintaining an internally pure faith.

In his analysis of the temptation to idolatry, Origen draws a distinction between bowing to an idol and worshiping it. In a Roman courtroom, for instance, a Christian on trial might succumb to fear and bow to a Roman idol, while not genuinely revering it. Yet Origen considers bowing itself as a grave sin. Had not Israel committed fornication with the daughters of Moab by bowing to their idols (Num 25:1)? The Israelites' willingness to bow to foreign deities was a sure sign that their love for the God of Israel had been seriously compromised. Israel's rapid descent into sin with Moabite women quickly revealed the fault lines in Israel's faith as they were tested, tried, and scrutinized in the wilderness.[35]

Origen argues that apostasy is just as serious a sin as idolatry. To deny Christ—the "evil word" spoken in apostasy—must be avoided at all costs, "for how great an abomination must be the evil word of denial, the evil word of public recognition of another god, and the evil oath taken by the fortune of men, a thing that does not endure!" To swear that one is not a follower of Christ is, for Origen, a clear violation of Jesus' teaching against taking any oaths (cf. Mt 5:34).

Natural fears and demonic temptations. Origen warns that during persecution Christians are subjected to both natural fears and demonic temptations. Is the momentary worship of a creature really all that serious? Surely not, the devil tempts. Yet Origen contends that "in no way may we bow down to the creature in the presence of the Creator who sustains all and anticipates their prayer." Origen pictures the soul as a bride united to God. To worship any aspect of the created order is to fornicate "with demons and pretended gods. . . . In my opinion, just as he who is joined to a harlot is one body, so he who bears witness to someone, especially in a time of persecution and trial of faith, unites and joins himself to him to whom he bears witness. And he who denies is by the denial, just as by a sharp sword, separated from him whom he denies."[36]

Origen lists a variety of factors that could induce a Christian to commit apostasy under the duress of persecution:

1. "Indecision."
2. Verbal "taunts," "insults," "mockery"; "It is probable that we shall be insulted by our neighbors, and certain people we associate with will turn up their noses and shake their heads at us as though we were mad."[37]
3. "Pretended" or feigned "pity" meant to induce apostasy.
4. Familial considerations: love of children and mother.[38]

Origen exhorts those who face persecution to "give" themselves "entirely to God and to life with Him and near Him with a view to sharing union with His Only Begotten Son and those who have a share in Him: then we can say that we have filled up the measure of bearing witness."[39]

Union with Christ and the church. The strength to bear witness faithfully, Origen teaches, comes from union with Christ and with his community, the church. This union, in turn, is grounded in the covenantal relationship that the church and each Christian possesses with God. Origen encourages martyrs to remember "that we have received the so-called covenants from God in virtue of agreements we made when we accepted the Christian way of life." From the beginning of their relationship with Christ, believers understand and agree that their life of discipleship includes the willingness to bear a cross on which they one day might well be crucified.

Though we appear to lose our soul in martyrdom, "we shall achieve for it its true salvation." Origen warns that the opposite is also true. If we deny Christ,

we shall be told that it profits nothing to gain the whole material universe at the price of our own destruction or loss. Once a man has lost his soul or forfeited it, even if he gain the whole world, he cannot give that world in exchange for his soul that is lost. For that soul, created to be the image of God, is more precious than all material things. One alone can redeem our soul if it is lost—He who purchased us with His precious blood.[40]

Origen's spiritual hermeneutic. Origen buttresses his arguments by applying his well-known spiritual hermeneutic.[41] Christ summons martyrs as the special friends of God to a divine encounter and accompanying knowledge that is "face to face." "For His friends see things as they are, and not in a dark manner or through mere book knowledge of words and expressions, symbols and types." Paul himself had been caught up to the third heaven, where he heard inexpressible words. Yet he had to once again descend to earth. The martyr will hear similarly wondrous words but never have to descend to earth again. "If you remain united with His followers, you, too, will pass into the heavens, passing beyond not only the earth and its mysteries but the heavens and all that concerns them. For in God as in a treasury are stored up wonders much greater than those mentioned, which cannot be grasped by a nature joined to a body until it has put off all that is of the body."[42]

Fullness of blessing. Through faithfulness to Christ, the martyr experiences "that certain special and greater fullness of beatitude," if he comes "through the combat without faltering." Origen interprets Jesus' response to Peter in Matthew 19:27-29 as a promise to faithful martyrs. The martyr, like Peter, has "left all things" and followed Christ. In return, the martyr is assured that she will "receive many times more, or as Mark says, a hundredfold more, which indeed is much more than the little—even if it were multiplied by a hundred—that we shall give up if we are called to martyrdom."[43]

Spiritual children, the spectacle, and spiritual discipline. A martyr's faithful witness births children to God, though the martyr is asked to leave wife, children, and house behind. "In exchange for these, they have become fathers of the fathers of the patriarch Abraham and other patriarchs. For it is obvious that martyrs who leave their children behind them and bear witness, become fathers, not of children, but of fathers," fathers who will beget children for the kingdom.[44] "They beget a hundred times more children and receive a hundred times more lands and houses."[45]

Martyrs play a role in a spectacle performed before the eyes of human beings, angels, and demons. Hence, the outcome of the martyrs' faithfulness or apostasy has ramifications far beyond what is visible in this world. "The whole world . . . all the angels on the right and on the left, all human beings, both those on the side of God and the others—all will hear us fighting the fight for Christianity. Either the angels in heaven will rejoice over us . . . or—and God forbid that it should happen—the powers of the lower world will gloat over our crime and will be glad."[46] Though the strife be painful and exhausting, the martyr's struggle is part of the spiritual discipline necessary for the soul. Indeed, the present life is an arena of "humiliation" and "affliction for the soul."[47]

The example of Eleazar and the Maccabees. Thankfully, those called to martyrdom have many faithful ancestors to study and imitate. For who "could be more deserving of praise than he who of his own choice elected to die for his religion?"[48] Origen, Chrysostom, Gregory of Nazianzus, Ambrose, and Augustine all point to Eleazar and the Maccabees[49] as outstanding examples of faithful martyrdom.

The Maccabees were faithful witnesses to the God of Israel as they were martyred in a horrific fashion by Antiochus Epiphanes, events narrated in detail in 2 Maccabees. Origen singles out the family patriarch Eleazar as the ideal martyr, precisely because Eleazar by "*his own choice elected to die for his religion*" (emphasis added). What motivated and strengthened Eleazar to die as a witness to his faith in the God of Israel? Origen lists a number of contributing factors to Eleazar's faithfulness in the midst of great trials and sufferings.

Eleazar's *long life of faithfulness and spiritual discipline*, aided by "excellent upbringing from childhood" and immersion in the law of God, gave him the insight to discern the danger and falsehood of dissembling before others simply to prolong his life. Denying his faith might have given

Eleazar a few more years of life, but at great cost to Eleazar's own soul and to those who were watching him. A lack of faith at the point of crisis and witness would only serve to deceive "the heathens" who were testing Eleazar, in a manner of speaking, to see what genuine faith actually looked like.

Not only so, but God was observing the scene, ready to reward or judge in accordance with Eleazar's faithful witness or denial of his faith. Other "young men" of Israel were also watching, to whom Eleazar was called by God to bear faithful witness with his words and his blood. In Eleazar's words, "Such pretense is not worthy of our time of life . . . for many of the young might suppose that Eleazar in his ninetieth year had gone over to an alien religion, and through my pretense, for the sake of living a brief moment longer, they would be led astray because of me, while I defile and disgrace my old age" (2 Maccabees 6:24-25). Eleazar's deep reverence or "fear" of God strengthens him for the suffering to which he is divinely called.[50]

After Eleazar's death, the narrator of the Maccabean revolt describes in horrendous detail the martyrdom of an entire family—a mother and her seven sons—who refuse to eat swine's flesh forced on them by Antiochus Epiphanes. The faithful death of this family, Origen explains, illustrates further key elements of Christian martyrdom.

Consistent, courageous faith. All eight martyrs demonstrate *constancy of faith* in the midst of their suffering. Though their bodies are mutilated and seared in a frying pan, they "remained constant in their religion. . . . They not only endured tortures in their own persons, but showed also a virile tenacity of faith when they had to look at the sufferings of their brothers."[51] "When he refused to change his purpose, he was made to endure the whole series of tortures, but he maintained his constancy to the last breath."[52]

The martyr as the Lord's athlete. The theme of the martyr as an athlete of the Lord stands out in the narrative. As one of the brothers dies in the frying pan, the vapor of "the most noble *champion of faith*" rises from his body. Origen comments that though these brothers lost tongues, hands, and feet in their martyrdom, they will receive them back "from God in such condition as God certainly will return them to His loyal athletes."[53]

Love for God and God's law. Love for God and God's law is a third prominent theme in the narrative of the eight martyrs. For instance, the first brother endures mutilation "as others endure the circumcision ordained by the divine law, for he believed that in enduring this he was also carrying out the word of God."[54] The martyrdom of the eight, then, demonstrates intense and faithful love for God and God's truth as revealed in the law of Moses.

God's sovereign providence. God's overarching providence is a significant fourth theme in the narrative of the Maccabean martyrs. If one judges on the basis of appearances, God seems to have abandoned this faithful family into the hands of wickedness personified—Antiochus Epiphanes—and appears unconcerned about the unfolding horrors. Not so, Origen insists. *Contrary to appearances,* the suffering brothers are aware of what is happening behind the scene, invisibly and powerfully. God is also aware of what is happening, though he is not choosing to intervene. This special family, Origen writes, consoled

> themselves with the thought that God saw all these things. The conviction that the eye of God was watching over their sufferings was sufficient assurance for their constancy. And the Judge of the champions of faith comforted them, comforted Himself, and, so to say, rejoiced with them for struggling against such great sufferings. If we find ourselves in like pains, it would be well for us to say what they said to one another: "The Lord God looks upon us and takes pleasure in the truth in us."[55]

The transformation of the martyr. All of us will suffer; occasionally our suffering will be directly related to our faith in the God of Israel and his Son, Jesus. In the midst of our suffering we can rest assured that God does not abandon his people. In the accounts of the martyrs, Christ's athletes suffer intensely, but simultaneously their suffering transforms them more deeply into the divine image, Jesus himself. In the martyrs' transformation they are pictured as cleansed from sin in the fire of their suffering, a theme that reoccurs often in patristic discussions of martyrdom. By way of contrast, persecutors such as Antiochus Epiphanes—the persecutor par excellence—experience the judgment of God, "for he indeed fights against God who fights them that are made divine by the Word."[56]

The furnace of suffering burns away sin's rust from the martyrs' character; increasingly, often on the spot, they grow in holiness and love. Natural loves and attachments, such as that of a mother for her children, are enveloped, immersed, and transformed by the love of God in the midst of the martyr's vocation to love, trust, reverence, and persevere. In the martyrdom of Eleazar's family, supernatural empowerment and transformation explain a mother's ability to not only witness the death of her seven sons but to actually encourage her children to complete their task faithfully and courageously. "For the dew of piety and breath of holiness did not allow the fire of a mother's feelings, which inflames many mothers in the presence of most grievous ills, to be kindled within her heart."[57] Human weaknesses and fears dissipate in the midst of a situation of terror and stress, dispelled by God as enemies "alien from the whole soul. And this weakness has become powerless in the case of one who can say, 'The Lord is my strength and my praise,' and 'I can do all things in Him who strengthens me, Christ Jesus, Our Lord.'"[58]

The resurrection of the dead. The last significant theme highlighted by Origen in the story of the eight Maccabean martyrs is the reality of the resurrection of the dead. The resurrection of the dead demonstrates a surprising and encouraging reversal of fortune. In the resurrection, Antiochus the king will be judged and shamed, while the faithful martyrs will receive back their bodies healed and whole. As the fifth brother dies he also affirms his firm faith in the resurrection of the just and the judgment of the unjust. He tells Antiochus "to his face that he" is "only a mortal man. . . . In the midst of his sufferings he also declared that 'his people was not abandoned by God,' who would presently torment Antiochus 'and his seed.'"[59]

Martyrdom and thanksgiving for God's goodness and benefits. At this juncture in his treatise, Origen leaves his exegesis of Maccabees 6–7 behind and develops other aspects of martyrdom's significance. Those called to martyrdom possess "a special sense of honor" and wish "to give a recompense for the benefits conferred" on them "by God." Origen does not argue that martyrs attempt to buy their salvation through the sacrifice of their own bodies to God. Rather, martyrs' hearts are filled with a sense of wonder over the gift God has given them in Christ's salvation and view their martyrdom as a response of love, one similar to Christ's own willingness to embrace his cross in love and obedience to the Father.[60]

Origen's thoughts turn to Psalm 115, where the psalmist poses a "rhetorical question": "What shall I render to the Lord for all the things that He has done for me?" The psalmist then answers his own question: "I will take the chalice of salvation, and I will call upon the name of the Lord." Just as the psalmist in responsive love lifts up the chalice of salvation, so the martyr imitates the love of Christ in drinking from Christ's chalice, the cup he offers for the salvation of many.

Origen's thought then turns to the mother of James and John. The mother of these key apostles has asked a favor of Jesus, requesting that her sons, James and John, sit at Jesus' right and left in his kingdom. Jesus responds with a question of his own, one posed directly to James and John. "Are you able to drink the cup that I am about to drink?" (Mt 20:22). Christ's cup is his crucifixion, and the cup he offers his disciples, Origen believes, is the cup of martyrdom.

Though the cup of Christ is painful to drink, demanding the ultimate sacrifice love offers, this gift of love leads to a wonderful place of honor in Christ's kingdom. "And again learn," Origen comments, "that he who drinks the chalice that Jesus drank will sit, reign, and judge beside the King of Kings. Such, then, is the chalice of salvation: he who takes it will 'call upon the name of the Lord,' and whoever 'shall call upon the name of the Lord shall be saved.'"[61]

At this point in Origen's treatise on martyrdom, his Christology and soteriology are muddled as Origen much too closely identifies the salvific benefit of Christ's death and the death of martyrs. Origen seems to believe the baptism of blood involved in martyrdom also has an atoning effect for sin.

> Note also that the baptism of martyrdom, as received by our Savior, atones for the world; so, too, when we receive it, it serves to atone for many. Just as they who assisted at the altar according to the law of Moses seemed to procure for the Jews remission for sins by the blood of goats and oxen, so the souls of believers that "are beheaded for the testimony of Jesus," do not assist in vain at the altar of heaven, but procure for them that pray the remission of sins.[62]

Origen errs at this point by blurring the distinction between Christ as our unblemished high priest and the priesthood he sees martyrs performing on behalf of the world and the church. Origen rightly understands that Jesus as "High Priest" "offered Himself in sacrifice" for us. Origen swerves off course, though, in writing that martyrs also serve as unblemished high priests. "Who then is the priest without blemish who can offer a victim without blemish, if not he who bears witness to the last and fulfills every requirement of martyrdom?"[63] Here Origen has crossed a line in the sand that should never be traversed. His profound admiration for the martyrs of the church, a vocation he himself will courageously fulfill, has pushed him into a theological no-man's land. Origen has much to teach us about martyrdom, but at this point he unwisely blurs christological and soteriological distinctions that the church must maintain clearly and unreservedly.

A fundamental choice. Origen correctly notes that the fundamental choice for the martyr in Origen's day was between death in allegiance to Christ and the worship of false gods. Satan, "the Enemy," attempts "to force" idolatry on the church through his attack on its members. The choice for Christians facing this demonic attack is clear and weighty: faithfulness to Christ or idolatry. In fact, the idols themselves are in reality demons.[64] "How monstrous is it to give up the 'sweet yoke' of Christ 'and His light burden' to submit oneself once more to the yoke of demons and to carry the burden of the gravest sins!"[65]

Origen's mind is drawn to the story of Shadrach, Meshach, and Abednego in the book of Daniel. Just as Nebuchadnezzar warned these three witnesses that a refusal to worship the idol he had created would result in death in a fiery furnace, so "now too, Nebuchadnezzar speaks the same words to us—the true Hebrews, the Hebrews of the world to come." And like Shadrach, Meshach, and Abednego, the faithful martyr must say, "I will not place human glory above the glory of the God of Israel."[66] Jesus himself had warned his disciples that they would be handed over to tribunals and put to death because of their faithful witness to him.[67] Yet martyrs can be assured that "no one comes to the combat of martyrdom without Divine Providence," a reoccurring theme in Origen's treatise.

Not only does God's providence guarantee the ultimate safety of those who die for the faith, but the promised resurrection of Jesus' faithful followers guarantees a glorious future, another prevalent theme we have encountered in Origen's treatise. "They that kill us, therefore, kill only the life of the body, as is clearly signified by the words, 'do not fear them that kill the body'—expressed in the same terms by Matthew and Luke. When they have slain the body, they cannot, even if they wished it, slay the soul: 'they have no more that they can do.'" Christ "will bear witness in heaven to him who has borne witness to Him on earth."[68]

Origen believes more controversially, though, that those who deny Christ will in turn be denied by him. "If a man thinks of denying before men, let him remember Him who said without any lie, 'I will also deny him before my Father who is in heaven.'" Faithful witness is crucial, for the martyr "bears witness to the Son before men" and in so doing "recommends so far as he can Christianity and the Father of this Christianity to those in whose presence he bears witness."[69] "What are we to say," then, "of them who, tested in the furnace of temptation, have denied Him?" Those who deny Christ, Origen believes, will be denied by Jesus before the Father and the angels in heaven.[70]

The Absolute Centrality of the Resurrection

We must stress that apart from Christ's resurrection from the dead, Christian martyrdom makes little sense for the church fathers. Athanasius argues in *On the Incarnation* that the willingness of Christians to die for their faith is proof of the "destruction of death" accomplished by Christ's cross and resurrection. "All the disciples of Christ despise death; they take the offensive against it and, instead of fearing it, by the sign of the cross and by faith in Christ trample on it as on something dead." Through Christ's resurrection, "death is no longer terrible, but all those who believe in Christ tread it underfoot as nothing, and prefer to die rather than to deny their faith in Christ, knowing full well that when they die they do not perish, but live indeed, and become incorruptible through the resurrection."[71]

Who could doubt the reality of the resurrection, Athanasius asks, in light of so many Christians' willingness to die rather than deny Christ?

> Even children hasten thus to die, and not men only, but women train themselves by bodily discipline to meet [death]. . . . Death has become like a tyrant who has been completely conquered by the legitimate monarch; bound hand and foot as he now is, the passers-by jeer at him, hitting him and abusing him, no longer afraid of his cruelty and rage, because of the king who has conquered him.[72]

Athanasius believes the martyr's witness is no "slender proof" of Christ's "victory" over death. Martyrs are empowered by the reality of their Lord's resurrection so that their natural love for life, a love planted within them by their Creator, is overcome.

> Is it a slight indication of the Savior's victory over [death], when boys and young girls who are in Christ look beyond this present life and train themselves to die? Everyone is by nature afraid of death and of bodily dissolution; the marvel of marvels is that he who is enfolded in the faith of the cross despises this natural fear and for the sake of the cross is no longer cowardly in face of it.[73]

Death, at one time "strong and terrible," is now transformed into a means of glorifying Christ. Jesus, "mounted on the cross," has "destroyed and vanquished" death. Not only is Christ's crucifixion a monument to his victory over death, but "he daily raises monuments to His victory in His own disciples" as they freely choose to follow the martyr's path. "How can you think otherwise, when you see men naturally weak hastening to death, unafraid at the prospect of corruption . . . not shrinking from tortures, but preferring thus to rush on death for Christ's sake, rather than to remain in this present life?"[74]

Athanasius describes death as a "snake" and "lion" that the martyr mocks on the basis of Christ's cross and resurrection. "No one in his senses doubts that a snake is dead when he sees it trampled underfoot, especially when he knows how savage it used to be; nor, if he sees boys making fun of a lion, does he doubt that the brute is either dead or completely bereft of strength."[75] In the light of Christ's cross and resurrection, what was once dreaded can now be embraced if necessary for the extension of the kingdom, for Christ's sake and his alone.

How Should We Respond?

How might the ancient church's thoughts and practice concerning martyrdom relate to the experience of modern Christians in the world today? The church fathers' own experience of martyrdom—I think of Polycarp, Ignatius of Antioch, Cyprian, and many others—will encourage and inspire Christians in our modern setting suffering at the hands of groups such as ISIS and Boko Haram. The thousands of Christians who daily experience threats, violence, and death at the hands of persecutors have learned, in Susan Bergman's words, "that something matters more than life,"[76] and a study of the church fathers' thoughts on martyrdom can further deepen this awareness.

For affluent, safe, and comfortable Christians living in the West, though, the world of the ancient Christian martyrs may appear foreign and—dare I say—irrelevant to the issues they face as they seek to live faithful and holy lives before God. As much as modern Western

Christians might desire to identify with the martyr's perspective on life, how can we do so living in areas of the world where persecution is much less prevalent, if not nonexistent? For instance, how might a Western evangelical's understanding of martyrdom be hindered by growing up in the wealthy, comfortable suburbs of Philadelphia?

If we do not live in an environment in which we will suffer significant loss if we are faithful to the gospel, what steps can we take to deepen our awareness of the demands and sacrifices that apprenticeship to Jesus entails? Is our study of ancient Christian martyrdom simply an exercise in church history that may provide a moment's pause for reflection in the busy schedule of a businessperson or stay-at-home mom or dad? How can we become deeper, more sensitive people to aspects, contours, and demands of the gospel that other Christians discern and experience if the water we habitually swim in is shallow, if the seas we sail remain calm and inviting?

Consider these words from David Platt, who writes that Western Christians "are giving in to the dangerous temptation to take the Jesus of the Bible and twist him into a version of Jesus we are more comfortable with."

> A nice, middle-class, American Jesus. A Jesus who doesn't mind materialism and who would never call us to give away everything we have. A Jesus who would not expect us to forsake our closest relationships so that he receives all our affection. A Jesus who is fine with nominal devotion that does not infringe on our comforts, because, after all, he loves us just the way we are. A Jesus who wants us to be balanced, who wants us to avoid dangerous extremes, and who, for that matter, wants us to avoid danger altogether. A Jesus who brings us comfort and prosperity as we live out our Christian spin on the American dream.[77]

Similarly, Dallas Willard comments, "more Christians have died as martyrs in the twentieth century than in all the period from the beginning to 1900." Yet the

"Western" segment of the church today lives in a bubble of historical illusion about the meaning of discipleship and the gospel. We are dominated by the essentially Enlightenment values that rule American culture: pursuit of happiness, unrestricted freedom of choice, disdain of authority. The prosperity gospels, the gospels of liberation, and the comfortable sense of "what life is all about" that fills the minds of most devout Christians in our circles are the result.[78]

Of course, there are aspects of human suffering that are inescapable regardless of where we live. Western Christians are not immune from loss, sickness, financial stress, family disruption and conflict, and death itself. For many Western Christians, though, Platt's and Willard's words ring true. They do for me as I examine my own life. What is one to do when the pressing issue of the day is not impending arrest for my faith, but a hectic schedule that must stretch far enough to cover two afternoon soccer games, homework assignments for the kids, and an evening Bible study with our home group?

If we recall that the central issue for the ancient martyr was not suffering but *allegiance*, things may clarify for the modern, Western Christian. Ancient martyrs suffered and died because they refused to bow the knee to the Roman demand to worship the emperor as a god. Early Christians realized—like many martyrs of the twentieth and twenty-first centuries—that their primary allegiance and loyalty must be to Christ, not to the demands of competing political and religious ideologies.

In the United States the issue of allegiance—of ultimate allegiance—always faces the Christian, though it is often not recognized. Our difficulty in facing this problem clearly and honestly is surely related to the cultural pressure to remain loyal to American values—political, economic, and social—even when those values contradict or conflict with the values of Christ's kingdom. This is especially true as we live in a time of global terrorism and war. The question of ultimate allegiance confronted me on a recent vacation visit to San Diego with my wife, Debbie.

One day we visited the USS Midway, a huge aircraft carrier now moored in San Diego's harbor, a carrier that has served in a variety of combat settings, including the Gulf War. During our visit to the Midway I was particularly moved as I remembered my dad's experience flying off the USS Yorktown as an eighteen-year-old Helldiver pilot during World War II.

Our visit to the Midway coincided with a moving on-board ceremony celebrating the retirement of a naval officer. A crowd stood silently, indeed, reverently as the officer was "whistled" off the deck as he retired from active service. Few eyes remained dry as people stood at attention and a Navy band played the "Star Spangled Banner." An American flag was folded with care and reverence, soon to be presented to the retiring officer. Shortly before the presentation ended, another officer read a poem, words honoring devotion to the flag and the country it represented.

As I listened to this poem, a testimony to love for country and a remembrance of great sacrifice, a lump formed in my throat. I thought of my dad flying over vast stretches of the South Pacific, alone in his Helldiver, searching for his target and accompanied only by his tail gunner. And then came the poem's next words, speaking of the American flag itself. "We worship you." I was caught off guard by these words as I faced an unexpected line in the sand I should not—must not—cross. Respect and honor? Yes. Worship? Absolutely not.

Here, perhaps, is where the Western—in this case American— Christian can learn the most from the martyrs of the ancient church, and from their modern counterparts in countries such as Egypt, Syria, and the Sudan. Each martyr, then and now, faces a fundamental, crucial, inescapable question. Where does my ultimate allegiance lie? To whom, finally, will I bow the knee? This is a question always facing the Christian, from the American mother sending her child off to school to the Iraqi Christian hiding from ISIS troops marching down the street, seeking those whom they may destroy.

Our allegiances are often reflected in our attitudes and behaviors toward money and toward the poor. We will be turning to this important topic in our next chapter.

Property that is beneficial to our neighbors is not to be thrown away, for possessions (being a possession) and property (being property) are supplied by God for people to use. They have been made available to us and placed under our control as means and instruments to be used well by those who understand.

CLEMENT OF ALEXANDRIA, WHO IS THE RICH MAN
WHO IS SAVED?[1]

A love of possessions is caused by three things: a love of pleasure, vanity, and a lack of faith. . . . I have mentioned three. The fourth kind is the frugal steward. Only this last clearly acquires money correctly, in order that there may always be enough to help those in need.

MAXIMUS THE CONFESSOR, CHARITY[2]

T W O

"A SOLID DROP OF GOLD"

Wealth and Poverty

WEALTH, POVERTY, AND CHRISTIAN RESPONSIBILITY

What did the church fathers think, teach, and practice on the thorny issues of money, the acquisition of property, and the responsibility of the rich for the poor? I think of John Chrysostom. John agonized over the human need that confronted him on a daily basis, thought deeply and preached loudly over Christ's call to care for the poor scattered through the city streets and country lanes of the ancient world. Chrysostom's words are lively, strong, insistent, and discomforting: the "rich and greedy" are "a kind of robbers lying in wait on the roads, stealing from passers-by, and burying others' good in their own houses as if in caves and holes."[3]

Roughly 150 years earlier than Chrysostom, Cyprian wrote of the challenges and possibilities for North African Christians who possessed great wealth; he did so in the context of persecution. In Roman culture wealth represented both material well-being and social status. Refusal to sacrifice to the emperor, then, often meant the choice "between the Christian and the imperial cultures." Cyprian "promoted generosity to the poor as an exercise of faith that prepared Christians for the confession of Christ and even martyrdom by requiring them to cast all their hope upon Christ."[4]

Both Chrysostom and Cyprian urge us to heed Jesus' call to respond to the needs of our poor neighbors, both near and far. And so we must ask, in very concrete terms, how are disciples of Christ—apprentices of Christ—to live economically wise, kind, grace-filled lives? How would Christ have us respond to our prosperity—or our poverty? What of the choices we make daily as to how we spend our money, how much we save, how much we give? What are our specific responsibilities to the poor, the millions who begin each day longing for a piece of bread, shoes to wear, a chance to send their children to school, to live in an environment free from the constant threat of violence—even war? What of the gap that continues to grow between the rich and poor? What of the issue of private ownership of property?

And what of the knotty question of greed? How does this particular vice manifest itself in a fallen human heart? Does greed have certain identifiable symptoms? When does the quest for sufficiency in material things cross the line into greed, the unquenchable desire for "just a little bit more"? How is one to tell? We are not the first Christians to ask these questions. The ancient Christian community faced the same issues.

Similar Cultures, Similar Problems

The church fathers have much to teach us about wealth, poverty, greed, and giving. They lived in a world of great disparities, a pre-industrial environment in which the gap between rich and poor was as wide and deep as the Grand Canyon.[5] The life of the poor in the Roman world was short, bitter, wretched. Most people lived from hand to mouth, struggling to survive.[6]

Helen Rhee guides us skillfully into the life of the poor in the Roman world. The poor were the "vast majority" of the Roman population and surely those most likely to suffer during times of famine, disease, political unrest, and war. In addition, the poor suffered from the Roman social stigmas attached to poverty.

Roman authors typically presented the urban poor as the idle mob whose grievances and moral defect (such as laziness) led them to crimes, riots, and sedition. They were seen as a threat to social harmony and stability, and could only be controlled by satisfying their insatiable cravings for "bread and circuses." Cicero described the poor as *"sordem urbis et faecem,"* "the poverty-stricken scum of the city."[7]

The poor were invisible to the eyes of many, including too many Christians. Peter Brown comments that in "Antioch and Constantinople, the rich were urged by a preacher such as John Chrysostom to look over the edge of a social precipice into a swirling and anonymous crowd of beggars, buffoons, and homeless immigrants gathered around them in a great city."[8] If Chrysostom had to urge his congregation to look over the precipice, there must have been many who were not looking—or were unwilling to do so.

As we listen to the voices of these ancient Christians addressing the range of complexities and confusions surrounding wealth and poverty in their cultural and ecclesial context, notice how fervently, how loudly the church fathers tend to speak. They are turning up the volume, trying to catch people's attention, for the rich in their churches and in Roman society at large too often turned a blind eye to the horrendous need facing them on a daily basis. People weren't listening. People weren't seeing.

To be fair, wealthy Roman Christians of the time can't be blamed entirely for their blindness to the poor, for they had grown up in a cultural environment of extravagance, luxury, self-indulgence, and profound social stratification. Wealthy Romans were not only rich but were expected to flaunt, to parade their wealth as a sign of their standing, power, and prestige. In *Reading Scripture with the Church Fathers*, I introduced readers to the Roman emperor Vitellius, formerly the male prostitute of Tiberius, an avid gambler, master of ceremonies for Nero's debut on the Roman stage, and notorious glutton. Suetonius describes a feast given by Vitellius's brother to celebrate the emperor's entry into Rome, an emperor whose reign lasted only eight months:

> 2,000 magnificent fish and 7,000 game birds are said to have been served. Yet even this hardly compares in luxuriousness with a single tremendously large dish which Vitellius dedicated to the goddess Minerva and named "Shield of Minerva the Protectress." The recipe called for pike-livers, pheasant-brains, peacock-brains, flamingo-tongues, and lamprey-milt; and the ingredients, collected in every corner of the empire from the Parthian frontier to the Spanish Strait (Straits of Gibraltar), were brought to Rome by warships.[9]

Though Vitellius's tastes were extravagant and viewed as such by many in the Roman elite, they reflect Roman society's admiration for wealth as a status marker, the first and most important sign of power and prestige. It is important, too, to note that while the vast majority of ancient Christians were severely to moderately poor, extremely wealthy Christians were peppered throughout Christian congregations in both the West and East. The wealthy Christian lived in both the church and the upper echelons of the Roman world; to navigate both environments well was a challenging task, one with both great opportunities and great temptations.

Consider the example of Melania the Younger. Melania, a wealthy Roman matron, received an annual income of 120,000 gold solidi; a single *solidus* "was a solid drop of gold. In the reign of Constantine, a pound of gold yielded seventy-two gold coins." Melania's annual income, then, was equivalent to around 1,660 pounds of gold.[10] Melania was an extremely generous person, yet toward the end of her life she related the tempting vision she once received of her vast wealth, a mental picture she believed was inspired by the devil. "The inner chambers of her palace, where a part of her wealth had been stored in the form of gold coins and ingots of pure gold, prior to distribution to the poor, had seemed to shimmer with an unearthly glow. A thought sent from the Devil crossed her mind at that moment. How could *any* kingdom—even the kingdom of heaven—equal such wealth?"[11]

Melania's vision—one she considered demonic—reflects a fundamental ambivalence toward wealth that we will encounter in many of the church fathers and ancient Christian communities. Christians rarely considered wealth as inherently evil. In Melania's case, wealth was a wonderful blessing. It could be distributed to the poor; she was an extremely generous woman and gave away the equivalent of millions of dollars over her lifetime. Yet in a heartbeat—as Melania clearly understood—the desire to use wealth for good purposes could morph into a love for money in and of itself.

To be Roman and rich was to naturally parade one's wealth before others. "To be rich was not simply to have an income. It was to advertise the fact, all the time, in as assertive and as visible a manner as possible. To possess and to show *splendor*—éclat—was what being rich was all about. To be poor (whether as an unsuccessful professor, an impoverished country gentleman, or a pauper—it was all the same) was to lose this éclat."[12]

Should we be terribly surprised to find wealthy Christians imitating these Roman cultural patterns—and churches accommodating their desire to do so? The Christian elite had much to give and often did so. Brown observes, "Christian women from the aristocracy could load a church with silk veils and altar coverings made from textiles from her private wardrobe. A noble woman could finance the foundation of an entire basilica in the middle of Rome through the sale of her jewelry alone."[13] Yet wealthy Christians often expected to be recognized publicly for their generosity.

During Sunday worship services wealthy Christian benefactors walked up the aisle to present their gifts on "special tables placed near the altar. The deacons would bring these offerings to the altar to be offered to God with a moment of thanks and blessing by the priest." At this moment of thanks, "the names of those who brought donations would be read aloud to the acclamations of the congregation."[14] Sharing between rich and poor was indeed occurring, but within the larger context of ingrained Roman communal habit patterns, some of which supported Christian values, while others severely undercut them.

We find wealthy Christians not only donating significant gifts to the church, but also sponsoring—with an enormous expenditure of funds—secular events such as the extremely popular Roman games. Christian noble families sometimes "presided at the Circus Maximus and the Colosseum over spectacles that were as thrilling, as cruel, and as calculated to cause the raw, pre-Christian adrenalin of worship for the city and the empire to flow in their veins as were those laid on by any pagan family," information we obtain through examining the bronze tokens coined for these events.[15]

Augustine comments on similar events in Carthage, funded by wealthy Christian families:

> Puffed up with pride . . . they even wish to lose their fortunes by giving—giving to actresses, giving to cabaret artists, giving to wild-beast hunters, giving to charioteers. They pour forth not only their inherited resources, but their very souls. They draw back with disgust from the poor, because the People do not shout for the poor to receive largesse. But the People roar for the *venator*—the matador—to have his prize. . . . Crazy expenditure is treated as a source of glory and works of [Christian] mercy—*opera misericordiae*—are held in derision.[16]

A CASE STUDY: CHRYSOSTOM'S SERMONS ON THE RICH MAN AND LAZARUS

St. John Chrysostom was well aware of the constant danger of spiritual viruses infecting the bloodstream of his congregation, both in Antioch and later as he served as bishop in Constantinople. While a priest in Antioch, Chrysostom preached a series of sermons on Jesus' parable of the rich man and Lazarus, sermons designed to rebuke a troubling tendency in his parishioners to miscalculate what was of lasting value. These sermons provide some of Chrysostom's richest insights on the issue of wealth, greed, and poverty, and they are worth exploring in some detail. As we do so, we will weave in the insights of other church fathers on the key points Chrysostom is making.[17]

Chrysostom begins the first sermon in the series by moving quickly to the heart of the matter, "the condemnation of luxurious living." For, John states, "As long as this feast [Saturnalia] continues, and the devil goes on wounding the souls of the drunkards with drink, our duty is to go on applying the remedies."[18] Chrysostom directs his congregation to Jesus' parable of the rich man and Lazarus—found in Luke 16:19-31—a story that vividly demonstrates the dangers of luxury and self-indulgence.

The blindness of the rich man. What was the wickedness of the rich man? How had he reached such a place of deep moral blindness? What had created such striking dead zones in his soul? How could he so easily pass by the suffering of Lazarus? For one thing, the rich man had not been "tested by any misfortune, but everything flowed to him as if from a fountain." His wickedness was manifested in a lifestyle of indulgence and self-centeredness; he himself experienced little "distress" or "disturbance."

The curse of his undisturbed, pampered life was the rich man's blindness to human need and suffering, right before his very nose. He simply didn't see Lazarus lying in utter destitution at his gate. Lazarus was invisible to him.[19] Jerome, a contemporary of Chrysostom, makes a similar point on the same parable, sharply commenting that the social distance between Lazarus and the rich man was no excuse for the rich man's blindness and insensitivity.

> Lazarus was lying at the gate in order to draw attention to the cruelty paid to the body and to prevent the rich man from saying, "I did not notice him. He was in a corner. *I could not see him.* No one an-

nounced him to me." He lay at the gate. You saw him every time you went out and every time you came in. When your crowds of servants and clients were attending you, he lay there full of ulcers.[20]

If the rich man's wealth, comfort, and security blinded him to Lazarus, an abject case of tremendous human need, whom else was the rich man overlooking? If Lazarus could not move him to pity, who possibly could? A carefree, comfortable existence had hardened the rich man's heart and blinded his eyes.

Cyprian, writing over a hundred years before Chrysostom, identifies the same blinding effect of riches on human perceptions. "You that are rich cannot do good works in the church, because your eyes, saturated with blackness and covered with the shadows of night, *do not see* the needy and poor."[21]

Less than human. The rich man's behavior is beastlike rather than human. Who would have imagined that a comfortable, undisturbed life could transform a human being—God's image bearer—into a ravening beast? Chrysostom repeatedly accentuates the rich man's savage, beastly nature. The rich man was a "savage man." He had locked up his heart. Rather than his own good fortune nurturing a concern for others, "that man was not improved by his prosperity, but remained beastly, or rather he surpassed the cruelty and inhumanity of any beast in his behavior."[22] As Chrysostom expresses in his homilies on the Gospel of Matthew, "He who lives for himself only and overlooks all others, is useless, he is not even a man, he does not belong to the human race."[23]

Lactantius, writing many years before Chrysostom delivered his sermons, also warns against the dehumanizing, beastly character of selfishness, cruelty, and greed.

Therefore, men who harm other men, men who spoil, torture, kill, exterminate others against human kindness and every right, should be considered as ferocious beasts. Because of this bond of brotherhood, God teaches us always to do good, never evil. He himself tells us what to do good means: to aid the lowly and the unfortunate, to give food to the needy. Because God is merciful, he wishes that men should live in society and that we should see in each human being our own nature. We do not deserve to be set free in dangers if we do not help others; we do not deserve aid if we refuse it to others.[24]

Basil the Great, a contemporary of John Chrysostom, graphically describes both the horror of starvation and the ferocious, beastly nature of those who can pass by easily and uncaringly those suffering so terribly.

> The pain of starvation, from which the hungry die, is a horrible suffering. Of all human calamities, famine is the principal one, and the most miserable of deaths is, no doubt, that by starvation. . . . Hunger . . . is a slow torture which prolongs the pain; it is an infirmity well established and hidden in its place, a death always present and never coming to an end. . . . The flesh clings like a cobweb. The skin has no color. . . . The belly is hollow, contracted, formless, without weight, without the natural stretching of the viscera, joined to the bones of the back. Now, what punishment should not be inflicted upon *the one who passes by such a body?* What cruelty can surpass that? How can we not count him among the fiercest of fierce beasts and consider him as a sacrilegious person and a murderer? The person who can cure such an infirmity and because of avarice refuses his medicine, can with reason be condemned as a murderer.[25]

With one voice the church fathers declare that to fail to *see* and to *respond* to human need is indeed to act in an inhuman, animal-like fashion. Gregory of Nyssa pictures such behavior as worse than that of wolves and wild dogs:

> But if one man should seek to be absolute possessor of all, refusing even a third or a fifth to his brothers, then he is a cruel tyrant, a savage with whom there can be no dealing, an *insatiate beast*

gloatingly shutting its jaws over the meal it will not share. Or rather he is more ruthless than any beast; wolf does not drive wolf from the prey, and a pack of dogs will tear the same carcass; this man in his limitless greed will not admit one fellow-creature to a share in his riches.[26]

Don't judge by appearances. The rich man, if one judges by appearances, possesses all he could possibly need. He has a "ship full" of valuable cargo, but because he lacks "discretion," does not understand how to unload it. Oblivious to the perils surrounding him, he is sailing full speed into disaster. "The rich man had his ship full of merchandise, and it sailed before the wind. But do not be surprised: he was hastening to shipwreck, since he refused to unload his cargo with discretion."[27] *What is discretion?*

In all likelihood, Chrysostom has a specific monastic virtue in mind, one that Jason Byassee describes as "knowing how to apply what spiritual teaching to whom and in what way." A person of discretion, in this specifically Christian sense, is much like a physician. "She must know all the potential cures at her disposal, with all the technical skill necessary to know their possible applications. But medicine is not formulaic. She must also know how to 'read' her patients, to know what should be applied and how."[28]

Discretion is a specific virtue, a gift of the Holy Spirit that enables God's image bearer to discern how the Spirit is moving in a specific situation or particular human life. Discretion, indeed, is linked to seeing, to discerning, to interpreting the meaning of a situation well and then responding accordingly. Chrysostom faults the rich man for failing to discern or understand why he has been given his wealth by God. He is not perceiving his situation well. He is blind, not only to Lazarus lying in front of him every day, *but to the purpose of what God has given him.*

It is this lack of discernment—a dead zone in the rich man's optic nerve—that causes the rich man's foolish, unreflective response to God's blessing on his life. As Clement of Alexandria puts it, the foolish rich don't know "how to use the good things given them."[29] The rich man never asks, "Why was I given this wealth? Why has God blessed me in this way? To what purpose? For what reason?" Instead, he lives on the surface of things, never discerning possibilities God is offering daily, if only he had eyes to see. By all appearances he is blessed, but his blessing mutates into a curse through his lack of discretion.[30] Again, Clement hits the center of the target: "Wealth, like a snake, twisting in the grasp . . . can cling to the hand and bite unless a man rises superior to it and uses it with discretion."[31]

By way of contrast, at first glance the situation of Lazarus appears absolutely horrific, but Chrysostom believes a closer, penetrating, discerning look will unveil hidden blessings. Though Lazarus "endured chastisements nine in number," the purpose of these hardships was not to punish but to lead to glory.

Each chastisement or discipline is worth a closer look. The benefit of each is not immediately discernible, yet Chrysostom argues that each discipline plays a specific role in the spiritual formation of Lazarus's character. The "chastisements" are not punishments; Lazarus has done nothing wrong for which his poverty is a punishment from God. Rather, these disciplines are learning tools, concrete means God is using to hone and shape Lazarus's praiseworthy character. To judge solely on the basis of appearances would be to respond without discretion, to misread his situation. Just as the rich man misunderstood the meaning of his wealth, so Lazarus would misunderstand the meaning of his poverty.

Nine disciplines. The first discipline in Lazarus's life is *poverty itself.* Chrysostom acknowledges openly that poverty "is truly a dreadful thing, as everyone knows who has experienced it; for no words can describe how great the anguish is which those endure who live as beggars without knowing wisdom."[32] The last phrase, "without knowing wisdom," is an essential qualifier for Chrysostom, as it is for the church fathers in general. While poverty is dreadful, a wise disposition can glean fruit from its bitter stem. As we will see, *how to form this disposition* occupies much patristic reflection.

The second discipline is *Lazarus's illness*, a sickness Chrysostom describes in vivid terms: "Lazarus was so much weakened that he could not even shoo the dogs away, but he lay like a living corpse, watching them coming without strength to protect himself from them." In Lazarus's case, poverty and sickness have linked hands, multiplying his suffering: "if each of these by itself is dreadful and unbearable, when they are woven together, is he not a man of steel who can endure them?"[33]

The third discipline? *Loneliness*. Lazarus is an invisible man, seen by no one. Day after day he lies at the rich man's gate in full public view, but invisible and unrecognized by the surrounding world. "For if he had endured such sufferings and been neglected while lying in a desert and uninhabited place, he would not have felt so much distress." To be present in a public place, but to be unnoticed and ignored—as though one did not exist—daily multiplies Lazarus's agony.

Human presence but lack of care represents Lazarus's fourth discipline. People were "present but unwilling to stretch out a hand. . . . For there was no one to console him with a word or comfort him with a deed, no friend, neighbor, or relative, not even any onlooker, since the rich man's whole household was corrupt."[34]

Not only was Lazarus suffering, but he was *forced to observe daily the good fortune of others*, and *the comparison hurt*. Here is Lazarus's fifth discipline. Chrysostom insists that Lazarus is neither "envious" or "wicked." He is simply human. "We all naturally perceive our own misfortunes more acutely by comparison with others' prosperity."[35] Such comparison, natural though it is, became even more painful when Lazarus *observed the wicked lifestyle of the rich man*, a sixth discipline. The wicked rich man continued to prosper, while the situation of the virtuous Lazarus only appeared to get worse.

> For if the man had been just, if he had been good, if he had been admirable, if he had been laden with every virtue, he would not have grieved Lazarus; but since he lived in wickedness, and had reached the height of evil, and was demonstrating such inhuman-

ity, and treated him like an enemy, and passed him by like a stone shamelessly and mercilessly, and in spite of this all enjoyed such affluence: think how he was likely to sink the poor man's soul as if with a series of waves.[36]

Chrysostom's analysis of Lazarus's situation is not yet finished. Lazarus's seventh discipline is related to his deep loneliness. The misery of invisible suffering is amplified by *the lack of fellow sufferers*. "He could not observe another Lazarus. We, for our part, even if we suffer a multitude of troubles, can at least gain sufficient comfort and enjoy consolation from looking at him. . . . But he could not see anyone else who had suffered the same trials as he had. . . . This is enough to darken one's soul."[37]

Chrysostom then compares Lazarus's suffering to that of the Christian. While Christ's suffering disciple can cling to the hope of the resurrection with its attendant glories, *Lazarus's Jewish perspective drastically limited his hope*. "He believed that the present situation was closed within the present life; for he was one of those who lived before the time of grace. . . . What was he likely to feel, deprived even of this anchor? He could not yet practice any such wisdom because the time had not yet come for these teachings."[38]

As if the first eight disciplines were not enough, Chrysostom adds a ninth. Chrysostom knew well how quickly people pass judgment on the sick, poor, and needy. *Day by day the reputation of Lazarus "was slandered by foolish people."* If Lazarus is suffering, it must be because he has done something wrong and deserved the punishment he is receiving. "For most people, when they see someone in hunger, chronic illness, and the extremes of misfortune, do not even allow him a good reputation, but judge his life by his troubles, and think that he is surely in such misery because of wickedness." For example, "if this man were dear to God, He would not have left him to suffer in poverty and the other troubles. This is what happened both to Job and to Paul." Job's foolish counselors quickly attributed suffering to "the penalty of sin and transgression." In a similar fashion, Paul's snakebite on Malta was viewed by many as a sign of God's judgment and wrath.[39]

Hidden blessings and punishments. A major tenet of Chrysostom's overarching perspective toward poverty, sickness, evil, and God's providence is that *appearances are deceptive*. While the rich man seems the fortunate party and Lazarus the unfortunate, the reality of the situation is quite different. Think, for instance, of the future. Even if the rich man experiences one thousand years of prosperity on earth, what is this compared to the vast reaches of eternity and the fate that awaits him there?

The logic of Chrysostom's spiritual mathematics magnifies the rich man's disadvantage when compared to Lazarus. In the rich man's future punishment and infinity loom. "As a little drop is to the boundless sea, so much a thousand years are to that future glory and enjoyment. What would one need to say more than that it has no limit and knows no end; and as much as dreams differ from the truth of reality, so much this condition differs from that hereafter?"[40]

Not only will the future punishment of the rich man more than balance accounts, but the rich man is actually already suffering beneath the disguise his wealth afforded him. For, unseen to others, the rich man's conscience continued to torment him. Indeed, Chrysostom teaches, the human conscience is an "imperial throne," an internal "courtroom" in which we all sit as our own juror.

All the time that Lazarus lay on the rich man's doorstep, God carefully observed the "inner dramas" at play within the rich man's mental and moral world as his conscience, his interior moral compass, judged his insensitive lifestyle. To return to the image of the conscience as courtroom and jury, "There is no way to corrupt that court. Even if we do not seek virtue, we still suffer anguish, when we are not seeking it; and if we seek evil, we still experience the anguish when we cease from the pleasure of the sin."[41]

Chrysostom repeats that the spiritually discerning person will refuse to be deceived by appearances as he views the respective situation of Lazarus and the rich man. Though Lazarus's body was covered with sores, his soul was "more precious than any gold—or rather not his soul only, but also his body." How so?

> A person is not loathsome if he has this kind of wounds on his body, but if he has a multitude of sores on his soul and takes no care of them. Such was that rich man, full of sores within. Just as the dogs licked the wounds of the poor man, so demons licked the sins of the rich man; and just as the poor man lived in starvation of nourishment, so the rich man lived in starvation of virtue.[42]

What is the meaning of Lazarus's poverty? At this juncture we come to a crucial aspect of Chrysostom's understanding of God's providence and its relationship to the issue of wealth and poverty. The larger lens provided by God's providential ordering of human affairs helps us avoid premature judgments concerning Lazarus's poverty and illness.

We would be wrong to view his struggles as a sign of God's displeasure and lack of love. Though Lazarus is materially poor, God's love is embracing him in the form of cleansing, stringent discipline. If we take a wider view, especially remembering the reality of the future judgment and the reversals that will occur there, we realize that Lazarus is actually the object of divine care. Yes, Lazarus is suffering, but consider the situation of a prosperous criminal. He lies in wait for the unsuspecting and grows rich on his dishonest gain. Would you willingly change places with him? Perhaps, if we judge on the basis of appearances alone. We would never deem a criminal genuinely prosperous, Chrysostom argues, if we remember that the boundaries of God's perspective and action *are not limited to this life.* "Nevertheless we do not call him [the thief] fortunate because of his present visible goods, but we call him miserable because of his future expected sufferings."[43] What is visible or mere appearance, then, is often illusory. This is a common patristic insight.

Highway robbery. Chrysostom is convinced that when the wealthy ignore the plight of the weak and poor, they are no better than the highway robbers they themselves would like to see prosecuted. The key question is this: Has God provided the rich with their wealth to facilitate lives of blind, cruel self-indulgence? Hardly. Chrysostom warns that the rich man has failed to ask why God has given him his wealth in the first place. Greediness, our dark response to God's material blessing of our lives, has blinded the rich man from discerning broader possibilities for the money God has entrusted to him; there are greater needs to meet than his own desire for security and self-indulgence. Greed's myopic vision focuses solely on its own small, self-centered world. The result? Highway robbery. Chrysostom states:

> Let us not therefore call them fortunate because of what they have, but miserable because of what will come, because of that dreadful courtroom, because of the inexorable judgment, because of the outer darkness which awaits them. Indeed, robbers often have escaped the hands of men; nevertheless, even knowing this, we would have prayed both for ourselves and for our enemies to avoid that life with its cursed affluences.[44]

Chrysostom makes similar points in his comments on Jesus' depiction of the rich fool in Luke 12. What characterizes the rich fool's foolishness? He never entertains the possibility that his full barns—God's blessing on his life—have been given to him for the sake of others rather than only himself. He foolishly, undiscerningly responds to divine blessing by immediately forming plans to build bigger barns. He will hoard what he has been given. And, from his perspective, the hoarding will provide safety and security. "There is nothing more wretched than such an attitude," Chrysostom exclaims to his congregation. "In truth he took down his barns; for the safe barns are not walls *but the stomachs of the poor*. He who had neglected these did not need to concern himself about walls."[45]

Wealth, poverty, and God's providence. In Chrysostom's sermons, neither wealth in itself nor poverty in itself is a blessing or curse. Blessing or cursing *depends on our response* to God's providence at work in our lives. We must avoid "thinking that wealth is worth anything without virtue," just as we must not think that poverty in itself "is any evil."[46]

These are tough words to accept, at least at first glance. Is not poverty inherently evil? Chrysostom, one of the greatest bishops in the history of the church in terms of his unremitting concern for the poor, answers *no*. Our response to poverty is what will determine the issue. Will those of us who are poor allow our poverty to be a means to draw closer to Christ in our dependence on him? Can we faithfully embrace the discipline of poverty as a means of cultivating patience, perseverance, and other virtuous gifts of the Spirit? Likewise, will those of us who are rich have eyes to see that our wealth is entrusted to us by God to alleviate the suffering of the poor? Just as Chrysostom is persuaded that poverty can be a teaching tool used by God for higher purposes, so he is convinced that everything possible must be done to alleviate poverty and its accompanying horrors.

Chrysostom repeats a fundamental principle that all the church fathers readily affirmed: "Let us learn from this man not to call the rich lucky nor the poor unfortunate." Rather, Chrysostom urges us, look more carefully at the reactions of human beings to circumstances of wealth and poverty, responses largely determined by the character of each person. "For we are accustomed to judge poverty and affluence by the disposition of the mind, not by the measure of one's substance."[47] In a word, how are we responding to what God is providentially allowing us to experience? What kind of people are we? Are we reading the world and God's providence well? Has our character been formed and shaped into Christ's image, with accompanying mental, emotional, bodily, and spiritual perspectives and practices that aid us in making sense of our world and what God is asking of us? Are we—am I—habitually responding to my circumstances as Christ responded to his, with a disposition of trust, dependence, receptivity, perseverance, and acceptance? "If you do not believe that poverty is productive of great wealth, think of the poverty of Jesus and you will be persuaded otherwise."[48]

Genuine poverty. Chrysostom warns against the danger of misreading what genuine poverty is. He insists that material poverty is an indifferent matter, much as a Stoic philosopher would, but frames his understanding of "indifference" within a broader and deeper Christian perspective. A poor person, for instance, may still be consumed "by many desires." Are we going to respond to our poverty with trust in God's provision or with a lack of faith? Chromatius of Aquileia comments: "Some who have no worldly resources continue in sin and live without faith in God."[49] Or, as Ambrose puts it, "For what does it do me to lack worldly goods, unless I am meek and gentle?"[50]

In turn, a person "who possesses many things" might well be the poorest of all, if the black hole of greed has darkened his vision of the surrounding world's needs. It is one thing to possess many things. It is another to wrap one's heart and mind around them. Clement of Alexandria notices that the rich man's sin is not the possession of wealth. It is "his notions about wealth, his excitement and morbid feeling about it, the anxieties, which are the thorns of existence, which choke the seed of life."[51]

Here Clement, like Chrysostom, draws on a Stoic commonplace and infuses it with Christian meaning. Wealth itself is an "indifferent thing" that becomes a good or evil depending on how it is used.[52]

Insatiable desire. Chrysostom is an expert in diagnosing and analyzing *the neurotics of insatiable desire*. Think, for example, of someone whose thirst can never be quenched. The moment he drinks a glass of water, his thirst returns.

> Just as we would not call a person healthy who was always thirsty, even if he enjoyed abundance, even if he lived by rivers and springs (for what is that luxuriance of water, when the thirst remains unquenchable?), let us do the same in the case of wealthy people: let us never consider those people healthy who are always yearning and thirsting after other people's property.[53]

Pity rather than envy of such a person is the fitting response. Surely, Chrysostom believes, there must be something disordered about such a person's life and perspective. How, Chrysostom asks, could a person suffering from greed ever become genuinely affluent? How would a greedy soul ever recognize when it has attained true wealth? "For if one cannot control his own greed, even if he has appropriated everyone's property, how can he ever be affluent?" Likewise, Ambrose writes, "The more you have, the more you want, and however much you win, in your own eyes you are poor still. *Rapacity is not quenched by gain; it is fanned the more. . . .* Holy Scripture shows us how wretchedly poor a rich man may be, how abject a beggar he may be."[54]

The great reversal. Ironically, the rich man had lived his life of luxury as within "a dream." Reality—the true state of affairs—snapped on him at the moment of death like a steel trap. Whereas Lazarus had frequently begged for a drop of water during his lifetime of suffering, it is now the rich man who assumes the role of the supplicant. "The situation was reversed," Chrysostom comments, "and everyone learned who was really the rich man and was really the poor man, and that Lazarus was the most affluent of all but the other was the poorest of all." Chrysostom draws on the actor's craft to accentuate his point. "For just as on the stage actors enter with the masks of kings, generals, doctors, teachers, professors, and soldiers, without themselves being anything of the sort, so in the present life poverty and wealth are only masks."[55] *Don't judge on the basis of appearances.*

The danger of deception. The present life, Chrysostom preaches, is much like a theater. As we look at the actors on the stage, we "see many rich people." Yet we don't "think that they are truly rich, but that they are wearing the masks of rich people." If the actor portraying a rich merchant were to take off his mask, he would quickly be identified by the audience as the local butcher or "coppersmith." *Mere appearances are always deceptive.* "Just as that man who acts the part of king or general on the stage often turns out to be a household servant or somebody who sells figs or grapes in the market, so also the rich man often turns out to be the poorest of all."[56] Poor in terms of material possessions? No, but surely poor in terms of virtue. Crack open the conscience of many rich people, Chrysostom is convinced, and you will uncover only withered remains, an internal destitution revealed at the moment of death and judgment.

The clarity of the age to come. Death, the afterlife, and the guarantee of divine judgment will reveal matters as they truly are. The time for playacting will have passed. No more masks. No more disguises. No more assumed roles. In the age to come *appearance and reality will correspond exactly.*

> Just as in the theater, when evening falls and the audience departs, and the kings and generals go outside to remove the costumes of their roles, they are revealed to everyone thereafter appearing to be exactly what they are; so also now when death arrives and the theater is dissolved, everyone puts off the masks of wealth or poverty and departs to the other world. When all are judged by their deeds alone, some are revealed truly wealthy, others poor, some of high class, others of no account.[57]

How different things will appear in the age to come! Whereas the rich man had every imaginable need and desire fulfilled in this present age, in the future even his desire for a drop of water will be denied. Here is genuine poverty, "so poor indeed that he was not master even of a drop of water, but had to beg for this and did not even obtain it by begging."[58]

Spiritual myopia and its sad effects. The issue of "seeing" frequently appears in Chrysostom's thoughts on the relationship between the rich man and Lazarus. One of the rich man's great sins is his failure to see Lazarus lying at his gate. Only in the afterlife does he actually see Lazarus, and then it is too late. "When Lazarus was near, he used to ignore him, and now when he is distant he calls to him. The man whom he did not see as often as he went in and out, now he sees clearly when he is far away."[59]

Why the striking lack of attention on the rich man's part while he was still alive? He had apparently decided that Lazarus's life and condition had little to teach him. What could possibly be learned from such a poor, miserable, unfortunate life? "Yes," the rich man seems to say to himself. "I'll admit that Lazarus has led a virtuous life. But where has his virtue got him?" "Why do I need piety and virtue? Everything flows to me as if from a fountain; I enjoy great abundance and great prosperity.

I do not endure any misfortune. Why should I seek virtue? This poor man who lives in righteousness and piety nevertheless suffers a multitude of troubles."[60]

The rich man settles unreflectively into the self-indulgent softness of the present moment, never considering the possibility that the circumference of reality's boundaries is much wider than he had ever dreamed. The future awaits. And when it finally, inexorably arrives, it includes the sudden realization that while Lazarus will enjoy great prosperity, the rich man will suffer continually. Wealth and comfort have blinded the rich man to the lesson God providentially sent to him in the life of Lazarus. "I sent the poor man Lazarus to your gate to teach you virtue and to receive your love; you ignored this benefit and declined to use his assistance toward your salvation."[61]

A CATALOGUE OF SIN

The rich man is guilty of a serious catalogue of sin, including theft. Not only Chrysostom but the fathers in general insist that to possess the means to help the poor and needy but to fail to do so is a form of theft. "See the man and his works: indeed this also is theft, not to share one's possessions. . . . The failure to share one's goods with others is theft and swindle and defraudation."[62]

Interestingly, early Christian texts indicate that *both those who give and those who receive may be guilty of theft. All depends on the issue of need.* In the Didache, sometimes dated as early as the late first century AD, those who receive from others are warned they should not accept gifts if their need is not genuine. "But woe to the receiver! If he receives because he is in need, he is guiltless. But if he is not in need, he will be required to show why he received and for what purpose."[63] The Shepherd of Hermas also warns those who receive that they will be held accountable. "Those who have received will give an account to God why they received and for what purpose. For, those who receive because they are in need will not be judged, but those who receive under false pretenses will be punished."[64]

The Didache also teaches that those who have more than enough bear a clear obligation to the poor. "Never turn away the needy; share all your possessions with your brother, and call nothing your own. If you and he share what is immortal in common, how much more should you share what is mortal!"[65] Sufficiency is the qualifying marker. That is, if your basic needs have been met and you have money remaining, that money has been given to you by God for a specific purpose, that of meeting the needs of others.

Such a perspective makes sense, the writer of the Shepherd of Hermas believes, when we remember that the Christian is simply a pilgrim headed toward home. Why would a pilgrim plant deep roots in a foreign land, as though she had already reached her final destination?

> Be careful therefore, while you live in a foreign land, not to acquire anything more than an adequate sufficiency. . . . Instead of fields, then, buy souls that suffer tribulation, according to your ability. . . . Spend your wealth and all your possessions you have received from the Lord on this kind of fields and houses. It is for this purpose that the Master has made you wealthy, to perform this ministry for him.[66]

Ambrose says much the same thing to a fourth-century AD audience. "Wealth is redemption if one uses it well; it is a snare if one does not know how to use it. For what is a man's money if not provision for his journey?" The Christian's journey home does not require an extravagant allowance. *Moderation will suffice.* "A great amount is a burden; a moderate sum is sufficient. We are pilgrims in this life; many are walking along, but we must make a good journey in order to have Christ as our fellow-traveler who spent his life on earth doing good."[67]

THE KEY QUESTION OF CHARACTER

Both Clement of Alexandria and Chrysostom recognize that the mere possession of wealth is not the fundamental problem facing the Christian. Yet, wealth is indeed dangerous and must be handled with care, much like a black mamba. The more fundamental issue, though, concerns human character. As Clement frames things, does the wealthy Christian possess the requisite virtue—in this case discretion—to handle wealth safely and sanely?

Issues of spiritual formation and the cultivation of Christian virtues are crucially linked to the possession and wise use of money. For instance, Clement asks why Jesus commands the rich young ruler to give away all his possessions if he is to follow Christ (cf. Mk 10:17-23). Is the young man's wealth the problem? Or the young man's character? Clement clearly believes it was the latter.

The young man's refusal to part with his possessions points to deeper character flaws that Christ desired to heal. Christ's command is "not, as some hastily interpret it, a command that he should throw away what he possesses and renounce his wealth. What he is told to banish from his soul are his notions about wealth, his attachment to it, his excessive desire for it, his morbid excitement over it, and his anxieties—those thorns of existence which choke the seed of true life."[68]

Clement wisely comments that to be poor is no guarantee of personal virtue. He points to many Christians who have given away all they possessed, yet remain infected with deep character flaws. "They became arrogant, boastful, vain, and contemptuous of other men, as if they had done something superhuman."[69] In addition, in an insight we will develop in coming pages, if all Christians divest themselves of all wealth through a wooden interpretation of Christ's command, how can the needs of the poor and destitute possibly be cared for? "How could one give food to the hungry, and drink to the thirsty, clothe the naked, and shelter the homeless (and those who fail to do so are threatened with fire and outer darkness), if no one has any of those things himself?"[70]

In an extremely helpful illustration, Clement compares wealth to a musical instrument. If you possess the skill to play the instrument well, you will produce wondrous melodies and harmonies. If you lack the musician's talent, a cacophony will result.

Wealth is an instrument of this kind. If you are able to make a right use of it, then it will serve justice. If it is wrongly used, then it will serve injustice. For its nature is to serve, not to rule. . . . So what is to be destroyed is not one's possessions but the passions of the soul, which hinder the right use of one's property. By thus becoming virtuous and good, a man will be able to make good use of his riches.[71]

THE CHRISTIAN AS STEWARD

The fathers consistently view all Christians—rich or poor—as stewards of their possessions rather than owners. Only God rightfully owns anything. Basil, commenting on the rich fool of Luke 12, states that "what ails his soul is much what ails the glutton, who would burst with cramming rather than give the poor any of his leftovers." What is the rich fool's fundamental problem? *A short memory.*

Man, remember who gives you these goods. And remember yourself—who you are, what you are steward of, from whom you had it, why you have been favored above most. You have been made the minister of a gracious God, steward for your fellow-servants. Do not suppose that all these things were provided for your belly. The wealth you handle belongs to others; think of it accordingly. Not for long will it delight you; soon it will slip from you and be gone, and you will be asked to give a strict account of it.[72]

Tertullian, writing years before Basil, makes similar points. "Even what seems to be our own belongs to another, for nothing is our own, since all things belong to God to whom, we, too, belong. Therefore, if we feel impatient when we suffer some loss, we show that we entertain a love for money, since we grieve for the loss of what is not our own."[73] Cyprian, another North African father, echoes Tertullian's sentiments and encourages his congregation to become imitators of God's justice. Whatever God possesses is given to human beings for the use of all, rather than a select few. Divine goodness and generosity should be reflected between God's image bearers.

This is truly to become a child of God by spiritual birth; this is to imitate God's justice by the heavenly law. For whatever belongs to God, is for the common use of all, nor is anyone excluded from his benefits and gifts, nor is the human race prevented from equally enjoying God's goodness and generosity. Whoever owns property and follows this example of equity, sharing his returns and fruits to his brothers and showing himself fair and just with his gratuitous bounties, is an imitator of God.[74]

Gregory of Nyssa also highlights the need to imitate the divine perspective and is saddened by how often we succumb to selfishness's temptations. "God himself is the prime author of beneficence, the rich and generous provider of all that we need. But we, who are taught in Scripture's every syllable to copy our Lord and Maker in so far as the mortal may imitate the divine and immortal—we snatch everything to our own enjoyment."[75]

THE QUESTION OF PRIVATE PROPERTY

The church fathers often demonstrate a deep suspicion of private property, though most were willing to live with the pitfalls private ownership poses. Many fathers—Chrysostom and Ambrose come to mind—are sure that private ownership inflames greed, foments strife, and leads to envy and violence. Chrysostom writes that "as soon as someone attempts to possess himself of anything to make it his own, then contention is introduced, as if nature itself protests against the fact that, whereas God brings us together in every way, we are eager to divide and separate ourselves by appropriating things, using those cold words 'mine' and 'yours.'"[76]

Ambrose comments similarly on the story of Naboth, observing that the rich too often act as though they alone "dwell on the earth." The gap between rich and poor did not always exist, for originally the earth "was for all in common, meant for the rich and poor alike; what right have you to monopolize the soil?" Ambrose argues that private ownership of agricultural resources goes against the grain of nature itself. "Nature knows nothing of the rich; all are poor when she brings them forth. Clothing and gold and silver, food and drink and covering—we are born without them all; naked she receives her children into the tomb, and no one can enclose his acres there." Among the dead all are equal.

> Who can tell class from class among the dead? Open the earth again and find your rich man if you may; excavate a tomb a short while after, and if you know the man that you see, prove by token that he was poor. The sole difference is that the rich has more to waste away with him; the silken garments and cloth of gold swath-ing his body are lost for the living without helping the dead. Being rich, he has perfumes lavished on him, but that does not stop the stench; he wastes the sweetness that might be used by others and is none the sweeter for it himself. And he leaves behind him heirs to bicker.[77]

Exactly what can we claim before God as our own possession? Basil specifically mentions a common Christian response to the issue of own-ership, one modern Christians might well support: "I am wronging no one. I hold fast to my own, that is all." Basil will have none of this. "You are like a man who takes a seat in a theatre and then keeps out newcom-ers, claiming as his own what is there for the use of everyone."[78]

The key principle for Basil centers on the purpose of our possessions. In a word, why has God chosen to bless us materially? So that we may be-come self-indulgent and greedy, with hearts closed to the needs of those around us? Too often, Basil argues, the rich "seize what belongs to all and claim the right of possession to monopolize it."

Chrysostom, too, in his homilies on 1 Timothy, argues that "wealth is not a possession, it is not property, it is a loan for use."[79] How can we regard something as our own property, Chrysostom asks, if on our death what we possess passes on to others, and on their deaths, to others, ad infinitum? "We are all sojourners," rich or poor. In fact, the tenant of a house is in a more advantageous position than its legal owner. Even if the owner of the house dies, the tenant will continue to occupy it, enjoying it year after year, yet free from worrying about its upkeep. "Property, in fact, is but a word; we are all owners but of other men's possessions."[80]

Chrysostom is utterly convinced that the only property worth keeping is what we take with us into the future, the eternity beyond death's door. "Only the virtues of the soul are properly our own, as almsgiving and charity." "External" goods such as fields and cattle will be ours for only an instant. It is wiser to focus on "internal" goods such as love and kindness. "This is what we should say to our houses and all our goods. Virtue alone is able to depart with us, and to accompany us to the world above."[81]

WHEN IS ENOUGH ENOUGH?

The fundamental principle? "All you might help and do not—to all these you are doing wrong."[82] Basil repeatedly stresses that "goods in and of themselves are not evil." If they were, "they could have in no way been created by God." The problem lies with those who fail to "administer" their goods well. "The one who is condemned is condemned not because he possesses things, but because he makes a bad use of what he possesses."[83]

Of course, the question of enough immediately raises its head. How can we determine when our basic needs have been supplied? How can we discern when wise stewardship has mutated into greed? *When is enough enough?*

Augustine addresses the issue of enough by drawing a distinction between sufficiency and self-indulgence. He supports *those who wish to advance in the world, as long as their ambition is fueled by a desire to* "do good by providing for the welfare of those who live under them." Ambition engendered by "empty pride of self-esteem, or useless ostentation, or hurtful vanity," though, is to be avoided. As for the financial gain that usually accompanies promotion in "rank and authority," Augustine's guideline is "what is sufficient for the necessaries of life." And exactly what is sufficiency? "This sufficiency is not an improper desire in whoever wishes this and nothing more; whoever does wish more does not wish this [simple sufficiency], and therefore does not wish properly."[84]

Generally speaking, the church fathers do not provide detailed codes and laws for answering the question of sufficiency and need. Instead, they spend much more time describing *the kind of person* who can possess and administer goods safely and wisely. Basil speaks of the need for a "detached attitude" for "earthly" possessions combined with a "respect" for what they can accomplish.

The Real Impossibility

Chrysostom goes so far as to say it is "impossible" for a genuine Christian not to care for others. "For as the natural properties of things cannot be made ineffectual, so it is here: the thing is part of the very nature of the Christian. Do not insult God." How so? "To say that the sun cannot shine would be to insult him. To say that a Christian cannot do good is to insult God and call him a liar. For it is easier for the sun not to give heat or not to shine than for the Christian not to send forth light; it is easier for the light to be darkness than for the Christian to be so."[85] *A generous Christian is a genuine Christian.*

For the Christian to fail to respond to the poor is to act unnaturally, an indication that our human nature is unraveling. Under the bondage of covetousness, human beings mutate into "wild beasts," a point Chrysostom made in his first sermon on the rich man and Lazarus. Considerations of "conscience, friendship, or association, or the salvation of their own soul" fall to the wayside as we become the slave of diseased, disordered desires. "Moreover, the dreadful part of this very bitter slavery is that it even persuades them to feel grateful for it, and the more they become enslaved in it, so much the more will the pleasure they take in it increase. As a result, the disease becomes incurable, the beast becomes hard to tame."[86]

Augustine skillfully analyzes the relationship between human character and the possession of wealth. Some people possess the character and associated ability to use wealth wisely. Others do not. Once again, the fault does not lie with wealth itself. "Some men make evil use of these things, and others make good use. And the man who makes evil use clings to them with love and is entangled by them (that is, he becomes subject to those things which ought to be subject to him, and creates for himself goods *whose right and proper use require that he himself be good)."*[87] As a person's character improves, so his possessions "become better because of him."

The wise and loving person's possessions are an extension of himself to those in need. Don't blame wealth itself for the distortions and cruelties its possession sometimes produces. "You do not think, do you, that silver or gold should be blamed because of greedy men, or food and wine because of gluttons and drunkards, or womanly beauty because of adulterers and fornicators? And so on with other things, especially since you may see a doctor use fire well, and the poisoner using bread for his crime."[88]

CHRYSOSTOM'S FRUSTRATION

Chrysostom is particularly frustrated by his congregation because they have allowed their wealth and comfort to shield them from poverty's sharp bite. They lack mercy because they lack the will to identify closely with the poor in their midst. In a biting commentary, Chrysostom compares the predicament of the poor with the comfortable lifestyle of the rich. As evening falls, Chrysostom comments, the poor man moves "about the market place," "not knowing where he is going to spend the night. How can the unhappy fellow sleep, with pangs in the belly, tortured by hunger, while it is freezing and the rain coming down on him?" Meanwhile, the wealthy Christian is "coming home from the bath, clean and dandy, dressed in soft clothes, full of contentment and happiness, and hastening to sit down to splendidly prepared dinners."

Something is terribly wrong with this situation. "When therefore, you have returned home, when you lie down on your couch, when the lights around your house shine bright, when your table is well prepared and plentiful, at that time remember that poor miserable man wandering about like dogs in the alleys, in darkness and in mire."

His bed for the night will be a lonely one. No house. No wife. Only a "pile of straw, like those dogs which we hear baying all through the night."[89] *Self-indulgence has strangled mercy.* The will to help, Gregory of

Nyssa's definition of mercy, has been suffocated by self-indulgent comfort and culpable separation from the poor.

MERCY'S FUNDAMENTAL PARADIGM

Gregory of Nazianzus points his audience to the incarnation of the Son of God as the fundamental paradigm for mercy toward the poor. The genuine Christian is the disciple of "the meek and merciful Christ who carried upon himself our infirmities." In the incarnation, the Son of God humbled himself to the extent of "assuming our human condition and made himself poor to clothe himself with our flesh and dwell in this earthly tent . . . so that we might be enriched by his divinity."[90] *We are called to imitate the pattern of our Lord.* If Christ is humble, merciful, and compassionate, so must be his apprentice. In turn, our vision and field of action will widen. People we habitually overlook, much like the rich man blindly passed by Lazarus each day, will assume form and shape.[91]

CHRIST AMONG THE POOR

Gregory takes matters a step further. Not only does the incarnation of the Son of God concretely demonstrate God's love for the poor, the helpless, and the vulnerable, but *Christ is uniquely discovered among the poor.* As Origen observes, when we clothe the naked, "we have woven a garment for the cold and shivering Christ."[92]

At the last judgment, Gregory believes, many will be judged who have never committed adultery or theft. Their judgment will be based not on what they have done, but on what they have failed to do. They have failed "to care for Christ himself in the person of the poor."

> While there is still time, let us visit Christ, let us take care of Christ, let us feed Christ, let us welcome Christ, let us honor Christ, not only by inviting him to our table, as some have done (Lk 7:36), not only with ointments, like Mary (Jn 12:3), not only with burial, like Joseph of Arimathea. . . . No, the Lord of the universe asks for mercy rather than thousands of lambs. Offer them to him, then, through the poor and those who are spread through-

out the earth, so that, when we leave this world, we will be welcomed by them into the eternal dwelling with the same Christ, our Lord, to whom be glory forever and ever. Amen.[93]

To fail to recognize Christ in the poor is to eviscerate the fundamental message of the gospel and to cripple the church's witness to the broader watching world. Why should the pagan world accept Christ's gospel, Chrysostom asks, if Christ's own body, the church, lives as though this present world is its permanent residence? "This is the reason why the pagans do not believe what we say. Our actions and our works are the demonstrations which they are willing to receive from us."

If the church's actions consistently undercut its words, why would anybody bother to take the gospel seriously? "When they see us building for ourselves fine houses, and laying out gardens and baths, and buying fields, they are not willing to believe that we are preparing for another sort of residence away from our city."[94] Rather than resembling a pilgrim community headed toward home, Chrysostom complains ironically, the church looks more like settlers putting down permanent roots in the wrong location. A likely pagan response to the Christian community's skewed perspective and practice, Chrysostom fears, will be an ever stronger attachment to the present life, with little regard for the future.

Consider Chrysostom's catalogue of the rich man's character malformations and skewed, habitual responses to the wealth God had given him in trust:

+ the pursuit of luxury (self-indulgent living)
+ licentiousness
+ laughter (a cynical, pseudo-sophisticated humor that laughs at things that simply are not funny)
+ self-indulgent relaxation
+ gluttony
+ drunkenness
+ a self-centered hoarding of wealth ("the madness for money")
+ exaggerated concern with clothing

Though by all appearances the rich man possesses all he needs for a comfortable, carefree life, in reality he lacks the most essential things. Paradoxically, his prosperity serves as a physical, emotional, and spiritual anesthetic, numbing him to the needs and horrors of his environment. "He was drowned every day by the waves of evil and did not take notice of it. He was torn to pieces every day by wicked desires and enjoyed himself."[95] To employ a phrase coined by Neil Postman in his description of late twentieth-century North American culture, the rich man entertained himself to death. Rampant self-indulgence accomplished its desensitizing work, creating dead zones in his soul. "In his delusion, so to speak, he kept on walking the easy road, driven along toward the very brink without being aware of it because of his drunkenness. His prosperity in all aspects of this life drowned his reasoning, and blinded the eye of his mind; and as if deprived of his sight thereafter he went on walking without knowing where he was going."[96]

Chrysostom finds no ground for rejoicing in the rich man's fate; indeed, Chrysostom pictures Abraham as "moved to pity by seeing the severity of his punishment, but . . . is not able to do anything else for his assistance. . . . Abraham all but apologizes to him."[97] For the rich man, *the failure to remember the most important things* during his time on earth results in the lengthy, eternal memory of the irretrievable past.

A CALL TO MODERATION, PROPORTION, AND DISCRETION

To sum up the parable and this chapter as a whole: the rich man's fundamental error, one we repeat when we fail to respond to wealth and prosperity with *discretion*, is his failure to identify the purpose for which God had given him his wealth. He views his prosperity as good "without qualification." Chrysostom exhorts his parishioners to enjoy the goods given to them by God "in due proportion," always remembering they are stewards, not owners. If we have "sustenance for our life," sufficient prosperity "to overcome the weakness of our bodies," we should rest satisfied.[98]

The goodness of wealth depends on *how we respond to our prosperity.* If we respond to God's blessing foolishly and self-indulgently consume God's gifts to feed skewed appetites and passions, wealth will "indeed cause our destruction." We will never find what we are searching for. We will become increasingly insensitive to the needs of those around us. Ironically, *our humanity will be diminished through what was given to bless others.* When wealth is enjoyed "in moderation," with the rest distributed "to the stomachs of the poor," then the purpose of wealth will be fulfilled in our lives—and in the lives of others.

Our response to our wealth or to our poverty, the church fathers argue, is a sign of faithful discipleship or hollow apprenticeship. What we do with our bankbook tells others so much about the state of our heart. The same can be said when we encounter evil. How are we to respond to our enemies? Can Christians, for instance, serve in the military? The thoughts of the church fathers on this question might surprise you. We'll explore them in the next chapter.

Consider the scale of those wars, with all that slaughter of human be-ings, all the human blood that was shed! Those wars are now past history; and yet the misery of these evils has not yet ended. . . . If I were to try to describe, with an eloquence worthy of the subject, the many and multifarious disasters, the dour and dire necessities, I could not possibly be adequate to the theme.

AUGUSTINE, CITY OF GOD[1]

The question is whether a believer can become a soldier and whether a soldier can be admitted into the faith, even if he is a member only of the rank and file who are not required to take part in sacrifices or capital punishments. There can be no compatibility between the di-vine and the human sacrament, the standard of Christ and the stan-dard of the devil, the camp of light and the camp of darkness. One soul cannot serve two masters: God and Caesar.

TERTULLIAN, IDOLATRY[2]

THREE

"THE MISERY OF THESE EVILS"

War and Military Service

How did the church fathers interpret Jesus' and the apostles' teaching concerning resistance to evil, killing, and warfare? Did Christians ever serve in the Roman legions? Did early Christian perspectives on war, violence, resistance to evil, and service in the military change over time? Or did they remain consistent? Are patristic perspectives on war and violence applicable in the twenty-first century, the age of global terrorism and—always lurking in the background—the nuclear weapon?

A SAD STATE OF AFFAIRS

A look at the extent and frequency of war in human history is sad and sobering. James Waller relates that since the wars of Napoleon, human beings "have fought an average of six international wars and six civil wars per *decade*." Since 1900, at any given moment, "three high-fatality struggles" have been occurring. Since the end of World War II, human beings have enjoyed a total of twenty-six days of world peace, not counting, Waller notes, "the innumerable internal wars and police actions." He somberly observes, "Buried in the midst of all of our progress in the twentieth century are well over a 100 million persons who met a violent death at the hands of their fellow human beings. That is more than five times the number from the nineteenth century and more than ten times the number from the eighteenth century."[3]

As Christ's disciples, as Christ's apprentices and image bearers, how are we to respond to human evil? In what manner and to what extent may we resist? How are we to interpret Jesus' words in the Sermon on the Mount? "You have heard that it was said, 'Eye for eye, and tooth for tooth.' But I tell you, do not resist an evil person. If someone slaps you on the right cheek, turn to them the other also. And if anyone wants to sue you and take your shirt, hand over your coat as well. If anyone [a Roman soldier] forces you to go one mile, go with them two miles" (Mt 5:38-41 NIV).

The basic question facing the church fathers was this: What was Christ modeling for his body on earth—the church—as he taught about resistance to evil and patterned that opposition and confrontation in his habitual behaviors and precise actions? What could be more relevant for our lives as Christ's apprentices today, as the radical, militant Islam of ISIS rumbles through the Middle East, leaving in its wake scores of Christian martyrs, as well as the suffering and death of thousands of others?

Of course, questions of resistance to evil in the twentieth and twenty-first centuries can't be limited to the present situation with ISIS. Think, for example, of other twentieth-century horrors: the Holocaust in the 1930s and early '40s, the Cambodian genocide in the 1970s, the Rwandan genocide in 1994. Think of the millions who have died in the Congo in recent years. Sadly this litany of suffering can be extended still further. Waller reminds us, "At the close of the twentieth century, a third of the world's 193 nations were embroiled in conflict, nearly twice the Cold War level."[4]

If ancient Christian leaders such as Tertullian, Cyprian, Chrysostom, Basil, Athanasius, and Augustine were invited on a guided tour of Auschwitz, how would they respond after seeing the gas chambers and hearing the numbers—seventeen thousand image bearers going up in smoke each day? Would they respond with one voice concerning resistance to evil on this scale? Would they end up disagreeing with one another? What word would they speak to us today as Christ's church, Christ's body in the midst of this present evil age?

A central date we will keep in mind is AD 312, the year of the "conversion" of the Roman emperor Constantine. A commonplace in patristic studies, one with a significant degree of validity, is that with the power shift that occurred in 312 Christian ideas and practices slowly but surely began to morph into new patterns. Was such the case with the church fathers' perspective on war and service in the military? To answer this question, we will first survey ancient Christian attitudes and practices regarding war, killing, and military service in the pre-Constantinian period, from the first century AD up to 312. We will then analyze developments after the acceptance and advocacy of Christianity by the Roman emperor.

Pre-Constantinian Perspectives

One of the earliest references to military life in Christian literature occurs as a metaphor in an ancient Christian letter, the First Letter of Clement, written sometime during the last two decades of the first century AD. In his letter, Clement utilizes a military example to make a spiritual point concerning church discipline and order, much like New Testament authors such as the apostle Paul. In Ephesians 6, for instance, Paul dresses the Christian in a Roman soldier's armor to illustrate the reality of spiritual warfare with the powers of darkness. Similarly, Clement uses military imagery to illustrate that the church is composed of many gifts, abilities, and positions and that ecclesiastical discipline should be maintained:

> So let us serve as soldiers, brothers, will all seriousness under his faultless orders. Let us consider the soldiers who serve under our commanders—how precisely, how readily, how obediently they execute orders. Not all are prefects or tribunes or centurions or captains of fifty and so forth, but each in his own rank executes the orders given by the emperor and the commanders. The great cannot exist without the small, nor the small without the great.

There is a certain blending in everything, and therein lies the advantage.[5]

Justin Martyr, writing some fifty years after Clement of Rome, emphasizes in his defense of the Christian community before the Emperor Antoninus Pius that Christians are loyal subjects, pay their taxes, and pray regularly for the emperor. Yet Christians, Justin explains, also follow the teaching of Christ and live in the era predicted by the prophet Isaiah, one characterized by a "new ethic" wrapped around the teaching of Jesus.[6] Justin refers to Isaiah's prediction of a time when swords will be beaten into plows and spears into pruning hooks; war will finally come to an end. This time of peace, Justin believes, had begun with the coming of Christ, the promised Messiah. More importantly, Justin emphasizes that followers of Christ "refuse to make war" on those who oppose them. Rather, they willingly accept death as faithful witnesses to the truth they have beheld and embraced.

> And that it did so come to pass, we can convince you. For from Jerusalem there went out into the world, men, twelve in number, and these illiterate, of no ability in speaking: but by the power of God they proclaimed to every race of people that they were sent by Christ to teach to all the word of God; and we who formerly used to murder one another do not only now refrain from making war upon our enemies, but also, that we may not lie or deceive our examiners, willingly die confessing Christ.[7]

The challenge facing the ancient Christian community was daunting. How could Christian leaders convince the Roman authorities of their loyalty while simultaneously refusing to engage in or be entertained by acts of violence?[8] Justin insists that the Christian community refuses to "rebel." Yet Christians now follow a new leader, Christ, who does not want Christians "to imitate the wicked, but . . . has exhorted us, by our patience and kindness, to guide all people out of shame and desire for evil." In a striking phrase he writes, "We have proof of this in the many examples of those who used to be on your side but who have turned from the way of violence and tyranny, who were overcome by observing their neighbors' steadfast way of life, or by observing the strange patience of their fellow travelers when they were taken advantage of."[9]

Athenagoras, another second-century AD Christian apologist, like Justin stresses the loyalty of Christians to the Roman state. "We pray for your reign in order that the succession may pass from father to son, as is most fitting, and that your sway may increase and expand as everyone becomes subject to you. Such a development benefits us, too, inasmuch as we can both lead a life of quiet and peace, and do willingly everything that is enjoined upon us."[10]

Yet the Christians' loyalty to the state was clearly bounded. The teaching of Jesus, what Athenagoras calls "the particulars of our doctrine," was the compass that guided the church's attitudes and actions. Jesus' teaching was clear: "Love your enemies and pray for those who persecute you" (Mt 5:44).

Athenagoras specifically responds to the charge of cannibalism—a Roman slander based on rumors surrounding the celebration of the Eucharist—by insisting that the Christian refusal to kill makes such charges ridiculous. "For when they know that we cannot endure even to see a person put to death, though justly; who of them can accuse us of murder or cannibalism?"[11] Indeed, Christians avoided attending gladiatorial contests and wild-beast combats, specifically because to watch these events was to participate in them. "To see a person put to death is much the same as killing him. . . . How, then, when we do not even look on, lest we should contract guilt and pollution, can we put people to death?"[12]

Though Athenagoras does not directly address the question of war and military service, his vivid portrayal of the early Christian community's aversion to violence and killing is surely relevant to our topic.[13] For instance, he writes, "We have learned not only not to return blow for blow, or to bring to court those who plunder and rob us, but to those who strike us on the one cheek to offer the other, and to those who take away our shirt to give also our coat."[14]

Swimming against the current. The early Christian community was clearly swimming against strong Roman cultural currents in the second and third centuries AD. Celsus, a strong opponent of Christianity in the late second century AD, chides Christians for their stubborn resistance to honor the divine status of the Roman emperor. "If everyone followed your example, nothing would prevent his [i.e., the emperor's] being left all alone and deserted while all earthly affairs fell under the sway of the most lawless and uncivilized barbarians."[15] To refuse to acknowledge the emperor's divinity—the common Christian response—was from a Roman perspective to make both a religious and a political statement, one with strong implications for military service. As Louis Swift notes, "Emperor-worship and defense of the realm went hand in hand; one could not refuse the one without endangering the other."[16]

The twelfth legion. Thus far, what can we conclude? Christians paid taxes to the government, prayed regularly for the emperor, and avoided public entertainments involving violence. These practices were grounded on Jesus' own teaching in the Sermon on the Mount. The question of Christians serving in the military, though, is complex. Consider, for instance, the story of the twelfth legion, a tale recounted by both Tertullian and Eusebius of Caesarea.[17]

In Tertullian's *Apology* 5, addressed to the Roman Senate, he urges his audience to examine the letters of Marcus Aurelius, "that most grave of emperors, in which he bears his testimony that Germanic drought was removed by the rains obtained through the prayers of the Christians who chanced to be fighting under him."[18] Eusebius goes into even greater detail in book five of his *Ecclesiastical History*, relating that while Marcus Aurelius, the brother of Antoninus, was "about to engage in battle the Germans and Sarmatians, he was in great trouble on account of his army suffering from thirst." It was "the so-called Melitene legion," Eusebius writes. Disaster was averted as Christian members of the legion "kneeled on the ground, as is our custom in prayer, and engaged in supplications to God." In response to these prayers, "a shower refreshed the army of those who had called on God, all of whom had been on the point of perishing with thirst."[19]

Eusebius acknowledges that non-Christian interpreters of the apparently miraculous deliverance of Marcus Aurelius and his troops credited their escape to deities other than the god of the Christians. "The miracle has been presented by writers outside the faith, yet, inasmuch as they were strangers to the faith, it was not confessed that this happened by the prayers of our people." Some Roman historians attributed the miracle of the lightning and rain to the intervention of Egyptian magician Arnuphes, while Aurelius's biographer Capitolinus favored the prayers of the emperor himself as the most adequate explanation for the wondrous event.

Though disagreement among ancient historians concerning the cause of the miracle is evident, we can reliably conclude on the basis of this incident that Christians were serving in the Roman army in the second century. That Christians were serving in the twelfth legion, though, does not signal that the church at large approved of this service—or disapproved. Louis Swift concludes that the presence of these Christian soldiers "created no apparent scandal."[20] Other historians, such as Ron Sider, remind us that while the ancient sources inform us of Christian service in the legion, they do not tell us whether "they were already Christians when they enlisted, or became Christians while in the army." In fact, as Sider observes, these sources do not indicate how many Christians were actually serving in the army.[21]

A closer look at Tertullian. A closer look at Tertullian's thoughts on service in the military will serve us well. Tertullian acknowledges the presence of Christians in the army in the late second century. In his *Apology* (AD 197), Tertullian labors to show that Christians are a benefit to the Roman state, rather than a seditious group. To assure the Senate that Christians have no interest in subverting Rome's authority, he points to Jesus' teaching. "If we are enjoined, then, to love our enemies . . . whom have we to hate? If injured, we are forbidden to retaliate, lest we become as bad ourselves."

Yet, in the same chapter of the *Apology*, Tertullian mentions the growth of the Christian community throughout the empire and comments on the presence of Christians within "the [military] camp itself." What are we to think? Tertullian later in the same chapter observes, "For what wars should we be not fit, and ready even with unequal forces, we who so willingly yield ourselves to the sword, *if in our religion it were not counted better to be slain than to slay?*"[22]

As Tertullian continues to ponder Christian service in the military, his position clarifies. Whereas in his *Apology* he strained to demonstrate Christian loyalty to Rome, in other works he clearly opposes service in the military. Why? We can summarize Tertullian's argument along the following lines:

Jesus' teaching clearly forbids the use of the sword by Christians.

But now inquiry is made about this point, whether a believer may turn himself to military service, and whether the military [man] may be admitted to the faith, even the rank and file, or each interior grade, to whom there is no necessity for taking part in sacrifices or capital punishments. . . . Indeed how will [the Christian] serve in the army even during peacetime without the sword that Jesus Christ has taken away? Even if soldiers came to John and got advice on how they ought to act, even if the centurion became a believer, the Lord, by taking away Peter's sword, disarmed every soldier thereafter. We are not allowed to wear any uniform that symbolizes a sinful act.[23]

Enrollment in the army or service in the Roman government inevitably involves the Christian in idolatrous practices.

A dispute has arisen of late whether a servant of God can hold a position of honor or authority as long as he can stay free of any appearance of idolatry by means of some special grace or his own cleverness after the manner of Joseph and Daniel. . . . We may grant that somebody could hold a position in a purely honorary way if you can believe that it is possible for him to avoid sacrificing or authorizing sacrifices, paying for victims, managing the upkeep of temples, taking care of temple taxes, putting on shows at his own or at public expense, or presiding over the staging of shows, issuing solemn pronunciations or edicts or even taking an oath.[24]

Acts of violence and idolatry are inescapable in the life of a Roman soldier.

Will a son of peace who should not even go to court take part in battle? Will a man who does not avenge wrongs done to himself have any part in chains, prisons, tortures and punishments? . . . At night will he protect those [demons] that he has exorcised during the day, leaning and resting all the while on the spear that pierced the side of Christ? Will he carry the standards that rival Christ's? . . . Will he be cremated according to the usual practice when this has been forbidden him and when he has been freed by Christ from the punishment of fire? By looking around one can see how many other forms of wrongdoing are involved in fulfilling the duties of military camps, things which must be considered violations of God's law. Carrying the title "Christian" from the camp of life to the camp of darkness is itself a violation.[25]

Tertullian admits that the situation of a soldier who converted to Christ after his enrollment in the army is different from that of a Christian who enrolled after conversion. Still, Tertullian argues, soldiers who became disciples of Christ must expect to suffer, even to the point of martyrdom. *There were simply certain things Christian soldiers could not do.* To plead one was only following orders would not wash.

There is no allowance for a plea of necessity. No necessity for wrongdoing is incumbent on those for whom the only necessity is to avoid wrongdoing. Someone, you say, is pressed into sacrificing or officially denying Christ by the inevitability of torture or punishment. All the time, Church discipline does not wink even at that kind of necessity because the necessity to fear denial and to suffer martyrdom is greater than the necessity to avoid martyrdom and to make the required offering.[26]

Tertullian's position on Christians serving in the military did not arise in a vacuum. The Apostolic Tradition, an early third-century document, acknowledges the presence of Christians in the Roman army and severely limits what they can and cannot do. Canon 16 reads:

> A soldier in the lower ranks shall kill no one. If ordered to do so, he shall not obey, and he shall not take an oath. If he does not want to comply with this directive, let him be dismissed [i.e., from the church]. If anyone exercises the power of the sword or is a civil magistrate who wears the purple, let him give up the office or be dismissed. A catechumen or a member of the faithful who wants to join the army should be dismissed because he has shown contempt for God.[27]

This canon reflects an ecclesial perspective providing guidelines for the church as it attempted to live in two worlds: the kingdom of God and the Roman state. The canon recognizes that military service and engagement in warfare pose dangers to central Christian tenets. Were, as Swift asks, more and more Christian men failing to see any conflict between Christian beliefs and military service? If so, there was a distinct need for the church to prescribe carefully what Christian soldiers could and could not do. "How workable such arrangements were in actual practice we have little way of knowing, but the prohibition at the end [of canon 16] against volunteering reveals that the Church in Rome was still throwing all its weight behind efforts to discourage Christians from having anything to do with the service."[28]

Other second-century voices. In Tertullian we have encountered a clear opposition to military service by Christians. What of other second- and third-century Christian leaders such as Cyprian and Clement of Alexandria?

Cyprian is unambiguous in his opposition to the killing of human beings, whether by individuals or by the state, sarcastically commenting in a letter to his friend Donatus:

> Observe the roads blocked by robbers, the seas beset by pirates, wars spread everywhere with the bloody horrors of camps. The

world is soaked with mutual blood, and when individuals commit homicide, it is a crime; *it is called a virtue when it is done in the name of the state.* Impunity is acquired for crimes not by reason of innocence but by the magnitude of the cruelty.[29]

The killing that occurs in the Roman games is especially condemned by Cyprian, as is the training gladiators receive in the art of killing. "Man is killed for the pleasure of man, and to be able to kill is a skill, is an employment, is an art. Crime is not only committed but is taught."[30] Can we logically extend Cyprian's condemnation of the games and the gladiators' honed killing skills to the Roman legionnaire, a well-known, highly disciplined killing machine? In the case of the gladiator, we have a warrior killing for sport in state sponsored games; in the case of the legionnaire, we have a warrior killing on behalf of the state. In both cases human beings, God's image bearers, are violently losing their lives. Yet is battle on the field morally equivalent to battle in the arena?

Perhaps the most direct comment of Cyprian on military service occurs in the context of his work *On the Good of Patience.* Patience, Cyprian writes, "not only keeps watch over what is good, but it also repels what is evil." A number of vices undercut patience: adultery, fraud, and homicide. For those who practice patience, adultery will not pollute the body, nor will fraud stain innocence, "nor, after the Eucharist is carried in it, *is the hand sullied by the blood-stained sword.*"[31]

What sword is in view, and put to what use? The sword of the murderer? The sword of the soldier? Or, for Cyprian, is the soldier who kills guilty of homicide, as is the gladiator? In Cyprian's letter to Demetrian, an ardent opponent of Christianity, Cyprian reminds him that Christians "always ask for the repulse of [Rome's] enemies."[32] By praying for Rome's enemies to be repulsed, is Cyprian also praying for Rome's armies to be successful? Such seems to be the case, though this stance in prayer would not necessarily indicate Cyprian's support for Christians serving in the military. As George Kalantzis rightly observes, "whatever the disposition of a writer (Christian and non-Christian alike) towards war and military service, strong military language and imagery conveys the urgency and gravity of a situation."[33]

Insights from Clement of Alexandria. When we turn to Clement of Alexandria, we find little in terms of direct comments on war, though, like Cyprian, Clement's work is filled with military metaphors and demonstrates fairly detailed knowledge of Roman military practices. In one instance, Clement illustrates a spiritual principle by pointing to military custom. "This is the proclamation of righteousness: to those that obey, glad tidings; to those that disobey, judgment. The loud trumpet, when sounded, collects the soldiers, and proclaims war. And shall not Christ, breathing a strain of peace to the ends of the earth, gather together His own soldiers, the soldiers of peace?"[34]

Clement clearly admires Moses' abilities as a military leader, acknowledges "the appropriateness of certain military practices in the Old Testament," and approves "the Jews' despoiling the Egyptians on the grounds that it was the usual practice in war or a legitimate means of seeking reparation."[35]

In an intriguing passage, one that may have implications for Clement's views on Christian service in the military, he comments that an individual's vocation should not prove a roadblock to "the knowledge of God." "If you are a farmer, we say, till the earth, but acknowledge the God of farmers; if you love seafaring, sail on, but remember to call upon the celestial Helmsman. *If you were in the army when you were seized by the knowledge of God, obey the Commander who gives just commands.*"[36] A farmer who becomes a Christian can continue to till the earth, as a sailor who believes can continue to sail the oceans. In the third case, though, that of a soldier who converts while serving in the army, Clement's thought shifts. You are now under a new commander. Act accordingly. The question is, what would the new commander order?

Does Clement take it for granted that Christians would know what their new commander—Christ—would allow and forbid? We simply don't have records of Clement's writing in greater detail on the question of war and military service, and we are left to extrapolate from the meager commentary we do have in his writings.[37]

Origen's resistance to war and military service. In Origen, the student of Clement of Alexandria, we have a much wider field to glean for insights into ancient Christian perspectives. The ambiguity present in Clement—perhaps because he never addressed the issue of military service and Christian engagement in war directly—is largely absent in Origen. In Origen's *Against Celsus*, an apologetic treatise written circa 246, we find a number of suggestive comments concerning war, service in the military, and killing in general.

The pagan philosopher Celsus composed a discourse against second-century Christianity around AD 178. In the treatise, Celsus sharply criticizes the Christian community as a subversive group seeking to undermine the welfare of the Roman state through religious and political practices that could only be viewed as seditious. Why else would Christians enter "into secret associations with each other contrary to law"? In addition, rumors abounded concerning rampant sexual immorality at Christian "love-feasts"; perhaps even cannibalism was occurring as the body and blood of the Christian god were consumed. Was the early Christian community loyal to the Roman state or not?

As Origen responds to Celsus's criticism of the church, his task is twofold. He must demonstrate the church's loyalty to Rome while simultaneously defending the church's strong aversion to military service. Origen's tactic is to argue that Christians do serve and defend the Roman Empire, not by serving in the military but through the spiritual warfare Christians engage in on behalf of Rome. "To be sure, the more pious a man is the more effectively does he assist the emperors—more so than the troops that go out and kill as many of the enemy as possible on the battle line. This would be our answer to those who are strangers to our faith and who ask us to take up arms and to kill men for the common good."[38]

In what Swift describes as a "bifocal view," Origen is willing to acknowledge that the emperor may at times have to fight wars to maintain the peace and defend the empire from attack. Christians can aid the emperor by praying for the success of the legions. But Origen is adamant in his refusal to accept the possibility that Christians could themselves wield a physical sword on behalf of Rome. To do so would openly disobey Christ's commandment against taking human life. "[Jesus] considered it contrary to his divinely inspired legislation to approve any kind of homicide whatsoever."[39]

What of the Old Testament teaching on military service? Of course, if Origen is to defend a consistent pacifist position, he faces the problem of the Old Testament. God often instructs the Israelites to take military action, at times even commanding them to kill women and children. How can the Christian exegete reconcile such passages with Jesus' command to love one's enemies? Origen takes a twofold approach in responding to this difficult question.

1. The Jews, under the terms of the old covenant, "were allowed to take up arms in defense of their possessions and to kill their enemies."

> But in the case of the ancient Jews, who had a land and a form of government of their own, to take from them the right of making war upon their enemies, of fighting for their country, of putting to death or otherwise punishing adulterers, murderers, or others who were guilty of similar crimes, would be to subject them to sudden and utter destruction whenever the enemy fell upon them; for their very laws would in that case restrain them, and prevent them from resisting the enemy.[40]

Christians, however, under Christ's leadership, are "the entering wedge of the eschatological kingdom"[41] and as such are to wage spiritual rather than physical warfare. Origen refers approvingly to Isaiah's prediction of a time when swords will be transformed into pruning hooks and sees that time as fulfilled in Christ. "To those who ask about our origin and our founder we reply that we have come in response to Jesus' commands to beat into plowshares the rational swords of conflict and arrogance and to change into pruning hooks those spears that we used to fight with. For we no longer take up the sword against any nation, nor do we learn the art of war any more."[42]

2. Origen frequently allegorizes texts in the Old Testament that command Israel to wage war against its enemies. Passages advocating war and violence possess a "two-fold sense," Origen argues, "the one literal, the other spiritual." Psalm 101, for instance, contains "the noblest thoughts and purposes," yet also promotes ideas that cannot be interpreted literally if Christ's teaching is to be obeyed faithfully.

> Judge, then, from the words and spirit of the speaker, whether it is conceivable that, after having in the preceding part of the Psalm, as anyone may read for himself, uttered the noblest thoughts and purposes, he should in the sequel, according to the literal rendering of his words, say that in the morning and at no other period of the day, he would destroy all sinners from the earth, and leave none of them alive.[43]

Thus if every morning the just man "slays his enemies in the land," the "land" must represent "the flesh whose lusts are at enmity with God," an interpretation Origen believes is congruent with "the true idea and conception of God, which makes it to be admired by all who look upon it." Enemies given up to destruction in Old Testament texts are transformed into "vices" to be eradicated, including children dashed against the rock (Ps 137), with these children symbolically representing the "early beginnings and promptings of evil."[44]

To summarize the territory we have covered thus far: up to the conversion of Constantine the early Christian community likely opposed Christians serving in the Roman army. If Christians did serve, the activities the church allowed them to perform were significantly restricted, often to the extent that most options for military service were eliminated.

How closely the church's restrictions were followed by Christian soldiers is another question. As we have seen, Christians were serving in Marcus Aurelius's legions in the second century AD, and it is unlikely that all were willing or allowed to restrict their service to noncombat activities. In fact, we find Christians serving in the Roman army in the second half of the third century AD and occasionally suffering during the periodic persecutions that increasingly intensified early in the fourth century.[45]

We have listened to strong pacifist voices such as Tertullian and Origen. For teachers such as these, Christ's instructions were crystal clear concerning the killing of human beings, whether in combat or through the executions Roman soldiers occasionally carried out. As Lactantius puts it, writing in the first decade of the fourth century:

> For when God forbids killing, he is not only ordering us to avoid armed robbery, which is contrary even to public law, but *He is forbidding what men regard as ethical.* Thus, it is not right for a just man to serve in the army since justice itself is his form of service. Nor is it right for a just man to charge someone with a capital crime. *It doesn't matter whether you kill a man with the sword or with a word since it is killing itself that is prohibited. And so there must be no exception to this command of God. Killing a human being whom God willed to be inviolable, is always wrong.*[46]

As Rome gradually morphed into a Christian nation-state under the leadership of Constantine and succeeding emperors, however, we find the perspective of the Christian community dramatically shifting.

Post-Constantinian Perspectives on Service in the Military

With the conversion of the Roman emperor Constantine to Christian faith in AD 312, perspectives toward military service changed significantly. Whereas for most of the church's first three centuries it had experienced an adversarial relationship with the Roman government, with the accession of a Christian emperor Christians now found one of their own as head of the Roman state *and of the Roman legions.*

Were there principles in the gospel that the church would now see less clearly from its new position of privilege and dominance? Or were there aspects of the good news that Christians would be forced to analyze more carefully and thoroughly in light of the necessity of much deeper involvement in the governance of the Roman world? Specifically, what were key aspects of the change now facing the church with the conversion of Constantine? Two key points come to mind:

1. Attitudes toward the use of violence and coercion by Christians will have to be reviewed, in light of the many Christians who will be serving Constantine in his governance of the empire.

2. The relationship between the church and the Roman government will have to be rethought.

As Swift reminds us, the idea "that Christianity and the empire were conjoint works of God intended to be mutually supportive now became a commonplace idea."[47] How were each of these "conjoint works of God" to support one another? What was allowed? What was forbidden? If the lines between church and state became too blurred, what would result? The reflections of church fathers living in the Constantinian world on the issue of war and military service demonstrate their struggle to navigate the drastically new state of affairs between the church and the Roman government. How were the principles of Christ's teaching to intersect faithfully and wisely with the new world in which a Christian led the Roman government, a government that by necessity wielded the sword?

Eusebius's two-lifestyle approach. Eusebius of Caesarea provides an important example of how Christian leaders responded to the new Constantinian world. For Eusebius, the conversion of Constantine was a sign of God's blessing and future plans for the Roman Empire. Eusebius effusively praises Constantine in a panegyric offered in AD 336, an address in which he clearly connects the accession of Constantine to the Roman throne with biblical prophecies:

> One God was proclaimed to all the world; one Roman empire flourished everywhere, and the implacable and undying hatred that had always existed among enemy nations was completely swept away. As knowledge of the one God spread to all men and with it the saving teaching of Christ, which is the path of true piety, at that very time a single ruler sprang up for the whole Roman

empire, and a deep peace embraced the whole world. By the command, as it were, of the one God, two blessings sprouted forth simultaneously, that is, the Roman Empire and the doctrine of true piety. . . . Thus, the pronouncements of the ancient oracles and the sayings of the prophets were fulfilled.[48]

If Constantine and the Roman Empire are signs of the fulfillment of biblical prophecy, i.e., definite instances of God's express will and kingdom manifesting itself on earth, a specific question immediately poses itself: Can Christians then serve in the military of the Roman state, much like Israelites served in the army of Israel?

The direction of Eusebius's thought and historical developments during Constantine's lifetime indicate an increasingly positive attitude among Christian leaders toward military service and the possibility of just wars. Christian symbols such as the *labarum* began to appear on Roman military standards and were introduced in battle if events began to go awry.[49] Not only so, but for the first time we have Christian bishops invited to accompany Constantine's troops who, in Eusebius's words, "fight together with him by means of their prayers to God."[50]

At first glance Eusebius's comment appears to line up exactly with the perspective of Origen, who had also encouraged prayers on behalf of the emperor, while forbidding Christians from actually taking part in combat. Yet Eusebius sees matters differently. In a striking move, Eusebius argues that there are "two life styles . . . established in the Christian church." The lifestyle one practices depends on the role and position God has given a particular individual in the church. Clergy, for instance, are a distinct grouping within the church and practice a role that "goes beyond nature and the usual manner of life, is not involved at all with marriage, children, property, or an abundance of possessions. Out of an extraordinary love for things heavenly it departs from the common and customary pattern and is devoted wholly to the worship of God."[51] Service in the army, then, would continue to be out of bounds for those whose lives were particularly devoted to God.

Others, those of the second lifestyle, are "more concerned with human affairs," marriage, the procreation of children, home management, and so on. Most importantly for our present discussion, Eusebius adds that this second, subordinate lifestyle "lays down practical rules for those fighting in a just war. . . . For such individuals there is a secondary state of perfection which is suitable in its own way for their kind of life."[52]

Canon law on service in the military. Eusebius's two-lifestyle approach to resolving the problem of war and military service represents only one response of the post-Constantinian church. Heated disagreement among Christians continued. The Synod of Arles (AD 314), for example, declared that those soldiers—presumably Christians—"who throw down their arms in time of peace are to be separated from the community." Yet what exactly does a "time of peace" mean? Some scholars, as Swift observes, believe the synod's canon refers to Christians serving in the army during a time of peace, when soldiers acted much like police. Christians who refused to serve in this capacity, the canon declares, would be subject to church discipline. Yet how could one serve in the Roman police force and avoid the use of lethal violence? "The physical violence involved in both activities [the army and the police] is indivisible, and the idea of Christians serving during periods of relative calm but deserting when war threatened is simply not credible. No emperor, either Christian or pagan, could endorse or tolerate an arrangement of that kind."[53]

Instead, the canon promulgated at Arles more likely refers to the duty of Christians to serve in the Roman legions "when there is no persecution, i.e. when no threat of idolatry exists." Apparently Christian service in the military became a much more viable option, at least in the view of some, if the danger of idolatry was eliminated. A major hurdle to military service seemed be eliminated, and perspectives and practices accordingly shifted. Or so at least the canon passed by the church leaders gathered at Arles appears to indicate.

Other canons of the early fourth century reflect the divided mind of the church. Consider canon 12, passed by the Council of Nicaea in

AD 325: "Those who responded to the call of grace and initially ex-pressed their faith by putting off the military belt, but who subsequently acted like dogs returning to their vomit when they offered money and gifts in order to get back into the army, must remain among the hearers for three years and then among the supplicants for ten more."[54] At first glance, canon 12 appears to punish Christians who return to military service. Yet is it military service or service in a particular Roman army that the canon condemns? Swift speculates that this canon is specifically addressing the case of Christian veterans who had served in the army of Valerius Licinius, a rival to Constantine who "had abandoned Christi-anity and was engaged in persecuting the Church." To serve in Licinius's legions was to expose oneself once again to idolatrous practices and hence, such service was prohibited.

Both the canon passed by the Council of Arles and that passed by the Council of Nicaea indicate that Christians were serving in some capacity in the military, that the church felt uneasy about such service, and that the church was attempting to adjudicate the thorny problem of church and state, Christians and war, and so on, in the midst of a fairly fluid situation.

One thing is clear. The church continued to oppose Christian sol-diers using the sword to carry out their various duties. A canon passed around AD 340 demonstrates the continuing attempt of the church to regulate what must have been fairly common practice:

> A Christian should not voluntarily become a soldier unless com-pelled to by someone in authority. He should have a sword, but he should not be commanded to shed blood. If it is ascertained that he has done so, he should stay away from the mysteries at least until he has been purified through tears and lamentation. He should fulfill his obligation without deceit and in fear of God.[55]

Basil of Caesarea faced similar situations involving Christian soldiers who had taken human life while serving in the military. In dealing with the pastoral issue of what to do with a Christian who has used the sword,

Basil draws a distinction between killing and murder, while still insisting that church discipline be applied. "Our predecessors did not consider killing in war as murder but, as I understand it, made allowances for those who fought on the side of moderation and piety. Nonetheless, it is good to admonish those whose hands are unclean to abstain just from communion for three years."[56]

The implications of Basil's decision to discipline Christian soldiers who took life in battle are important to consider. Three years' exclusion from the Eucharist is a significant length. As John McGuckin comments, "Basil's arrangement that the returning warrior may stand in the Church (rather than the narthex, where the other public sinners were allocated spaces) but refrain from communion makes the statement that a truly honorable termination of war, for a Christian, has to be an honorable repentance."[57]

Augustine of Hippo. Augustine constructs a theological model of peace and war that is multifaceted. His views on the reality and depth of human sin, God's providential control over human history, the Christian's call to acknowledge the role of human government in maintaining peace, and the relationship between the kingdom of God and the kingdoms of this world shape his understanding of war and Christian service in the military. Augustine's "assumptions concerning man's present condition in the created world and the role of the state in human society," in Louis Swift's words, were the "hinge" on which Augustine's thoughts on war and peace turned.[58]

Because of humanity's rebellion in Adam and Eve, human nature itself is now skewed, warped by a *libido dominandi* or "lust for domination" that inevitably leads to the clash of human wills and the conflict of war. "Even with the advent of salvation in Christ man's tendency to follow his own selfish interests and lower appetites remains all but irresistible, and this fact threatens the very structure of human society."[59] Hence, Augustine argues, the absolute need for governmental and societal structures designed to preserve peace and maintain order.

> Surely it is not in vain that we have such institutions as the power
> of the king, the death penalty of the judge, the hooks of the execu-
> tioner, the weapons of the soldier, the stringency of the overlord
> and even the strictness of a good father. All these things have their
> own method, reason, motive and benefit. When they are feared,
> evil men are held in check, and the good enjoy greater peace among
> the wicked.[60]

Human beings, Augustine teaches, are inherently social beings. "The
philosophies hold the view that the life of the wise man should be social;
and in this we support them much more heartily." The city of God itself
depends on the social nature of human beings for its life and various
functions. "How could that City have made its first start, how could it
have advanced along its course, how could it attain its appointed goal if
the life of the saints were not social?"[61]

The relationships between human beings, though, as a result of
Adam and Eve's sin, are now infected with a disease that seeps into all
social relationships and structures. "There is nothing so social by nature
and so discordant by its perversion as the [human] race."[62] Sin's crip-
pling, distorting effect manifests itself even within the intimate, loving
context of the home and within the warmest, most loving of human
friendships. The "disorders of love" are rampant. "Have they not everywhere filled up the story of human experience? Are they not of frequent
occurrence, even in the honorable love of friends? The story of mankind
is full of them at every point; for in that story we are aware of wrongs,
suspicions, *enmities and war—undoubted evils these*."[63]

Crime and its accompanying violence presently haunts all social life,
its vicious force manifesting its presence from the most intimate human
relationships to the crowded social life of the Roman city.

> If, then, safety is not to be found in the home, the common refuge
> from the evils that befall mankind, what shall we say of the city?
> The larger the city, the more is its forum filled with civil lawsuits
> and criminal trials, even if that city be at peace, free from the

alarms or—what is more frequent—the bloodshed, of sedition and civil war. It is true that cities are at times exempt from those occurrences; they are never free from the danger of them.[64]

Augustine writes that the citizens of the city of God take

no issue with that diversity of customs, laws, and traditions whereby human peace is sought and maintained. Instead of nullifying or tearing down, she preserves and appropriates whatever in the diversities of diverse races is aimed at one and the same objective of human peace, provided only that they do not stand in the way of the faith and worship of the one supreme and true God.

The Christian community should actively support the efforts of human government to preserve and extend peace, for peace itself nourishes the church's life. "Thus, the heavenly City, so long as it is wayfaring on earth, not only makes use of earthly peace but fosters and actively pursues along with other human beings a common platform in regard to all that concerns our purely human life and does not interfere with faith and worship."[65]

In turn, the citizens of the earthly city should wisely draw on the wisdom of the city of God as they employ force to preserve peace, maintain order, and restrain evil.

If the earthly city observes Christian principles, even its wars will be waged with the benevolent purpose that better provision might be made for the defeated to live harmoniously together in justice and godliness. Anyone whose freedom to do evil is curtailed is subject to a beneficial kind of restraint since nothing is less fortunate than the good fortune of sinners.[66]

Can an "evil" such as coercive force or war still avoid the label of "sin"? Augustine answers yes, because he considers the use of force, whether in the courts or on the battlefield, as only sinful if *the intent* of the judge or the soldier is to cause harm maliciously. "All these serious evils our philosopher does not reckon as sins; for the wise judge does not act in this way through a will to do harm, but because ignorance is unavoidable—and yet the exigencies of human society make judgment also unavoidable." If sin did not exist, the necessity to judge it would necessarily be absent. Sadly, though, sin does exist, infects human relationships, and must be judged. "Here we have what I call the wretchedness of man's situation, at any rate, even if it is not to be called the wickedness of the wise man, in his judicial capacity."

The duty of judgment is unavoidable and necessary and will occasionally entail evils but not sins. These evils, though, should never be considered goods.

> Yet if it is through unavoidable ignorance and the unavoidable duty of judging that he tortures the innocent, are we to be told that it is not enough to acquit him [the judge of sin]? Must we grant him happiness as a bonus? How much more mature reflection it shows, how much more worthy of a human being it is when a man acknowledges this necessity as *a mark of human wretchedness*.[67]

The reality of war, even just wars, is a demonstration of humanity's wretchedness. Yes, through the expansion of the Roman Empire many peoples have been united, including the union of "peace and fellowship" enabled by the sharing of Latin as a common language. Yet "the cost of this achievement" has been great. "Consider the scale of those wars, with all that slaughter of human beings, all the human blood that was shed!" Though the wars of expansion have ended, "the misery of these evils has not yet ended."

The reality of injustice. Augustine believes—with sadness—that occasionally "the wise man" will be forced to "wage just wars." Still, "if he remembers that he is a human being, he will rather lament the fact that he is faced with the necessity of waging just wars." Why the necessity of such wars? The reality of injustice. "For it is the injustice of the opposing side that lays on the wise man the duty of waging wars; and this injustice is assuredly to be deplored by a human being. . . . And so everyone who reflects with sorrow on such grievous evils, in all their horror and cruelty, must acknowledge the misery of them." Indeed, Augustine argues, "a man who experiences such evils, or even thinks about them, without heartfelt grief, is assuredly in a far more pitiable condition, if he thinks himself happy simply because he has lost all human feeling."[68]

What Augustine describes as "the earthly city" possesses "its good in this world," a lesser good than that of the eternal city, but still a good that we can participate in "with such gladness as can be derived from things of such a kind."[69] The good manifested in the earthly city, however, is apt to cause "frustrations to those enamored of it" and is likely to lead to "litigation," "wars," and "battles."

Still, Augustine insists, "it would be incorrect to say that the goods which this city desires are not goods, since even that city is better, in its own human way, by their possession." Conflict may occur over the good present in the earthly city, but conflict and war are not necessarily evil. It is possible that one of the parties in a conflict may indeed be fighting for "the juster cause," with the result that the peace won through victory "is a matter for rejoicing." Can anyone question, Augustine asks, whether "the resulting peace is something to be desired? These things are goods and undoubtedly they are the gifts of God."[70]

To seek after a lower good in the earthly city is praiseworthy, but only if the "higher goods" are not "neglected." Augustine warns, "If these goods are neglected and those other goods are so desired as to be considered the only goods, or are loved more than the goods which are believed to be higher, the inevitable consequence is fresh misery, and an increase of the wretchedness already there."[71]

Our present life. Augustine describes our present life as a "situation of weakness" into which evil is inevitably woven. It is a situation of tension, mistrust, conflict, and worry. The "anxiety produced" in such times, though, provides believers the opportunity to seek peace even more fervently. We occasionally will taste, if only briefly, the fruit that we will feast on fully in "the ultimate bliss, the end of ultimate fulfillment that knows no destructive end." We would be naive, however, to think that in this present time of partial fulfillment, full peace is attainable. "Such blessedness as this life affords proves to be utter misery when compared with that final bliss."

The wonder and breadth of salvation, though, assure us that the virtues to be fully manifest in the life to come can yet be put to good use in this present life, even in a context where evil is manifestly present. The virtues produced by the Spirit can "turn" evil into a good, more comprehensive usefulness. "Even when we do not possess that peace, virtue turns to a good use even the ills that man endures."[72]

The church's responsibility. The church is not exempt from involvement in the maintenance of peace and order. Nor should it be. Because the city of God lives in the midst of the city of this world, issues of law, peace, war, crime, and so on deeply affect the well-being of the citizens of the city of God. Swift comments that the "inhabitants of the two 'cities' are divided from one another by the objects of their love as well as by their goals, habits and ultimate destiny. However, since the two 'cities' are intermingled with one another in the world of time, and the inhabitants are not easily distinguishable, the welfare of the City of God is inextricably bound up with that of the earthly city."[73]

Praise for Constantine. Augustine praises the Christian emperor Constantine for his robust defense of Christian Rome, including Constantine's willingness to wage war against Rome's enemies. "Constantine had a long reign, and as the sole Augustus he ruled and defended the whole Roman world; he was victorious, above all others, in the wars which he directed and conducted; fortune favored his efforts in the repression of usurpers; and he died of sickness and old age after a long life, leaving the throne to his sons."[74]

Not only does Augustine praise Constantine, a Christian emperor, but Augustine defends the actions of earlier pagan Roman emperors as they waged war in response to "unprovoked attack." In a rosy interpretation of Roman history, Augustine argues that "the Romans had a just excuse for undertaking and carrying on those great wars. When they were subjected to unprovoked attacks by their enemies, they were forced to resist not by lust for glory in men's eyes but by the necessity to defend their life and liberty. . . . That Rome grew great by such conduct was nothing to be ashamed of."[75]

For Augustine, Constantine is a sparkling example of a "happy" and just ruler. Among other things, happy rulers

> rule with justice. . . . They are not inflated with pride, but remember that they are but men; if they put their power at the service of God's majesty, to extend his worship far and wide. . . . If they take vengeance on wrong because of the necessity to direct and protect the state, and not to satisfy their personal animosity. . . . It is Christian emperors of this kind whom we call happy; happy in hope, during this present life, and to be happy in reality hereafter, when what we wait for will have come to pass.[76]

And when Christian emperors wage just war—following the stringent guidelines Augustine provides—their actions are praiseworthy and worthy of the support of the Christian community.

Augustine does not write a blank check to the Roman government to wage war whenever the emperor's heart desires. He clearly foresees the possibility that war may be waged unjustly and links unjust war to the activity of demons or "malignant spirits," beings who engender and stimulate the human wickedness all wars entail. "Can anyone fail to see and understand . . . what efforts these malignant spirits use, to give by their example a presumed divine authority to criminal acts?" Behind the pagan reading of an animal's entrails or an oracle from a pagan temple to wage war lie the inspiration and actions of evil spirits. Demonic and human pride join hands to foment "shameful battle," "loathsome battles," "frightful bloodshed," and "abominable warfare."[77]

Can we ever justify killing another human being? Augustine draws careful distinctions concerning the question of homicide, as do other church fathers such as Athanasius. Not all killing should be classified as murder. Augustine believes God has ordained that in certain circumstances human life may be rightfully forfeited. "There are some whose killing God orders, either by a law, or by an express command to a particular person at a particular time." When the state carries out the penalty for a capital crime, it is not the state who is killing the criminal, but God through the state carrying out his intent that justice and order be maintained, a position we have seen rejected by other church fathers earlier in this chapter. Indeed, many of Augustine's arguments regarding war and killing are significant modifications of the church's tradition.

When Augustine argues that "one who owes a duty of obedience to the giver of the command does not himself 'kill'—he is an instrument, a sword in the user's hand," he is writing against the grain of the church's earlier position in the second and third centuries on capital punishment and killing in general.[78]

A closer look at the possibility of just war. When can war justly be waged? Augustine encourages the Roman ambassador Darius to wage war only after he has exhausted all other means of obtaining peace through diplomatic means.

> Preventing war through persuasion and seeking or attaining peace through peaceful means rather than through war are more glorious things than slaying men with the sword. If those who engage in combat are good men, they are undoubtedly striving for peace, but they do so by shedding blood; your charge, however, was to prevent bloodshed. That is your good fortune in contrast to the others who are required to kill.[79]

Augustine points to key individuals in the biblical narrative who were commanded by God to take human life, classifying Abraham's willingness to sacrifice Isaac and Samson's destruction of the Philistines as acts of obedience to God's command or the movement of God's Spirit. All other killing, Augustine believes, is murder, pure and simple. "With the exception of these killings prescribed generally by a just law, or specially commanded by God himself—the source of justice—anyone who kills a human being, whether himself or anyone else, is involved in a charge of murder."[80]

Augustine's debate with the Manichaean Faustus concerning the wars conducted by Moses is especially illustrative of Augustine's position on war and on God's providential ordering of human history. Faustus distinguished sharply between the God of the Old Testament, a God who was warlike, vindictive, and prone to displays of violence and anger, with the God revealed in the teaching and actions of Christ. Augustine will have nothing to do with such a division between the God of the old and new covenant and replies to Faustus at some length.

First, Moses did not wage war on his own behalf or at his own initiative. He was directly commanded to wage war by God. God, by definition, cannot act in an unjust manner or command others to do so. If God, who cannot sin, commanded Moses to wage war, such wars must be just. Similarly, if wars can be justly fought, so Christians can justly and honorably serve in the military. Old Testament luminaries such as Moses and David, and New Testament figures such as the Roman officer Cornelius, serve as examples of holy warriors. "Do not believe that it is impossible for anyone to serve God while on active duty in the army. Holy David, whom God was pleased with, was a military man, and so were a good many just men of his time. . . . The same is true of Cornelius."[81]

Augustine also points to the teaching of John the Baptist as evidence for praiseworthy Christian service in the military. When soldiers came to John and asked for guidance as to how they should carry out their vocation, John replied, "Do not strike anyone or make false accusations. Be content with your pay." Augustine concludes: "If he told them to be content with their pay, he certainly was not telling them that they could not be soldiers."[82]

Augustine believes John clearly distinguished between murder and the violence that necessarily occurs in serving the public good.[83]

> If this (i.e. that war is sometimes necessary and justified) were not true, when the soldiers came to John for baptism and asked "What are we to do," he would have replied, "Throw down your arms; leave the service. Do not strike, wound, or kill anyone." But recognizing that when they do such things as part of their military duty they are not guilty of homicide but are administering the law, that

they are not avenging private wrongs but protecting the safety of the state, he replied, "Do not strike anyone; do not make false accusations. Be content with your pay" (Luke 3:14).[84]

Only duly constituted governments may wage war, and only for specific reasons.

It makes a difference for what reasons and under whose authority men undertake wars that are to be waged. The natural order of things, which is designed for the peace of mankind, requires that the authority for waging war, and the planning of it, rest with the chief of state. Soldiers, in turn, for the sake of the peace and safety of all are obliged to carry out a war that has been decided on.[85]

Jesus' statements in the Sermon on the Mount concerning turning the other cheek to those who have harmed us, Augustine contends, are applicable "more to the interior disposition of the heart than to external actions, the idea being that we should maintain an interior spirit of patience and benevolence but do what seems most beneficial for those whose welfare we are bound to look out for."

Jesus himself was angered by those who unjustly struck him in the face at the time of his trial.

Thus, he did not follow his own command if we take that command literally because he did not turn the other cheek to his assailant but told him not to compound the injury. Nonetheless, Christ had come prepared not only to be struck in the face but to die by crucifixion for those who inflicted these sufferings on him. It was for them that he prayed while hanging on the cross, "Father, forgive them because they do not realize what they are doing" (Luke 23:34).[86]

Under what conditions can a just war be conducted? Augustine speaks frequently of *just* war and *just* punishment. Through Moses God punished evil peoples who rightly deserved such punishment. Wickedness warrants punishment by the state; it deserves this punishment. In turn, the fear of punishment deters evil people from doing evil things. "He [Moses] was inflicting *just punishments* and striking terror in the hearts of those *who deserved* it."[87]

The Israelites' military victories over the Amorites are an apt illustration of both God's providential purposes being fulfilled and "justifiable aggression."[88] "One ought to note how just wars were waged. Harmless passage, a right which ought to have been granted according to the most reasonable standards governing human society, was denied [by the Amorites to the Jews]. But, to fulfill his promises, God assisted the Israelites on this occasion since the land of the Amorites was to be given to them."[89]

Augustine argues that the *wars conducted under the old covenant* demonstrate the specific criteria for waging a just war, reasons that include the following:

+ to resist human beings who are actively attempting to harm others unjustly

+ to resist those who are vengefully harming others

+ to discipline people whose actions demonstrate an "implacable disposition" and a refusal to listen or respond to reasonable arguments for peace

+ to resist those who are rebelling against legitimate governmental authority

+ to resist those who are attempting to dominate others unjustly through the use of violent means. The attempt to expand one's borders forcefully is an apt example of unjust warfare. "What else can we call it but larceny on a grand scale," Augustine comments in the *City of God*.[90]

How must just war be waged? How war must be conducted and the means the military may employ in combat also come under Augustine's scrutiny. Peppered throughout Augustine's major treatises and letters are comments on conduct *in bello* (in war). Augustine has obviously studied carefully how the Israelites waged war. If, for instance, Joshua set up ambushes against his enemies, soldiers may justly do so in a more modern setting.

> This teaches us that such things are legitimate for those who are engaged in a just war. In these matters the only thing a righteous man has to worry about is that the just war is waged by someone who has the right to do so because not all men have that right. Once an individual has undertaken this kind of war, it does not matter at all, as far as justice is concerned, whether he wins victory in open combat or through ruses.[91]

Treaties must be honored and mercy shown to one's defeated enemies. "Just as we use force on a man as long as he resists and rebels, so, too, we should show him mercy once he has been vanquished or captured, especially when there is no fear of a future disturbance of the peace."[92]

Undergirding all of Augustine's arguments for the possibility of just war is the fundamental principle that *certain evils must be resisted, and to do so is to honor the precious value of human life*, even though lives will be lost as evil is resisted. "What is it about war, after all," Augustine asks, "that is blameworthy? Is it that people who will someday die anyway are killed in order that the victors may live in peace? That kind of objection is appropriate to a timid man, not a religious one."[93]

In Augustine's words,

> The reason why good men in the face of violent resistance even undertake wars at God's command, or the command of legitimate authority, is to inflict just punishment on things like these. That is to say, when they find themselves in that kind of situation in human affairs, right order constrains them to initiate such wars or to follow the commands of others in this regard.[94]

The "Israelite wars enjoined by God are incontrovertible evidence that not all wars, even in a Christian context, are immoral."

The voice of correction and the voice of mercy. Louis Swift observes that for Augustine there are "two voices throughout the Scriptures: the voice of correction and the voice of mercy. They operate in tandem with now one and now the other calling man to action."[95] Swift continues: "For Augustine there are evils connected with war which are worse than death, and it is to correct these that men are allowed and sometimes required to take up arms. Thus, war, as one modern commentator has expressed it, is both 'a consequence of sin and a remedy for it.'"[96]

To reiterate, Augustine does not believe that when a legitimate authority employs force or engages in war a violation of Jesus' teaching against returning evil for evil occurs. Such would only be the case if those waging war did so through the exercise of a vengeful or cruel interior disposition. Augustine views war as disciplinary action and emphasizes that one's disposition in the midst of war will often determine whether Jesus' prohibition against revenge can be preserved. "These precepts about patience that we have been discussing must always be observed with respect to one's interior disposition, and a spirit of benevolence must always permeate the will so as to avoid returning evil for evil." War will occasionally demand a "benign severity," but never a spirit of revenge or a delight in cruelty or violence.

Other post-Constantinian perspectives. Though Augustine's perspective on just war has deeply shaped Christian thought for hundreds of years, we would err in deducing from Augustine's towering influence that Christians were of one mind on warfare and military service, *during or after* Augustine's lifetime. Martin of Tours (mid-fourth century AD) is a striking example of a soldier who upon conversion felt that military service in the Roman legions directly contradicted the teachings of Christ. Paulinus, bishop of Nola (AD 409–431), also spoke out strongly against Christians taking up the sword.

The man who fights with the sword is an agent of death, and whoever sheds his own blood or someone else's will have death as his wages. He will be responsible for his own death or for the crime of bringing it on another because, of necessity, the soldier in war, even though he fights for someone else rather than himself, either meets death in defeat or attains victory through killing. One cannot be victorious except through shedding blood. For this reason the Lord says, "You cannot serve two masters" (Matt. 6:24), that is, both the one God and mammon, both Christ and Caesar, although Caesar himself now wants to be the servant of Christ in order that he might deserve to be ruler over certain nations. For no earthly king is king of the whole world. That belongs to Christ who is God because "all things were made through him, and without him nothing was made" (John 1:3). He is both the King of kings and the Lord of lords (Rev. 17:14). "He does whatever he wishes on the earth, in the sea and in the depths" (Psalm 135:6).[97]

Paulinus's words remind us that the perspective of Tertullian and Origen was still advocated strongly in the fifth century AD, one hundred years after the conversion of Constantine. The points Paulinus makes are well-nigh identical with those that Tertullian made against Christian service in the military three hundred years earlier. Both Tertullian and Paulinus emphasize that the killing soldiers must do to win in battle or to execute criminals violates the teaching of Jesus. Paulinus especially emphasizes that it is Jesus who is king, not Caesar, a courageous point to make when "Christian" emperors had been reigning for the last century. Tertullian's earlier concern about the idolatry that was inescapable in the life of a Roman soldier, though, is mainly irrelevant. It is largely Christian legions that are now serving the empire.

ISSUES TO PONDER

And so we must ask, What would Jesus have us do as we respond to the evil so prevalent in the world? As we've seen, ancient Christians such as Athenagoras, Tertullian, Origen, Martin of Tours, and Paulinus were firmly opposed to any use of violence in responding to evil and to Christian service in the military. Indeed, for hundreds of years the ancient church opposed service in the military, precisely because of what soldiers are required to do in their particular line of work. Jesus teaches that we are to love our enemies. Soldiers are trained to kill their enemies. For many ancient Christians this solved the issue. But not for all.

With the conversion of Constantine perspectives changed. It is not long before we discover church fathers such as Augustine advocating the legitimacy of Christian service in the military and the use of force by the state and the church in resisting evil. Thus the consensus we see in the church's great creedal traditions is lacking in the church fathers' perspective on warfare, military service, and resistance to evil, especially since the conversion of Constantine and Augustine's lifetime and writing. When the Roman world became a largely Christian world, views on the legitimate use of force shifted. The temptation to exercise power dramatically increased, including the use of the sword to achieve Christian ends.

In our next three chapters we will shift direction and focus on a wide constellation of issues related to the family, marriage, and human sexuality.

There is no relationship between human beings so close as that of husband and wife, if they are united as they ought to be. . . . This erotic love is deeply planted within our inmost being. Unnoticed by us, it attracts the bodies of men and women to each other, because in the beginning woman came forth from man, and from man and woman men and women now proceed.

JOHN CHRYSOSTOM, ON MARRIAGE AND FAMILY LIFE[1]

In general, let our affirmation about marriage, food and the rest proceed: we should never act from desire; our will should be concentrated on necessities. We are children of will, not of desire. If a man marries in order to have children he ought to practice self-control. He ought not to have a sexual desire even for his wife, to whom he has a duty to show Christian love. He ought to produce children by a reverent, disciplined act of will.

CLEMENT OF ALEXANDRIA, STROMATEIS[2]

We [Christians] consider that abstention from sexual intercourse is blessed when undertaken by those to whom God has given this state. We honor monogamy and the dignity of one marriage. . . . Both states—singleness and marriage—have their own distinctive ministries and services to the Lord. . . . Let each one therefore fulfill his ministry through the work in which he was called, in order that he might be free in Christ and receive the fitting reward for his ministry.

CLEMENT OF ALEXANDRIA, MISCELLANIES[3]

Two ways of life were thus given by the Lord to His Church. The one is above nature, and beyond common human living; it admits not marriage, child-bearing, property nor the possession of wealth. Like some celestial beings, these gaze down upon human life, performing the duty of a priesthood for the whole human race. . . . And the more humble, more human way prompts men to join in pure nuptials, and to produce children, to undertake government, to give orders to soldiers fighting for right; it allows them to have minds for farming, for trade and for the other secular interests as well as for religion.

EUSEBIUS OF CAESAREA, THE PROOF OF THE GOSPEL[4]

FOUR

"THE CLOSEST OF RELATIONSHIPS"

Sex and the Dynamics of Desire

Key Issues to Consider

A host of challenges, problems, opportunities, and questions faced ancient Christian families. Issues concerning marriage, widowhood, virginity, divorce, singleness and celibacy, and broader concerns about human sexuality immediately come to mind, issues that are of pressing interest and relevance for Christian image bearers in the twenty-first century. Occasionally the church fathers' thoughts and practices on these issues strike some readers as too stringent, foolishly narrow, short-sighted, misguided—the list of descriptive adjectives seems endless. Sometimes the adjectives may apply; I've yet to run across any period of the church's history where its leaders' vision was entirely pristine and pure. Yet, as I've argued in earlier volumes in this series, precisely because the church fathers lived in a time so far removed from our own, their insights can illuminate our blind spots; their favorite Bible texts might never appear on our iPad's selection of verses to memorize.

Eve Tushnet comments that our modern tendency to idolize marriage, "especially in the romantic and individualistic way we do today, isn't true to the much more radical Gospels. Jesus wasn't married. He didn't say, 'There is no greater love than this: to lay down one's life for one's wife,' or even 'one's children.'"[5] She's right. To support her point, Tushnet quotes a text that remains invisible to many modern Western Christians: "Whoever comes to me and does not hate father and mother, wife and children, brothers and sisters, yes, and even life itself, cannot be my disciple" (Lk 14:26). Tushnet then refers to the lives of St. Agnes and St. Lucy as examples of women who were martyred "for their refusal of marriage in favor of becoming brides of Christ."[6]

Tushnet's point, and mine in quoting her, is twofold: first, each age of the church's history has its strengths and weaknesses, its wisdom and its foolishness, its clarities and its blind spots. In the case at hand, is the modern West's—and particularly the Christian West in North America—idolization of marriage and the family a potential hairline fracture in the church's mind? Many evangelicals, for instance, have imbibed with their mother's milk that their number-one priority should be one's marriage, one's husband or wife, and of course one's children. The church fathers simply didn't think this way, though we often encounter great instances of deep familial love among them.

The church fathers took texts such as Luke 14:26 very seriously. Did Jesus not say—surely using hyperbole (purposeful exaggeration) for the sake of illustration—that if we are unwilling to "hate" our father or mother or wife or children or brothers or our own life, we cannot be his disciples? These words, the church fathers insist, must mean something. They should not die the death of a thousand qualifications.

The church fathers realized texts such as Luke 14:26 were hard to interpret well. Cyril of Alexandria believes the key to this text is the clause "more than me." "By adding 'more than me,'" Cyril argues, "it is plain that he permits us to love, but not more than we love him. He demands our highest affection for himself and that very correctly." Our love for God is "superior both to the honor due to parents and to the natural affection felt for children."[7]

The fathers are deeply concerned that marriages flourish, that children are raised in the faith, that single people are helped to live a holy, chaste sexual life, and that those called to the vocation of virginity are supported by specific church teachings and structures to help them fulfill that call.

The thoughts of the fathers—perhaps most strongly in the area of family life and human sexuality—will infuriate some readers and deeply attract others. My responsibility is to present their positions as clearly as possible. Let the chips fall where they may.

The quote from John Chrysostom that began this chapter illustrates the surprises that are in store for us. Chrysostom's words demonstrate that not all church fathers were uncomfortable with or disapproved of the joys of a sexually active, deeply fulfilling marriage. To repeat his words:

> There is no relationship between human beings so close as that of husband and wife, if they are united as they ought to be. . . . This erotic love is deeply planted within our inmost being. Unnoticed by us, it attracts the bodies of men and women to each other, because in the beginning woman came forth from man, and from man and woman men and women now proceed.[8]

To be honest, some church fathers might squirm in discomfort at Chrysostom's words, but not all.

What of those who never marry? Here I have in mind both persons who purposely choose not to marry for specifically Christian reasons—virgins by choice—and single people who would like to marry but, for one reason or another, never have the opportunity. The question of the single life surely remains with us today. How, indeed, are single people to live holy, sane sexual lives well before God? What advice might the church fathers offer?

More particularly, what did the vocation of Christian virginity represent and model in the ancient world of the church fathers? Why was celibacy so highly praised in the church? We will explore these issues in some detail in this chapter.

Preliminary Considerations

Chrysostom, among all the fathers, speaks most clearly and eloquently of the wonders, joys, and challenges of marriage. His words concerning erotic love between husband and wife and its fruit in the conception of a child are elevated and encouraging, and we will explore them in some detail.

At first glance, other ancient Christian writers appear much less enthusiastic in their comments on the relationship between the sexes. Tertullian comes to mind. He can be effusive in his praise and admiration for marriage. Yet the very same writer refers to women as Eve's imitators, bearers of Eve's guilt to the present day: "You are the devil's gateway: you are the unsealer of that (forbidden tree): you are the first deserter of the divine law: you are she who persuaded him whom the devil was not valiant enough to attack."[9] What are we to make of this? Are Tertullian's words simply a mad, misogynistic, rhetorical flourish? Or do they represent, as Elizabeth Carnelly puts it, both "the prejudices and concerns of his time"?[10]

How are we to interpret Clement of Alexandria's comment in the *Stromata* quoted at the beginning of this chapter? Clement writes that sexual intercourse rightfully occurs in marriage but seemingly advocates a view of sex that is passionless, void of desire, and simply an act of the will. I can imagine modern readers rolling their eyes in amusement.

Can Clement or other writers who appear so discomfited by the messy, heated, earthiness of sex—and its accompanying pleasures—have anything valuable to teach us in our contemporary context? Are ancient Christian writers like Clement simply sexually maladjusted men foisting their troubled ideas on the church? Or do we need to catch our breath, withhold premature judgments, ask careful questions, and empathetically listen to what Clement desires to teach us?

To understand Clement requires that we attempt to comprehend empathetically his language, his culture, and his philosophical and theological presuppositions—in this case concerning marriage and human sexuality. In short, we must work hard to enter the mind and world out of which Clement's comments emerge.

Clement has extremely positive things to say about *both* celibacy and marriage. Indeed, Elizabeth Clark writes that Clement's thoughts on marriage are "the strongest argument for the goodness of marriage to be found in the writings of the first three centuries."[11] Our introductory quotation is worth repeating:

> We [Christians] consider that abstention from sexual intercourse is blessed *when undertaken by those to whom God has given this state.* We honor monogamy and the dignity of one marriage. . . . Both states—singleness and marriage—have their own distinctive ministries and services to the Lord. . . . Let each one therefore fulfill his ministry through the work in which he was called, in order that he might be free in Christ and receive the fitting reward for his ministry.

Clement's teaching on celibacy is wise, sensitive, and measured. He longs for Christians "to be free in Christ." He quite evidently understands the strength of human sexual impulses, that God has created humans as sexual beings, and that to remain celibate is possible only through a special gifting and the grace of God. Abstention from sexual intercourse is "blessed" only under clearly defined circumstances; celibacy is not for all. To remain single or to marry each "have their own distinctive ministries and services to the Lord" and depend on the gifts God has given to each person.

Thus, discernment is necessary, a discernment that comes from the Holy Spirit. Vocation *and* gifting are key criteria to keep in mind as one seeks to discern whether to marry or remain a virgin. If we exercise wisdom in making these decisions, Clement believes, freedom will result. "Let each one therefore fulfill his ministry through the work in which he was called, *in order that he might be free in Christ.*"

To Desire or Not to Desire?

Clement's counsel is sensible, prudent, and even fairly earthy. Yet, we ask, isn't this the same man we encountered at the beginning of this chapter, the one who advised husbands to engage in sexual relations with their wives without passion or desire? "If a man marries in order to have children he ought to practice self-control. He ought not to have a sexual *desire* even for his wife, to whom he has a duty to show *Christian love*. He ought to produce children by a reverent, disciplined act of will."[12]

How in the world, we wonder, could Clement possibly think that sexual relations could ever occur without passion and desire? At this point—at least for many modern readers—Clement has morphed from a sensible, astute coach on celibacy, marriage, and sexual matters into an unbearable, unrealistic prude. Or has he?

Take another close look at the most provocative sentence in Clement's comment: "He ought not to have a sexual *desire* even for his wife, to whom he has a duty to show *Christian love*." In Clement's thinking, desire is the problem—in this case sexual *desire*—for desire is antithetical to Christian love. How so? Is desire the natural sexual attraction planted in human nature by God? Or is the desire Clement condemns dangerous, harmful, even sinister? And if so, why?

THE QUESTION OF DESIRE

Clement frequently contrasts desire and pleasure with self-control or self-discipline. Why does Clement insist that Christians practice self-control? He believes that the self in its present, sinful state desires or lusts after good things in a wicked, exaggerated, immoderate fashion.

To be direct: God's image bearers have gone bad (see Gen 2). The sad and shocking result is that in our present, sinful condition our appetites for good things—food, sex, friendship, entertainment, and so on—now run wild. We innately want too much of a good thing. In our sinful state, we are wired for excess.

To use Clement's vocabulary, we desire immoderately rather than moderately. Left to ourselves, we will gorge rather than eat, lust rather than love. Though one donut might do, I would much rather devour three or four and worry about the consequences later. I'm hungry, after all! Plainly, at least from Clement's perspective, our appetites—our desires—are askew. The unbridled self—the uncontrolled self—is a naturally skilled manipulator, exploiter, devourer. "You are there to meet my needs," the sinful self unabashedly exclaims. "I may be listening to you, but I'm thinking about me!"

Think of it this way: the sinful self—left to itself—is never satisfied. Its desires are never sated. Thus, Clement realizes—like Jesus and the apostle Paul—that the self in its present state *must be controlled*; it is like a runaway train, rolling down the tracks at high speed, in danger of flying off into oblivion at any moment. The tracks are meant to guide, stabilize, and control, but the train's furnace is blazing too strongly, producing too much energy to be controlled.

Desire, in the negative sense that so worries Clement, is the self's blazing furnace and the power it is generating. The tracks are meant to guide and harness this power. If they do their job, the train will reach its destination. Too much power, too much desire—what Clement calls "immoderation"—and the train will jump the tracks. The self ends up destroying the self—and often the object of its desires. In modern parlance, "Give me what I need, honey, or I'm going to have to move in a new direction."

The Need to Discipline the Self

Back to Clement: "Self-discipline [self-control] applies, not just to sexual matters, but to everything else for which the soul lusts improperly, because it is not satisfied with the bare necessities. Self-discipline applies to speech, possessions and their use, and to *desire* generally."[13]

Are human words *necessarily* evil? Or possessions? Or sexual desire? Absolutely not, Clement argues. Everything depends on the *nature of our desire* as we speak or write, seek to possess, and love our wives or husbands. Do we desire in the right manner and to the right degree? Is the nature of our desire life giving or death dealing?

To refer to Clement's specific example of sexual relations in married life, it is possible for me to have sexual relations in a manner and to a degree with my wife that manifests Christian love or in a manner and to a degree that destroys love and manifests lust. Sexual desire nurtures marriage and sometimes destroys marriage. If our desires are self-centered—the default position for sinful human beings—we end up misusing, exploiting, or harming those good things and people God offers to us for our flourishing and good. The tragic result is immeasurable pain for all involved.

AN ANCIENT AND MODERN-DAY OBSESSION

By way of example, consider the modern obsession with pornography, a vice that was also prevalent in Clement's world. Kyle Harper comments:

> In a society where "the work of Aphrodite" could always "be bought for a drachma," self-control was no trivial virtue. . . . The material environment of the Greco-Roman city was unusually adapted for stimulating the appetites. The high empire was the Indian summer of classical nudity, when prosperity carried the culture of public baths and gymnasia further than ever before and when frankly erotic art was ubiquitous in refined and popular media.[14]

The same is true of our global culture today. Dallas Willard refers to a *Christianity Today* survey conducted in 2000 that "found that 37% of pastors reported pornography as a current personal struggle and 57% of pastors listed pornography as the most sexually damaging issue in their congregations."[15] Barna Research indicates that 35 percent of men and 17 percent of women use pornography on a monthly basis. Somebody is making a lot of money. *Adult Video News*, an adult industry publication, reports 2006 revenues at $13.2 billion.[16]

Why are we so attracted to images (in Clement's day pornographic paintings, statues, dishes, drinking cups, and stage plays were commonplace) of human beings having sex? Well, as Clement would readily agree, we are sexual beings. Sexual activity naturally interests us. But more is involved in the vice of pornography than mere sexual attraction and activity. For pornography is generally an isolated, selfish affair for its viewer and a mainly impersonal affair for its producers and actors.

Are pornography's modern consumers genuinely involved with "real" people, people to whom they are lovingly giving as well as receiving? No.

They are simply watching and responding to images transmitted electronically to private viewing spaces. The viewer is never asked to contribute or sacrifice anything—except perhaps a credit card number. Pleasure is experienced, but it's purchased at a high price; the economic and sexual exchange is isolated, lonely, self-absorbed. An image demands nothing, requires nothing, gives nothing, receives nothing. As we all know, it's impossible to have sex with a photograph—unless we dramatically redefine what sex is. Porn promises to slake the viewer's thirsty, self-centered desire, but the promise is hollow. Lawrence Cunningham observes:

> The basic evil of pornography is not in its exhibitionism but in
> that it never satisfies the voyeur—which explains why, paradoxically, pornography is both boring and addictive; it is a species of
> gluttony that always promises *more*. The pornographic subject is
> an object (not a person), and the pornographic act is mechanical,
> but neither loving nor authentically human.[17]

In pornography and in a pornified culture—Clement's Roman world and much of the global world today—the sexual desire created by God to find its satisfaction in the "other," from a Christian perspective in one's wife or husband, and fulfilled in the giving of the self for the other, is drastically inverted. The self, twisted in on itself away from others, experiences increasing weakness—indeed, starvation—in its self-centered, isolated search for sexual pleasure and fulfillment. The pornographer feeds on sexually weak and fragile people, not strong ones. In Henry Fairlie's words: "Pornographic literature and movies do not incite us to strenuous emulations. On the contrary, they are substitutes, evidence not of the strength of our sexual feelings, but of their enfeeblement. . . . It is a substitute again for involvement with another person."[18]

False desires, false loves—in this case lust—desire much and obtain little. Those controlled by them fall prey to the ultimate shell-game. Yet these fallen desires' lure, their pull, is irresistible apart from power of God's grace at work in the life of his image bearer. Clement rightly insists that self-control is a "gift," "a divine power and grace of God." He also recognizes and emphasizes that we need one another if we are to live in a sane, self-controlled way. "We say that we ought to share in suffering and 'bear one another's burdens,' for fear that anyone who thinks he is standing firmly should in fact fall (1 Cor. 10:12)."[19]

The Problem of the Passions

Clement's vocabulary of desire includes another key concept we must thoroughly understand. We first encountered it in chapter one. I refer to the passions. "It is impossible," Clement writes, "for those who are still under the direction of their *passions* to receive true knowledge of God."[20] "We have learned to call freedom the freedom with which the Lord alone endows us, *delivering us* from pleasures, lusts, and *other passions*."[21] Is Clement thinking of passions in the same way a modern person would?

In the modern world, our passions are attached to what interests us, what deeply concerns us, what we enjoy, what we are devoted to, what we are willing to commit our time and our attention to. Some might be passionate about slavery and its eradication. Others are passionate about much less important things—for example, the Phillies. Frequently, if not always, strong *feelings* accompany our passions when pictured this way.

As we saw in chapter one, for ancient Christians a passion may have a strong emotional element or tone, but can just as often refer to "a state of mind, or even a habitual action. Anger is usually a passion, but sometimes forgetfulness is called a passion. Gossip and talking too much are also regularly called passions. . . . Depression, the very opposite of a passion as we usually use that term in our modern world, is one of the most painful passions."[22] The passions, then, are a "conglomerate of obsessive emotions, attitudes, desires, and ways of acting. . . . It is these passions that blind us in our dealings with ourselves, each other, and the world, and so pervert perfectly good and useful impulses *which take away our freedom to love*."[23]

Some passions, at least as understood by the ancients, can exhibit themselves in apathy, an emotional, intellectual, and moral deadness to things that genuinely matter. Think of the popular characters that entertained us in episode after episode of *Seinfeld* in the 1990s. They made us laugh—and still do on reruns—because the perspectives and behavior of Jerry, George, Elaine, Kramer, and Newman are outrageous, immature, and idiotic.

For instance, the *Seinfeld* gang are passionate about having sex as often as possible with as many people as possible. They are obsessed with sex. Their world revolves around sex. But the idea of long-term commitment to anyone horrifies them. The characters on *Seinfeld* have never grown up. They are emotionally and ethically stunted. As George asks Jerry after having sex on a desk in his office with the office housecleaner, a woman he has known for only a few minutes: "Was that wrong?"

The *Seinfeld* characters are emotionally apathetic; they are tone-deaf to circumstances and people that should normally elicit care, concern, sadness, or joy. Their passions run wild, leaving havoc in their wake. When George's longtime girlfriend Linda dies from licking poisonous envelopes, George's response is one of relief; commitment was closing in on him, suffocating him. In his own words, "George's world is collapsing." George's palpable relief when Linda dies makes us laugh because it is so incongruous with how an emotionally healthy person would react. No grief here; simply relief. And within hours George is on the prowl again in search of fulfillment.

Should we be surprised that one of the last episodes of *Seinfeld* takes place in a courtroom? One by one the characters we have encountered across the *Seinfeld* years point their fingers at Jerry and company and accuse them of thoughtlessness, self-centeredness, neglect, and indeed cruelty. Baboo, the Pakistani restaurant owner Jerry misguidedly coached concerning décor and cuisine, points his finger at Jerry and seemingly on behalf of the entire courtroom declares, "He is a bad man. A very bad man." Yet Jerry, George, Elaine, and Kramer simply don't get it. When finally convicted they still seem confused. We can almost hear them saying to each other: "Whatever."

Seinfeld amuses us because we know, in our heart of hearts, something is wrong here. When we laugh at Jerry and George, we're laughing at ourselves—and sometimes cringing.

The desert fathers and mothers—and writers such as Clement—believe the passions spring from the *logismoi* or *dialogismoi*. One ancient writer describes the *logismoi* as maggot eggs from which evil thoughts, motives, and actions spring and identifies them as the "seeds of the 'passions,' those suggestions or impulses that emerge from the subconscious and soon become obsessive."[24] From the perspective of the desert abbas and ammas, the passions "are blockages, usurpations, deviations. . . . They are forms of idolatry, of that 'self-idolatry' that deflects towards nothingness our capacity for transcendence."[25]

THE CALL TO APATHEIA

Cleansing from the passions is an indispensable first step toward the freedom to love one's spouse, children, friends, and enemies. Clement champions the practice of a specific type of response to the problem of the passions—what he calls *apatheia*—but what he means by the term is exactly opposite to the apathy displayed by Seinfeld and company.

Clement understands what it is to be deeply committed to a cause or person, though he also realizes that our strong feelings and devotions are not immune from the sinful infections running through our spiritual bloodstream. He, like church fathers in general, views the passions negatively. When he employs the term, he is not smiling. Why? The passions and their sidekicks—the desires—represent the cluster of *self-centered, self-indulgent* hopes, dreams, preoccupations, and obsessions that the human *ego* naturally generates in its sinful, skewed state.

When we are dominated by a "passion," as Clement understands the term, we inevitably misread reality. Our focus blurs, our seeking goes awry. The person controlled by his passions seeks pleasure for its own sake—to meets the need of an *ego* out of control in its quest for *self-satisfaction*. To employ a modern metaphor to illustrate the ancient dynamic, the sinful, passionate person is a nuclear reactor in meltdown, whose radioactive rays—the passions—contaminate and destroy.

Peter Brown describes the passions this way:

> The "passions" are best seen as tendencies built up within the *ego*, which could force the sage to overreact to any situation, to cathect [to invest with mental or emotional energy] it with a charge of

personal, egotistic significance that distorted its true meaning. The "passions" colored perceptions of the outside world with non-existent sources of fear, anxiety, and hope, or else bathed it in a false glow of pleasure and potential satisfaction. . . . Passions were not what we tend to call feelings; they were, rather complexes which hindered the true expression of feelings.[26]

A passionate person, then, in the ancient meaning of the term, might well be someone who by all appearances is emotionally flat, uninvolved and unengaged. Just as easily, a passionate person could be emotionally lively and vibrant. The mark of the passions in a human personality is not the strength or weakness of one's feelings. *It is rather the habitual misdirection of desire*, the tendency to identify things as important, as worthy of pursuit or emulation, that are genuinely unimportant and indifferent matters—if not downright detrimental to one's physical, emotional, and spiritual health.

The "passionate" person, Clement believes, *habitually misidentifies what is worth our love, commitment, and attention.* Certain values are indeed worth our emulation, protection, and devotion. In the passions' mumbo-jumbo, though, values that belong at the periphery of our attention migrate to the center because of the pleasure they seem to offer to us. Likewise, the passions drastically undervalue those things that are genuinely worthy of our pursuit and commitment. Things that belong at the center drift to the periphery. In a heartbeat, people driven by their passions can swerve sharply off course; the moral GPS of their lives continually adjusts to the north star of their passionate desires.

How often do we hear of a thirty- or forty-year marriage suddenly crumbling as a husband—or wife—announces, "You're simply not meeting my needs." Clement's point is that people trapped by their passions—desires intimately linked to the direct pursuit of pleasure—don't understand what their needs actually are. A husband tempted to adultery might have a greater need for rest and healthy leisure than a romp in his neighbor's wife's bed. Though Clement might raise his eyebrows at the idea of sport meeting a significant need, he would surely have understood the importance of rest and leisure. Again, when the important things are ignored or misunderstood, less important things—what Clement calls indifferent matters—rush in to fill the vacuum. Finally, life implodes.

The passions characterize foolish people, people who lack discernment and discretion, people who simply don't know how to live, folks such as our *Seinfeld* friends Jerry, George, Elaine, and Kramer. They are unable to discern when to speak, when to act, when to refrain from acting, when to cry, when to laugh, what to value, what not to value; people in the grip of the passions *don't know how to love.* They continue to make choices as each day passes, but the freedom exercised in these choices is false—indeed, enslaved by the reigning, sinful *ego*, a black hole whose gravitational pull sucks in all who get too near.

Surely such a state of affairs quenches human flourishing and destroys human relationships. Can the intimacy of marriage survive in such an environment? Thus, Clement's words and warnings—along with those of other church fathers—concerning the destructive effect of the passions. Without change, without a fundamental reorientation of perspective and practice, the obsessions of the self—the runaway, passionate *ego*—will consume the self and all within its orbit.

EVERYTHING BEGINS WITH THE GRACE OF GOD

The church fathers are of one mind that everything must begin with the grace of God. Clement takes his cue from the apostle Paul's teaching, insights Clement skillfully weaves with elements of Greek Stoic philosophy. In Paul's mind, self-control is a gift of the Holy Spirit: "The fruit of the Spirit is love, joy, peace, patience, kindness, generosity, faithfulness, gentleness, and self-control" (Gal 5:22-23). Clement reinforces Paul's point, writing that the self-control God's image bearers must exercise in overcoming the deleterious effect of the passions is "a divine power and grace of God."[27]

Self-control and self-discipline, virtues that initially may appear binding and restrictive, actually lead to freedom, "the freedom *with which the Lord alone endows us*, delivering us from pleasures, lusts and the other *passions."*[28] "It is not a matter of having desires and holding out against them," Clement writes, "but actually of mastering desire by self-control. It is not possible to acquire this form of self-control *except by the grace of God.* That is why Jesus says, 'Ask and it shall be granted to you' (Matt. 7.7)."[29]

As we have seen, for Clement *apatheia* is the ideal virtue the Christian philosopher or sage should pursue, what we might define as a healthy, sane, wise indifference to unimportant things. In a word, there are simply some things that are not all that important and that are surely not worth devoting our lives to.

Initially, the pursuit of *apatheia* seems counterintuitive. I should become "indifferent" *in order to love* my wife, my children, my friends, my enemies? All depends on the target of my indifference. If I have become so committed to my favorite baseball and football team that my sense of well-being and my ability to love those around me suffer when the Phillies or Eagles lose, something must change. If my wife is sitting on the porch as the sun goes down, longing for a conversation, and I continue to unconcernedly peruse my stamp collection—to which I've already devoted most of the afternoon—adjustments need to be made. If my kids fail to recognize me when I return from work in the evening and I have little to offer them because I am emotionally and physically spent, I need to ask a fundamental question: Why am I doing what I'm doing? How did I end up like this? What needs to change and how can I—by God's grace—begin to move in a new direction?

THE GOODNESS OF MARRIAGE

Allow me to be clear and direct: without doubt the ancient church affirmed the inherent goodness and beauty of marriage. Debates did occur, though, surrounding a constellation of issues. For instance, might ministers be married or not? The church would hammer on the anvil of this question for years, and sparks would fly.

Church historian Socrates, in his *Ecclesiastical History*, notes that at the Council of Nicaea (AD 325) the issue of clerical celibacy was a hot topic. Paphnutius, a desert monk, had long lived a celibate life. Yet at

Nicaea he vociferously opposed the idea of clerical celibacy as a requirement of the church for those set apart for ministry: "Roaring at the top
of his voice," Socrates writes, "he declared that 'all men cannot bear the
practice of rigid continence; neither perhaps would the chastity of the
wife of each be preserved.'"[30]

The council responded by agreeing with Paphnutius's position. David
Ford comments that "never again was mandatory clerical celibacy ever
considered in the Eastern Church."[31] Matters took a different direction
in the West, where celibacy for ordained clergy became a requirement.

The church strongly affirmed the goodness of marriage, sexual relations, and procreation; to do otherwise would be to deny the goodness of
the created order God established and declared to be very good. The
church's affirmation of creation's essential goodness in all its facets and
dimensions—including marriage and family life—occurred in the midst
of significant conflict with Gnostic teaching.

The Gnostic Threat

Gnostic teachers—many of whom desperately longed to be accepted
as legitimate members of the Christian community—denied the
goodness of matter and of all things composed of matter, including
human bodies.

Gnostic teaching proclaimed that a lesser, foolish god—sometimes
identified as the *demiurge* and occasionally equated with the God of the
Old Testament—had mistakenly birthed or aborted matter. What humans experienced daily as *embodied* selves—somatic experiences related
to taste, touch, sight, hearing, and so on—was inherently, necessarily
false, a misleading diversion from divine reality and our genuine past as
disembodied souls. Our true existence, Gnostic teachers insisted, is essentially spiritual, not material.

In the distant past, a time before stars, planets, seas, trees, butterflies,
or bodies, Gnostic leaders taught, as disembodied souls we understood
and experienced the spiritual nature of reality. We were entirely spiritual beings, unencumbered by material bodies. Alas, now as embodied

creatures we are unaware of what has happened. We have fallen into bodies and are presently entrapped in a prison of flesh, bone, blood, and brain. Enmeshed in material existence, we naturally engage in its rhymes and reasons—eating, drinking, marriage, sex, procreation, and family life—little realizing that to do so is to be ever more fully deceived regarding the nature of true reality. Little do we *know*, Gnostic teachers believed, what the truth is.

Salvation as understood by the Gnostics, the salvation Christian Gnostic teachers believed Jesus offered to all human beings, concerns knowledge (*gnosis*) of a very specific kind, knowledge revealed secretly to Gnostic teachers—either by the apostles or by direct revelation—and in turn shared by Gnostic teachers with those willing to become disciples of Gnostic masters such as Valentinian.

What is the heart and core of this Gnostic knowledge? *All reality is essentially spiritual.* If so, why would one marry, have children, and raise a family? Hadn't Jesus himself taught that there will be no marriage in heaven (Lk 10:27-35)? To marry, have sex, and procreate sadly and misguidedly introduces more "souls" into the illusions of a material world.

A FIRM NO TO GNOSTICISM

The church, led by gifted thinkers such as Irenaeus of Lyons, replied to Gnostic teachers with a firm *no*. As I stressed in some detail in *Worshiping with the Church Fathers*, Irenaeus understood that central, nonnegotiable aspects of Christian worship—the celebration of the Eucharist serving as the prime example—make no sense if Gnostic teaching is correct. "How can our human bodies be nourished by the Eucharist with the body and blood of Christ"—a given for Irenaeus—"if matter cannot become the means to communicate spiritual life as a gift of God?"[32] "How can they [the Gnostics] affirm that the flesh, which is nourished from the body and blood of the Lord, and is a member of him, is incapable of receiving the gift of God?"[33]

The Son has become incarnate in Jesus and thereby hallowed all matter. Matter is a good thing, a beautiful thing, a blessed thing, a holy thing. All embodied, material existence, from bodies to butterflies, is very good. *Incarnational thinking, the church fathers believe, weds the spiritual and the material.* The structures and practices that flow from God's love of matter are very good, including marriage, sexual activity within the perimeters and commitments of marriage, the procreation of children, and family life in general.

Two Ways of Life

Reread the introductory quotation from Eusebius. He speaks of "two ways of life" given by Jesus to his church. The first way is "above nature, and beyond human living." Characteristics that mark normal, everyday human life—marriage, sexual relations, the birth of children, the possession of property and wealth—have no place in this first way. Rather, the life Eusebius proposes is more angelic than human. Eusebius describes it as a life for "celestial beings," transformed humans who "gaze down upon human life," priests "for the whole human race."

The second way Eusebius mentions is "more humble, more human," one for human minds—and bodies—devoted to planting crops, bearing and raising children, business matters, and other "secular interests as well as for religion."

The first way is "celestial," the life of angels lived by a select group of God's image bearers, an angelic priesthood serving as mediators between God and the vast majority of humans. The second way, less elevated in its perspectives and practices, is the life most of us live: earthbound, enmeshed in daily life's ordinary, common rhythms; the second way has a religious aspect, but in a more human, less angelic manner than the first way. Does Eusebius's two-tiered model—some people "above nature" and others living more humbly within it—inevitably devalue aspects of human life that God has declared to be "very good"? We will ponder these issues in our discussion of the single life. We must ask: Did God create his image bearers to be humans—Jesus was and is human—or to be angels? How might Eusebius respond?

What of Those Who Never Marry?

What of those who never marry, either because they do not have the opportunity to do so or because they purposely choose to remain virgins?[34] We will consider this question for the remainder of this chapter, with John Chrysostom's praise of marriage following in chapter five. Ponder the following comment of Gregory of Nyssa (c. 335–c. 395), one in which he praises both marriage and virginity.

> The human nature that we all share is quite adequate to the task of speaking in defense of marriage. By itself, human nature instills in all of us a lower inclination to enter into marriage in order to beget, whereas virginity stands in the way of our natural proclivity in a certain manner. Since this is the case, writing a treatise praising or encouraging marriage is an unnecessary task. Its own pleasures are its best advocate and champion of its merits.[35]

Gregory praises marriage. "Its own pleasures are its best advocate and champion of its merits." Yet the tone of Gregory's praise is somewhat subdued. Human nature leads human beings to desire marriage, yet this is a "lower inclination." A higher path to pursue and defend—I see Eusebius nodding his head in agreement—is that of virginity, a way of life that "stands in the way of our natural proclivity in a certain manner." In a word, virginity requires an explanation and defense of its own that marriage does not need. We naturally know that marriage is a good thing; the decision to remain celibate will require some defending.

The Single Life

The last intense period of persecution against the early Christian community occurred in the first decade of the fourth century AD. With the conversion of Constantine in AD 312, persecution against the church largely died out, as did the age of the great martyrs of the faith. Boniface Ramsey comments: "As the age of persecutions drew to a close in the Empire and the number of martyrs diminished to relative insignificance, the Church realized that in some way something had been lost to it."

In a nutshell, Ramsey's thesis is this: as the age of the martyrs finished, it was "inconceivable" to the early church "that it should be without this charism." Hence, as we move into the fourth century *a new pattern of martyrdom emerges more fully*, that of virgins who have dedicated both body and soul in allegiance to Christ.[36] These folks represent the "celestial" people mentioned by Eusebius.

Ramsey's hypothesis is supported by fourth-century patristic works that accentuate the link between virginity and martyrdom. Ambrose, for instance, refers to martyrdoms throughout his treatise *Concerning Virgins*. First Ambrose points to Agnes, a twelve-year-old child, who was both a martyr and a virgin. Indeed, Ambrose preaches, Agnes is the prototype for a "new kind of martyrdom!" "She would not as a bride so hasten to the couch, as being a virgin she joyfully went to the place of punishment with hurrying step, her head not adorned with plaited hair, but with Christ."[37] Though many young men desired to marry Agnes, she remained single-minded in her devotion to Christ, both as virgin and as martyr. Agnes experienced, as Ambrose describes it, "a twofold martyrdom, of modesty and of religion. She both remained a virgin and she obtained martyrdom."

The connection that Ambrose makes between martyrdom and virginity is intentional and fits Ramsey's theory of virginity as replacing the gift of martyrdom so often present during periods of persecution. As the church's situation shifted from vulnerability to persecution to a position of religious and political power, the role the martyr played in the church's life and devotion increasingly shifted to the virgin. Consider, for example, the perspective of Methodius of Olympus, another church father who directly links martyrdom and virginity:

> Their (virgins') martyrdom did not consist in enduring things that pain the body for a short period of time; rather it consisted in steadfast endurance throughout their whole lifetime, never once shrinking from the truly Olympian contest of being battered in the practice of chastity. Because they stood firm against the torments of pleasure, fear, sorrow and other vices, they carry off the highest honors of all by reason of their rank in the land of promise.[38]

In the past, martyrs of the faith had sacrificially offered their bodies to Christ as a self-offering, literally dying to self as they died physically. Similarly, virgins die to self and its natural desires by offering their bodies solely to Christ. Again, we hear from Ramsey: "Virginity is not seen to be like martyrdom simply because it involves a comparable struggle but also because it produces the same effect, death to self, expressed through the image of bodily death."[39]

CHRISTIAN CELIBACY AND THE GRACE OF GOD

The church fathers generally view celibacy as a calling that directly and purposely challenges the normal rhythms and patterns of human life, a vocation possible only by the supernatural empowering given by God's grace. In Augustine's treatise on virginity (*De Virginitate*), he hammers home repeatedly that virginity is a gift of God's grace. Yes, it is a high and holy gift, yet there are no grounds for boasting; how could one boast in something given freely by God? "Wherefore let this be the first thought for the putting on of humility, that God's virgin should not think of herself as such, but that this best 'gift comes down from above from the Father of Lights, with whom is no change nor shadow of motion.'"[40]

No divine command, task, or vocation can be accomplished apart from a constant reliance on the grace of God. "Witnesses are those expressions of pious prayers in holy Scriptures, whereby it is shown, that those very things, which are commanded by God, are not done except by his gift and help, who commands. For we would be falsely asking for them if we could do them without the help of his grace."[41]

The life of the virgin, a gift freely given by God to some but not all, should lead to increased love rather than boasting. Humility, grounded on the awareness of the virgin's *graced* position before God and in the church, protects the virgin and those in relationship to her from pride's infection. "A virgin, therefore, has a subject for thought, such as may be of profit to her for the keeping of humility, that she not violate that charity, which is above all gifts, without which assuredly whatever other gifts she shall have had, whether few or many, she is nothing."[42]

Mary as Model

Mary appears constantly in patristic literature as the supreme model of virginity. Consider Ambrose's praise of Mary's purity: "The first thing that kindles ardor in learning is the greatness of the teacher. What is greater than the Mother of God? What more glorious than she whom Glory Itself chose? What more chaste than she who bore a body without contact with another body?"[43] Augustine expands on Ambrose's thought: Mary's virginity was "more pleasing and accepted" because before "He was conceived," he chose Mary's womb as "already dedicated to God, as that from which to be born."[44]

Ambrose, like Augustine and almost all church fathers, views Mary's character and body as specifically prepared by God for Christ's virginal conception. Patristic writers see Mary's virtues before Gabriel's visitation as a sign that God's grace already rested on her. "She was a virgin not only in body but also in mind. . . . Though the Virgin had other persons who were protectors of her body, she alone guarded her character." Mary "possesses the perfection of all virtues. . . . [She] attended to everything as though she were warned by many, and fulfilled every obligation of virtue as though she were teaching rather than learning. Such has the Evangelist shown her, such did the angel find her, such did the Holy Spirit choose her."[45]

Yet, Augustine emphasizes, Mary was "more blessed in receiving the faith of Christ, than in conceiving the flesh of Christ. . . . Her nearness as a Mother would have been of no profit to Mary, had she not borne Christ in her heart after a more blessed manner than in her flesh."[46] "Though she was the mother of the Lord, yet she desired to learn the precepts of the Lord, and she who brought forth God, yet desired to know God."[47]

Augustine teaches that Mary had already determined in her own mind, even before the annunciation, that she would remain a virgin for life. How so? Augustine points to Mary's response to the angel Gabriel's announcement that she would bear a child: "How shall this take place, since I am a virgin?"

Why would Mary mention that she was a virgin, Augustine asks, "unless she had before vowed herself unto God as a virgin"? The simple query, "How shall this take place?" would have sufficed in response to Gabriel. Mary's mention of her virginity, Augustine believes, informs the discerning reader that she had already taken the vow of virginity. Further, Augustine asks, would Mary have posed such a question to Gabriel if she were planning on leading a normal sexual life with Joseph?

Augustine reminds us that God does not command Mary to remain a virgin. While Protestant exegetes would see the lack of a command as a sign that after Jesus' birth Mary experienced an active sexual life with Joseph, Augustine interprets matters differently. Mary, whom God planned to be the model for future virgins dedicated to Christ and the church, freely chose to remain a virgin. God neither commanded nor coerced her to do so. "Thus Christ by being born of a virgin, who, before she knew who was to be born of her, had determined to continue a virgin, chose rather to approve, than to command, holy virginity. And thus, even in the female herself, in whom He took the form of a servant, He willed that virginity should be free."[48]

The Virgin as the Bride of Christ and Image of the Church

Mary's attitude and practice was the graced pattern for all virgins. Virgins need not "be sad" because their virginity prevents them from becoming mothers and bearing children. If Christian virgins live a life of faith and obedience to Christ, imitating Mary's faith, they "together with Mary are mothers of Christ." In fact, Augustine writes, Christ's "mother is the whole Church, because she herself assuredly gives birth to His members, that is, His faithful ones."[49]

Mary was the mother of Christ "after the flesh," "but after the Spirit she is both His sister and mother." Mary gives birth to Christ and is born again in Christ by the Spirit. The church through the Spirit follows the pattern of Jesus' conception in Mary's womb; in this case the Holy Spirit conceives many children—including Mary—in the womb of Christ's body, the church.

For it was necessary that our Head, on account of a notable miracle, should be born after the flesh of a virgin, that He might thereby signify that His members would be born after the Spirit, of the Church a virgin. . . . The Church, in the Saints who shall possess the kingdom of God, in the Spirit indeed is altogether the mother of Christ, altogether a virgin of Christ.[50]

Clement of Alexandria makes a similar point: "There is also one Virgin Mother, whom I love to call the Church. Alone, this mother had no milk, because she alone did not become a woman. She is virgin and mother simultaneously; a virgin undefiled and a mother full of love. She draws her children to herself and nurses them with holy milk, that is, the Word for infants."[51]

Virginity and the Incarnate God

Augustine grounds the life of virginity and its corresponding virtues on the model of the Son's incarnation: "All Christians have to guard humility, in view of the fact that it is from Christ that they are called Christians."[52] "Certainly we are to contemplate in Christ Himself the chief instruction and pattern of virginal purity. What further precept, then, concerning humility shall I give to the continent, than what he says to all, 'Learn of me, in that I am meek and lowly of heart.'"[53]

As we observed earlier, Augustine is clearly concerned that those called to the vocation of virginity may think too highly of themselves. Augustine stresses that Christ, a virgin himself, constantly warned of the insidious nature of pride. *Pride arrogantly claims that which only grace can give.* "Let these [virgins], by how much they are great, by so much humble themselves in all things, that they may find grace before you."[54] Virgins have received a wondrous gift through love's outworking. Let them remember to "violate not that love, which is above all gifts, without which assuredly whatever other gifts" they "shall have had, whether few or many, whether great or small," they "are nothing."[55]

Virginity as a Reversal of the Fall

Church fathers from the second century AD forward picture virginity as a reversal of Eve's sin in the Garden of Eden. Justin Martyr sees Mary and Eve as both similar and vastly dissimilar:

> [The Son of God] became man through a Virgin, so that the disobedience caused by the serpent might be destroyed in the same way it had begun. For Eve, who was virgin and undefiled, gave birth to disobedience and death after listening to the serpent's words. But the Virgin Mary conceived faith and joy; for when the angel Gabriel brought her the glad tidings that the Holy Spirit would come upon her and that the power of the Most High would overshadow her, so that the Holy One born of her would be the Son of God, she answered, "Let it be done to me according to your word" (Lk 1:38). Thus was born of her the [Child] about whom so many Scriptures speak, as we have shown. Through him, God crushed the serpent, along with those angels and men who had become like the serpent.[56]

Irenaeus further develops Justin's insights. A fallen angel deceives Eve. An archangel greets Mary. In turn, as Mary responds in faith to Gabriel's message and later gives birth to Jesus, she truly becomes Eve's advocate.

> Eve was seduced by the word of the [fallen] angel and transgressed God's word, so that she fled from him. In the same way, [Mary] was evangelized by the word of an angel and obeyed God's word, so that she carried him [within her]. And while the former was seduced into disobeying God, the latter was persuaded to obey God, so that the Virgin Mary became the advocate (*advocate*) of the virgin Eve.[57]

The Virgin Mary is the primary exemplar of this remarkable reversal, but others called to virginity imitate the same pattern of faith and obedience modeled by Mary. Origen perceives the design: "Every incorrupt and virgin soul, having conceived by the Holy Spirit in order to give birth to the will of the Father, is a mother of Jesus."[58]

Many church fathers believed that all who choose to imitate Mary's virginity and faithful response to God—women and men—*were proleptically living the life of heaven on earth*, as a preview of the coming attractions of the full manifestation of the kingdom of God. "Let us all, by God's grace, run the race of chastity, young men and maidens, old men and children, without abandoning ourselves to lust. . . . Let us not disregard the glory of chastity, which is the crown of the angels and a superhuman state of life! . . . Those who profess chastity are angels dwelling on earth. The virgins have their portion with the Virgin Mary."[59] Here we discover the rhyme and reason of Eusebius's teaching on the two ways of life, the celestial and the earthly.

QUESTIONS TO CONSIDER

What are we to make of Eusebius's two-lifestyles paradigm for the single life? And more broadly, what of the ancient church's understanding of virginity, a perspective that still deeply marks Roman Catholicism?

Protestants have generally struggled with patristic perspectives at this point. Why? The apostle Paul teaches that certain men and women are called by God to the single life through a specific spiritual gifting—he seems to have received this gift—but he also acknowledges that not all people receive this gift. Paul considers celibacy a gifting, not the requirement or accompaniment of a particular office or calling within the church (1 Cor 7:1-9).

In the Western church, though, the celibate or single life soon was linked to specific ecclesial offices—bishop, priest, and deacon come to mind. Ideally, vocation and the gift of celibacy would coincide. It was surely possible for someone with the spiritual gift of celibacy also to have a vocation to the priesthood. But what about situations where vocation and celibacy don't coincide?

Two sad results come from connecting celibacy to ecclesial vocations. First, many men and women called by God to pastoral ministry never had the opportunity to exercise their vocation. Why? They had not received the gift of singleness—and hence celibacy—that Paul refers to in 1 Corinthians 7.

Second, many men—I'm now thinking of Roman Catholic priests—
enter the ministry knowing they are to lead a celibate life, yet also aware
they do not have the spiritual gift of celibacy. The sad results of this decision have often demonstrated themselves across the church's history.[60]
The Orthodox Church has chosen a wiser path, with marriage allowed
for priests and celibacy required for bishops.

A two-lifestyles approach has also tended to create a laity-priesthood
split in which Paul's teaching on the spiritual gifting of all Christians
(1 Cor 12–14; Rom 12; Eph 4), with the corresponding responsibility of
all Christians to exercise their gifts, has been weakened.

We must ask a fundamental question: are some of God's image bearers created to live the life of angels on earth as a higher calling? Eusebius
and other church fathers believed that virgins within the life of the
church were modeling proleptically the life of the age to come, in
which—as Jesus taught—there will neither be marriage nor giving in
marriage (Mt 22:29-33). But is the future for God's image bearers in the
age to come to be the life of angels or the life of humans in a new heaven
and a new earth, even if marriage as we now experience it will no longer
exist? This is a question that both Protestants and Catholics must continue to ponder. If in the age to come, humans will live the life of angels,
the position of the church fathers makes sense. If in the future humans
will be humans and angels will be angels—with a clear distinction between the two—the Protestant position must be carefully considered.

More positively, the church fathers remind us that a single life can be
deeply satisfying and fruitful. Why should we be surprised that a Christian would choose to remain single to more effectively serve Jesus? Indeed, for the fathers, the single life is a blessing rather than a curse, an
insight that can help and encourage many modern Christians, whether
they have a clear call to the celibate life or not.

It is time to take a closer look at the goodness and beauty of marriage.
John Chrysostom will prove to be a wise and helpful guide.

How great is the marriage between two believers! They have one hope, one desire, one way of life, the same religion. They are brother and sister, fellow servants, divided neither in flesh nor in spirit.

TERTULLIAN, *TO HIS WIFE*

She had memorized the Scripture. . . . She urged me that she, along with her daughter, might read through the Old and New Testaments. . . . If at any passage I was at a loss and frankly confessed that I was ignorant, she by no means wanted to rest content with my reply, but by fresh questions would force me to say which of the many possible meanings seemed to me most likely. And I will say something here that perhaps will seem unbelievable to malicious people: from the time of my youth, I have learned the Hebrew language to some extent, through much effort and sweat, and I study it indefatigably so that if I do not forsake it, it will not forsake me. When Paula wanted to learn it, she pursued the project to the point that she chanted the Psalms in Hebrew and her diction echoed no trace of the distinctive character of the Latin language.

JEROME, *EPISTLE* 108[1]

FIVE

"ONE HOPE, ONE DESIRE, ONE WAY OF LIFE"

Life as Male and Female, and the Goodness
and Beauty of Marriage

THE ART OF LEARNING TO LOVE AND LIVE WELL

Clement and other church fathers teach that learning to love and live
well in the power of the Spirit is more an art than a science. They believe
it is truly possible to lead a beautiful—or an ugly—life. If the passions
reign, ugliness—disharmony—will distort our mental life (our ability to
think well), our physical life (our appetites will eventually harm our
bodies), and our spiritual lives (our ability to love God and our neighbor
will slowly but surely wither). Nothing will work right. Life will not
make sense. Misery on a vast scale will result.

Thankfully, though, as Peter Brown points out, church fathers such
as Clement, much in the pattern of Paul and Jesus, believe it is possible
to "'form' a life . . . a process as meticulous, as exacting, and as loving as
was the attention that a literary man (such as Clement himself) must
give to the right placing of every word, to the correct tone and balance of
every phrase. It was a polishing away of those ugly excrescences that
blurred the true, sharp form of the person."

Clement has little doubt that this is an exacting process. But it is very definitely not a process that demanded the repression of feeling. As we earlier learned from Brown, "Passions were not what we tend to call feelings; they were, rather, complexes which hindered the true expression of feelings."[2]

Marriage, with God's call to love in faithfulness, patience, kindness, perseverance, and so on, is a distinct relationship and a special learning space—one of great intimacy, tenderness, and yes, occasional conflict and anger—in which the skills and arts of apprenticeship to Christ can be learned, practiced, and demonstrated through the power of the Holy Spirit.

Gregory of Nazianzus captures beautifully the joy of living well before God as husband and wife. "Through marriage we become one another's hands, ears, and feet. Marriage doubles what had been weak. . . . Sorrows shared hurt less; joys shared are sweeter for both." Not only so, but marriage provides "a lock of self-control over desires and sets a seal on our natural need for friendship. . . . It is a drink from the household spring from which strangers cannot taste." Gregory emphasizes that the sexual and emotional fulfillment experienced in a healthy marriage nurture rather than cripple spiritual life. "The mutual love of those who are united in the flesh and are of one soul sharpens their piety to a fine point."[3]

Before we explore in detail the thoughts of Chrysostom on marriage, a broader look at male-female relationships in the ancient church might well be helpful.

Women in the World of the Fathers

The world in which the church fathers lived was, without doubt, deeply patriarchal. Occasionally, both the statements and tone of voice the fathers express when speaking of women can shock and exasperate us. Augustine, on one of his lesser days, struggled to find positive things to say concerning women, arguing that friendship reaches its greatest height only between men. "For how much better do two male friends live together, enjoying one another's company and conversation, than do a man and a woman! . . . Would anyone say that God was only able to make a woman from the man's side and not also a man if he had so willed it? Consequently I do not see what help a woman is to a man if not for childbearing."[4]

Yet the church fathers can also surprise us and encourage us. Gregory of Nazianzus movingly describes his mother and the spiritual leadership she provided for Gregory's father. His mother "was given by God to my father" and "became not only his co-worker—which is less wonderful—but even his leader, drawing him forward to the highest excellence by her influence in word and deed. She thought it best in all other respects to be excelled by her husband according to the law of marriage, but was not ashamed to present herself as his teacher with regard to piety."[5]

Or consider the words of Tertullian on the joys experienced between husband and wife:

> How great is the marriage between two believers! They have one hope, one desire, one way of life, the same religion. They are brother and sister, fellow servants, divided neither in flesh nor in spirit—truly "two in one flesh," for where there is one flesh there is also one spirit. They pray together; they prostrate themselves together; they carry out fasts together. They instruct one another and exhort one another. They are present in the church of God and at the banquet of God side by side; side by side they stand in difficulties and in consolations. Neither one hides anything from the other; neither one avoids the other; nor is either one a grief to the other. Freely the sick are visited and the poor sustained. Without anxiety, misgivings, or hindrance to one another they give alms, attend the sacrifices [of the church], and carry out their daily duties [of piety]. They are not secretive about making the sign of the cross; they are not fearful about greetings, nor silent in offering benedictions. They sing psalms and hymns to one another, challenging one another as to who sings better to God. When Christ sees and hears such things, he rejoices.[6]

CHRYSOSTOM AND OLYMPIAS

I have written elsewhere of the close and lasting friendship between John Chrysostom and the deaconess Olympias.[7] It demonstrates the love and support sometimes expressed between leading male and female leaders in the early church. We can discern the intimacy and care John and Olympias showed openly toward each other in the correspondence they exchanged during times of exile from their beloved church in Constantinople.

Chrysostom shares freely with Olympias his recent health problems and encourages her to investigate the possible use of a medicine he has lately found helpful for his own frequent bouts of nausea. "Pay great attention to the restoration of your bodily health," Chrysostom counsels Olympias. "For a few days ago when I suffered from a tendency to vomiting, owing to the state of the atmosphere, I had recourse to the drug which was sent me . . . and I found that no more than three days' application of it cured my infirmity." Chrysostom gently scolds his "most reverend and divinely favored deaconess Olympias. . . . If you would take the requisite care of yourself, you would be in a more satisfactory condition."[8]

It was Olympias's practice—she was a woman of some wealth—to share in providing for John's material needs in Constantinople, and she continued to do so during the last years of his life in exile. *The Life of Olympias, Deaconess* describes Olympias as possessing "an appearance without pretense, character without affection . . . a mind without vainglory, intelligence without conceit . . . character without limits, immeasurable self-control . . . the ornament of all the humble."[9]

MACRINA, GREGORY, AND BASIL

The life of Macrina, sister of Gregory of Nyssa and Basil the Great, is a remarkable example of theological acumen and practical spirituality. In fact, Macrina is often known as the "Fourth Cappadocian," in addition to Gregory of Nazianzus and her brothers Basil and Gregory.[10] Jaroslav Pelikan provides this description:

Not only was she, according to Gregory's accounts, a Christian role model for both of them by her profound and ascetic spirituality, but at the death of their parents she became the educator of the entire family, and that in both Christianity and Classical Culture. Through her philosophy and theology, Macrina was even the teacher of both of her brothers, who were bishops and theologians, "sister and teacher at the same time . . ." as Gregory called her in the opening sentence of the dialogue *On the Soul and the Resurrection.*[11]

Even as a young girl, Gregory tells us, Macrina studied the Scriptures, and especially the Song of Solomon and the Psalms. "She went through each part of the Psalm at its special time, when getting up, when engaging in work, when resting, when she took her meals, when she arose from the table, when she went to bed or arose for prayers; always she had the Psalms with her like a good traveling companion, not forsaking them for a moment."[12]

Both the quality of Macrina's life and the brilliance of her intellect deeply impressed her two brothers. The influence of Macrina convinced Basil to repent of his intellectual pride over his rhetorical abilities. As Gregory puts it, Basil "despised all the worthy people and exalted himself in self-importance above the illustrious men of the province." Macrina "drew him with such speed to the goal of philosophy that he renounced world renown."[13]

Even on her deathbed Macrina taught important lessons to her brother Gregory.

When she saw me come near the door, she raised herself on an elbow, not able to come towards me, for already the fever had consumed her strength. . . . She introduced topics on her mind and by asking questions, gave me a chance to talk. . . . She went through such arguments in detailed manner, speaking about natural phenomena, recounting the divine plan hidden in sad events, revealing things about the future life, as if she were possessed by the Holy

Spirit. As a result my soul seemed to lack little from being lifted outside human nature by her words, and with the guidance of her speech, to stand inside the heavenly sanctuaries.[14]

Basil, too, was later to recall the lasting effect of the teaching of both his mother, Emmelia, and his grandmother Macrina (the elder).

The teaching about God that I had received as a boy from my blessed mother and my grandmother Macrina, I have ever held with increasing conviction. On my coming to the mature years of reason, I did not shift my opinions from one to another, but carried out the principles handed on to me by my parents. Just as the seed when it grows is tiny at first and then grows bigger but always preserves its identity, not changed in kind though gradually perfected in growth, so I consider that the same doctrine has in my case grown through a development. What I hold now has not replaced what I held at the beginning.[15]

MARCELLA, PAULA, AND MELANIA THE ELDER

Other women served as models and mentors for key church fathers.[16] Think, for instance, of the Roman widow Marcella, one of the first female ascetics in Rome. Jerome praises both her devotion to Christ and her active, inquiring mind:

And because my name was then especially esteemed in the study of the Scriptures, she never came without asking something about Scripture, nor did she immediately accept my explanation as satisfactory, but she proposed questions from the opposite viewpoint, not for the sake of being contentious, but so that by asking, she might learn solutions for points she perceived could be raised in objection. What virtue I found in her, what cleverness, what holiness, what purity. . . . I will say only this, that whatever in us was gathered by long study and by lengthy meditation was almost changed into nature; this she tasted, this she learned, this she possessed. Thus after my departure, if an argument arose about some evidence from Scripture, the question was pursued with her as the judge.[17]

Jerome's closest personal female friend was Paula, whose wealth financed the construction of monasteries in Bethlehem.[18] Paula died there in AD 404. Jerome penned the following lines in his memorial letter to Paula's daughter Eustochium. He was especially touched by Paula's willingness to endure separation from her children for the sake of the gospel.

> Among the harsh fates of captivity, of being in the hands of enemies, none is more cruel than parents being separated from their children. She endured this with full confidence, though it is against the law of nature; yes, she sought it with a rejoicing spirit, and making little of the love of her children by her greater love for God. . . . I confess that no woman loved her children like this; before she departed, she disinherited herself of earthly things and bestowed all on them, so that she might find an inheritance in Heaven.[19]

Not only Paula's devotion caught Jerome's eye. In a letter written shortly after Paula's death, Jerome comments on Paula's sharp intellect.

> She had memorized the Scripture. . . . She urged me that she, along with her daughter, might read through the Old and New Testaments. . . . If at any passage I was at a loss and frankly confessed that I was ignorant, she by no means wanted to rest content with my reply, but by fresh questions would force me to say which of the many possible meanings seemed to me most likely. And I will say something here that perhaps will seem unbelievable to malicious people: from the time of my youth, I have learned the Hebrew language to some extent, through much effort and sweat, and I study it indefatigably so that if I do not forsake it, it will not forsake me. When Paula wanted to learn it, she pursued the project to the point that she chanted the Psalms in

Hebrew and her diction echoed no trace of the distinctive character of the Latin language.[20]

Finally, mention must be made of Melania the Elder, a woman renowned for her learning and intellect. Palladius comments that she "was very learned and a lover of literature. She turned night into day by going through every writing of the ancient commentators, three million lines of Origen, and two hundred fifty thousand lines of Gregory, Stephen, Pierius, Basil, and other excellent men." In fact, Palladius observes, Melania read each work "seven or eight times."[21]

JOHN CHRYSOSTOM ON THE BEAUTY OF MARRIAGE

Let us now turn our attention to marriage itself. In John Chrysostom, we discover a surprisingly strong proponent of the value, joys, and challenges of married life, from the inherent goodness and pleasure of sexual relations to the delights and difficulties of raising children. John's perspective was not always so positive.

John deeply valued his own calling to the single life of a celibate and in his younger days painted a negatively vivid picture of what awaited those who had chosen to marry. Marriage, viewed through the lenses of John's monastic vocation and its "new martyrdom"—life as a virgin—was "truly a chain, not only because of the multitude of its anxieties and daily worries, but also because it forces spouses to submit to one another."[22] John seems peevish, shortsighted, judgmental, harsh, immature.

Yet as the years passed and as John's thinking ripened in the context of his pastoral ministry in Antioch and later in Constantinople, his perspective on marriage and family relations changed dramatically. The man who had viewed sexual relations with seeming repugnance came to praise God's wisdom in creating his image bearers as sexual beings. The man who speaks so negatively as a young monk later writes that marital love is "a thing that no possession can equal; for nothing whatever, is more precious than to be thus loved by a wife and to love her."[23] So, as David C. Ford wisely coaches, when reading and interpreting Chrysostom it is best to consider his works "as a whole, when he is not specifically addressing monastics."[24]

ON MARRIAGE AND FAMILY LIFE

Across his lifetime, Chrysostom delivered hundreds—if not thousands—of sermons on a vast range of topics. His normal method was simply to preach verse by verse through the Bible, with his words transcribed by *amanuenses* or secretaries. Six sermons John delivered on marriage and the family have been translated by Catharine P. Roth and David Anderson and gathered into one volume, titled *On Marriage and Family Life.*[25] I will be developing themes from these sermons as we consider John's thoughts on marriage, sex, the family, and virginity. Other sermons of John will also provide valuable information and insight.

John addresses a broad range of issues that ought to concern and interest any Christian married couple—ancient or modern—and those people considering whether to marry or remain single. A sermon John preached on 1 Corinthians 7 contains his thoughts on highly relevant topics: marriage, sexual relations within marriage, and virginity.

As Chrysostom begins, he notes a change in Paul's tone in his letter to the Corinthian congregation. Up to this point Paul had been speaking directly, firmly, and sometimes angrily, for the Corinthians had fallen into serious sin: "unpleasant problems" had erupted among the Corinthians, including "factionalism," "incest," and "greed." These sins had to be rebuked and corrected with a strong apostolic word, and Paul does just that.

As Paul shifts his attention to key questions the Corinthians had asked about marriage in a previous letter, Chrysostom observes that Paul "speaks more gently." "He gives his audience a rest from such vulgarities" as greed and incest, and "inserts some advice and exhortation concerning marriage and virginity."[26]

SEXUAL RELATIONS IN MARRIAGE

The Corinthians were particularly concerned about sexual relations in marriage. Was it ever right to abstain from sex? At what times? Under what conditions? For what reason? Paul's response to the Corinthians is nuanced and sensitive, as is Chrysostom's interpretation of Paul. Paul

begins with a brief comment—"It is good for a man not to have sexual
relations with a woman" (1 Cor 7:1 NIV)—but then immediately quali-
fies his statement.

> But because of cases of sexual immorality, each man should have
> his own wife and each woman her own husband. The husband
> should give to his wife her conjugal rights, and likewise the wife to
> her husband. For the wife does not have authority over her own
> body, but the husband does; likewise the husband does not have
> authority over his own body, but the wife does. Do not deprive one
> another except perhaps by agreement for a set time, to devote your-
> selves to prayer, and then come together again, so that Satan may
> not tempt you because of your lack of self-control. . . . I wish that
> all were as I myself am. But each has a particular gift from God,
> one having one kind and another a different kind. (1 Cor 7:2-5, 7)

Chrysostom observes that Paul's comments occur within the broader
context of his teaching about virginity. The "best and most lofty path" is
not to marry at all. But Chrysostom, like Paul, realizes that many have
not been given the gift of celibacy. They have not been given this gift,
this strength, by God. So most people will marry and then face the many
issues married people encounter on a daily basis, including a cluster of
questions about sexual intimacy.

Chrysostom sensibly and earthily comments—any hints of prudish-
ness from his younger days seem long gone—that in any marriage "one
of two things is likely to happen; either the husband wants to have relations with his wife, but she does not, or vice versa." All married couples
can identify with this common dilemma. What is one to do? What is the
overarching principle to guide a couple when on a given day one wants
sexual intimacy and the other is uninterested, not in the mood, has
a headache?

As the NRSV translation puts it, "The husband should give to his
wife her conjugal rights, and likewise the wife to her husband." And,
Chrysostom asks, exactly what are these conjugal rights? "First, it means

that the wife has no power over her own body, but she is her husband's slave—*and also his ruler.* So, wife, if you want to abstain, even for a little while, get your husband's permission first. That is why St Paul speaks of conjugal rights as a *debt;* to show that *neither husband nor wife is his or her own master,* but rather are each other's servants."[27]

Both husband and wife must remember that their bodies are no longer their own. The wife's body belongs to the husband, and the husband's body belongs to the wife. Both are called to serve one another with their bodies. *Both are rulers. Both are slaves.* In the case of sexual relations—and the decision to abstain from them—Paul does not speak "of greater or lesser authority" between husband and wife. Though Chrysostom believes husbands have "greater responsibility in nearly every other concern," sexual fidelity "is an exception. . . . Husband and wife are equally responsible for the honor of their marriage bed."[28]

To deprive one another of sexual intimacy, Chrysostom argues, not only dishonors the marriage bed but promotes the sexual havoc he dealt with on a daily basis in the church he pastored: adultery, fornication, broken homes, and so on. To combat these sexual and familial disasters, Chrysostom urges that sexual intimacy in marriage be honored, preserved, and practiced to the mutual benefit and pleasure of both partners.

Here and elsewhere, Chrysostom is quite remarkable in his frank advocacy of sexual pleasure as the sweet ointment God has created to attract and cement his image bearers—male and female—together in a lifelong commitment. Of all the church fathers, Chrysostom most clearly and directly celebrates the inherent goodness of married love and life. In his comments on Ephesians 5:22-23, John states, "There is no relationship between human beings so close as that of husband and wife." Indeed, "The power of this love is truly stronger than any passion; other desires may be strong, but this one alone never fades." John celebrates the erotic love "deeply planted within our inmost being. Unnoticed by us, it attracts the bodies of men and women to each other, because in the beginning woman came forth from man, and from man and woman other men and women proceed."[29]

Or consider Chrysostom's celebration of sex and conception in his Homily 12 on Colossians:

> And how do they become one flesh? Just as if you should take the purest part of gold, and mingle it with other gold; so in truth here also the woman receiving the richest part fused by pleasure (*hedones*) nourishes and cherishes it, and contributing something from herself returns it back as a human being. And the child is a sort of bridge, so that the three become one flesh, the child connecting each other on either side. For as two cities, which a river divides through, become one city if a bridge connects them on both sides, so is it in this case—and yet more, since the very bridge here is formed from the substance of each side.[30]

What good is fasting and abstinence if the untimely, selfish practice of these spiritual disciplines results in cracking the love between husband and wife? "No good at all; it has broken love to pieces. How much abuse, trouble, and fighting have resulted from this!"[31] "Nothing is more important," Chrysostom insists, than the "harmony" that should exist between husband and wife.

> When husband and wife are at odds with one another, their household is in no better shape than a storm-tossed ship in which the captain and the pilot disagree. That is why Paul says: "Do not deprive each other except by mutual consent and for a time, so that you may devote yourselves to prayer. Then come together again so that Satan will not tempt you because of your lack of self-control" [1 Cor 7:5 NIV].[32]

Chrysostom emphasizes that Paul does not mean that sexual relations somehow pollute prayer. Rather, Paul is referring "to unusually intense prayer," a type of prayer that "can be intensified by abstinence. . . . He does not mean that sexual relations would make the prayer unclean." There is surely a time and place for such intense prayer, but this forceful, concentrated prayer is not the normal pattern followed by married couples. Husband or wife may engage in it, but only with the express permission of their partner and only for a specific, limited time span.[33]

A Profound Unity

The profound unity expressed in conjugal love in turn—with God's blessing—produces children. "What do we learn from this?" John asks. "The great strength of unity. The ingenuity of God divided one person into two at the beginning and, desiring to show that after the division they remained one, he did not leave one person sufficient for generating a child." The gift of a child becomes "a sort of bridge that connects each one to the other, so that the three become one flesh."

Still, Chrysostom is aware that some marriages remain childless. Does this mean that a married couple should eventually abstain from sexual intercourse because the fruit of their union fails to appear? Absolutely not. "What happens when there is no child? Does this mean that they remain two? The answer is quite clear: conjugal intercourse itself accomplishes this [unity] through the pouring forth and commingling of both bodies."[34]

Roth comments, "St. John is very far from the Augustinian view in which sexual pleasure is basically sinful but tolerated only for the sake of procreation. Here the union of husband and wife is recognized as good in its own right."[35] In fact, Chrysostom pictures sexual relations within a childless marriage as preserving "chastity." "These are the two purposes for which marriage was instituted: to make us chaste, and to make us parents. . . . We have as witnesses all those who are married but childless. So the purpose of chastity takes precedence, especially now, when the whole world is filled with our kind."[36]

Chrysostom forbids that a husband should use fear, intimidation, or coercion in attempting to gain his way with his wife. "But one's companion for life, the mother of one's children and the basis of all one's joy, must never be bound through fear and threats but through love and a good attitude. If the wife is afraid of her husband, what kind of a marriage can they have? What kind of a pleasure can a husband enjoy if he lives with his wife as though she were a slave instead of a free woman?"[37]

No, Chrysostom insists, instead of coercion or abuse, a husband is to love his wife as he naturally, instinctually loves his own body, a thought reflected in Paul's teaching in Ephesians: "In the same way, husbands should love their wives as they do their own bodies. He who loves his wife loves himself" (Eph 5:28).

Chrysostom reminds his congregation of the creation account in Genesis 2. When Adam sees Eve for the first time, a woman created from his own body, he exclaims, "This at last is bone of my bones and flesh of my flesh!" (Gen 2:23). Thus, in marriage and sexual union, Chrysostom sees Adam and his descendants nourishing and cherishing their own flesh, in a manner similar to Christ's love for the church as demonstrated in the incarnation.[38] "Christ was born from our matter, just as Eve was fashioned from Adam's flesh. Paul does well here to speak of flesh and bones, for the Lord has exalted our material substance by partaking of it Himself."[39]

Sexual intimacy in marriage, then, lovingly reflects the union between Christ and his body on earth, the church.

> Paul shows that a man leaves his parents, who gave him life, and is joined to his wife, and that one flesh—father, mother, and child— results from the commingling of the two. The child is born from the union of their seed, so the three are one flesh. Our relationship to Christ is the same; we become one flesh with Him through communion, more truly one with Him than our children are one with us, because this has been His plan from the beginning.[40]

Marriage is never to be disparaged, Chrysostom forcefully preaches, for to malign marriage is to dishonor the relationship between Christ and his church. "How foolish are those who belittle marriage! If marriage were something to be condemned, Paul would never call Christ a bridegroom and the Church a bride, and then say this is an illustration of a man leaving his father and his mother, and again refer to Christ and the Church."[41]

The Husband as the "Head" of the Wife

There is little doubt that the church fathers understood the husband to be the "head" of the wife and household in a hierarchical sense, a controversial position in some circles today. Chrysostom, however, delineates carefully the boundaries of the husband's headship. The wife is to respect the husband, precisely because the relationship between husband and wife reflects the relationship between Christ and the church. In turn, as Christ's love for the church is the fundamental pattern for the husband's relationship to his wife, Chrysostom teaches that the husband's headship must be grounded and demonstrated in sacrificial love. "To the husband he speaks of love, and obliges him to love, and tells him how he should love, thus binding and cementing him to his wife. . . . Do you not see, husband, the great honor that God desires you to give to your wife? He has taken you from your father and bound you to her."[42]

Chrysostom realizes that Roman Christian husbands desired and expected to receive fear and respect from their wives. *He is convinced, though, that a Roman cultural understanding of fear and respect does not fit the cruciform pattern of Christ's life and ministry*—a pattern to be imitated in Christian marriage. The Christian husband's wife was no slave. She was a free woman in Christ and to be honored as such. "And when you hear Paul say 'fear' or 'respect,' ask for the respect due you from a free woman, not the fear you would demand from a slave. She is your body; if you do this, you dishonor yourself by dishonoring your own body."[43]

Chrysostom, therefore, develops his understanding of marriage within a *creational, christological,* and *ecclesiological* context. Just as Christ loves the church and willingly sacrificed his life for her sake, so the husband must love his wife and willingly sacrifice himself for her. The exercise of the husband's authority over his wife *must reflect the pattern of the cross.* In addition, the family itself, with its various household structures, "is a little Church," with both the authority of the husband and the "secondary authority" of the wife serving to preserve "the welfare of the household."[44]

SAME-SEX RELATIONSHIPS AND BEHAVIORS

We close this chapter with a necessarily brief look at the church fathers'
perspective on same-sex relationships and behaviors. To do so, I'd first
like to introduce Wesley Hill, assistant professor of New Testament at
Trinity School for Ministry. Hill is a gay, celibate man and has written a
wise, helpful book, *Washed and Waiting: Reflections on Christian Faithfulness and Homosexuality*.[45]

I mention Hill's book because it is a moving account of his continuing, graced effort to live a faithful life of discipleship as a celibate homosexual in the twenty-first century. He does so in a North American
moral environment that views and promotes homosexual behavior and
relationships as normal and praiseworthy. Many of Hill's fellow West-
erners discount the possibility of a homosexual person living a celibate
life without enduring unending frustration, discouragement, disap-
pointment, and guilt.

Hill argues that a life of faithful discipleship in his sexual life is possible, though celibate life as a gay man surely entails times of deep challenge and significant sacrifice. I believe the church fathers would applaud Hill's effort to live a holy sexual life before God and would find
many of his arguments concerning same-sex celibacy to be valuable, life
sustaining, and strikingly similar to their teaching regarding the vocation of the virgin.

First, though, a word about the fathers' teaching on same-sex behaviors is necessary. I do not know of a single church father who expresses
approval of sexually active homosexual relationships. From very early
documents such as the Didache, to later writers such as Clement of Alexandria and Lactantius, opposition to same-sex relationships is uniform. Old Testament texts such as the story of Sodom and Gomorrah
and various Levitical commandments on same-sex activity were understood by ancient Christian writers as forbidding homosexual behavior.
Clement of Rome, for example, in a very early Christian letter, urges his
readers to be "cut off from the lusts of the world," and in his exhortation
to the Roman Christians refers directly to Paul's vice list in 1 Corinthi-

ans 6: "Neither the sexually immoral nor idolaters nor adulterers nor men who have sex with men will enter the kingdom of God."[46] Tertullian writes that "the coupling of two males is a very shameful thing."[47]

Praiseworthy, committed homosexual unions would be a foreign idea to the fathers, largely because they considered homosexual acts—whether in a committed relationship or not—to be against God's will and against nature's laws, and they believed their position to be in line with Paul's apostolic teaching in Romans 1:18-32; 1 Corinthians 6:9-10; and 1 Timothy 1:8-11. The fathers' teaching on homosexual behavior is direct and uncompromising.

Hill, like the church fathers, interprets Paul's teaching concerning homosexual behavior as clear and unambiguous.

> Paul, following the lead of his Jewish upbringing and of the nascent Christian communities through which he traveled, depicted homosexual unions as outside the bounds of God's desires for his new humanity, the church. Men who practiced homosexuality will not inherit the kingdom of God, he warned the Corinthians starkly (1 Corinthians 6:9, 10; see 1 Timothy 1:8-11). And in one of his greatest letters, the epistle to the Romans, he chose homosexual activity as a graphic illustration of Gentile idolatry and unbelief (1:18-32).[48]

The fathers would surely agree with Hill's understanding of these texts.

The church's traditional teaching on homosexual behavior, as Hill makes clear, has been uniformly consistent across hundreds of years, is grounded on Holy Scripture and patristic teaching and practice, and is still applicable today. Hill writes:

> In recent years, while considering what we now know of some persons having a virtually unchangeable "homosexual orientation," most of the church—Catholic, Orthodox, and Protestant—has continued to claim that homosexual practice is out of step with God's will. Acting on homosexual feelings and desires is contrary to God's design for human flourishing.[49]

Hill also refers to the 1986 Vatican Letter on Homosexuality: "As in every moral disorder, homosexual behavior prevents one's own fulfillment and happiness by acting contrary to the creative wisdom of God."[50]

Hill—and the church fathers before him—trust that if we know the will of God for any area of human life and choose through the power of the Holy Spirit to obey God's will, our lives will flourish, though in a manner that may well be veiled to the watching world. From the fathers' perspective, a flourishing life and a suffering life are not necessarily a contradiction in terms.

I'm reminded of Chrysostom's teaching to never judge God's providential will *on the basis of appearance*. Appearances can readily deceive. For Chrysostom the primary demonstration of this principle is the cross itself. By all appearances, death is victorious. Jesus' life has come to an ignominious end. The devil has triumphed. Yet, Chrysostom rightly teaches, what appears to be the greatest tragedy in the history of the world *is actually the most blessed event*. In turn, Chrysostom writes, Jesus invites his apprentices to the cruciform pattern of the cross as the fundamental design on which to model their understanding of God's work in their lives.[51] Hill does exactly this. He believes the sexual orientation God has chosen to allow him to experience is within, not without, God's providential love. Yet he also believes the behaviors correlated with his sexual orientation are outside God's will.

Hill explains that his life possesses great meaning and purpose. He is also honest concerning the sacrifice, courage, persistence, and spiritual discipline that obedience to Christ demands. The fathers would not be surprised. Words such as *sacrifice* and *discipline* often occur in the fathers' teaching on ethical issues, as we've seen throughout this book. They would be astonished and concerned to discover some modern Christians have erased this lively and demanding moral vocabulary from their personal ethical lexicon.

Hill quotes from a modern Orthodox writer, Thomas Hopko, who gently coaches modern gay Christians to view their homosexual desires as part of the cross Jesus offers to them in his providential love. These desires are a providential part of their struggle to glorify God and save their lives in a sinful world. They will view their same-sex attractions as a crucial part of their God-given path to sanctity . . . , both for themselves and potential sexual partners. And they will see their refusal to act out their feelings sexually as an extraordinary opportunity for imitating Christ and participating in his saving Passion. They will, in a word, take up their erotic sexual desires, with their desire to love and be loved, as an essential part of their personal striving to fulfill St. Paul's appeal: "I beseech you therefore, brethren, by the mercies of God, that you present your bodies as a living sacrifice, holy, acceptable to God, which is your reasonable service" [Rom 12:1].[52]

Hopko's teaching, profoundly patristic in its orientation, is tough. Indeed, its pattern is cruciform. Yet, the church fathers insist that living well before God in this present evil age always reveals a cruciform pattern. To give my money away when I would rather spend it on myself demands that I die with Jesus. To bless my enemy when I would rather kill him demands that I die with Jesus. To care for the unprotected, the sick who will never recover, the unrecognized and the invisible, demands that I die with Jesus. To remain in a marriage where love has died and hope of its resurrection seems a pipe dream is to die with Jesus. And to be born with sexual desires that can never be fulfilled is to die with Jesus. Hill understands this, as do the fathers.

Still, a cruciform life can be a flourishing life, one that drinks deep from the well of God's love. Hill writes:

When the earliest Christians spoke of their experience of God's love, they describe it as just that—an experience with a profoundly emotional quality. "God's love has been poured into our hearts through the Holy Spirit" . . . (Romans 5:5). "You have received the Spirit of adoption as sons, by whom we cry, 'Abba! Father!' The Spirit himself bears witness with our spirit that we are children of God" (8:15-16). "Though you have not seen him," another early

Christian wrote to fellow believers, "you love him. Though you do not now see him, you believe in him and rejoice with joy that is inexpressible and filled with glory" (1 Peter 1:8). In some profound sense, this love of God—expressed in his yearning and blessing and experienced in our hearts—must spell the end of longing and loneliness for the homosexual Christian. If there is a "remedy" for loneliness, surely this must be it. In the solitude of our celibacy, God's *desiring* us, is enough. The love of God is more valuable than any human relationship. And yet we ache. The desire of God is sufficient to heal the ache, but still we pine, and wonder.[53]

What Hill asks of his fellow believers is that we not forget him. His suffering and sacrifice as a gay, celibate Christian is part of the church's suffering as the body of Christ. Hill reminds us of the fathers' teaching on virginity and the role Christian community played in a virgin's life of love to God and neighbor.

Throughout much of Christian history, whenever Christians took on vocations of celibacy, they did so most often in community—in monastic orders, for example. Those committed to a life of sexual abstinence recognized that such a choice would be best undertaken not in isolation but with others and would be sustained by the rhythms of corporate worship and the mundane tasks of providing for one another's daily needs.[54]

All God's image bearers are of infinite value and should be deeply valued and loved. Too often they are neglected, forgotten, invisible. One thinks, for instance, of the unborn, the sick, the elderly. Are they our neighbor? We will explore this question in our next chapter.

For you do not allow the prostitute to continue as a mere prostitute, but you also make her a murderer. You see how drunkenness leads to sexual temptation, sexual temptation to adultery, adultery to murder; or rather to something worse than murder. For I have no name to give it, since it does not destroy a child, but prevents it being born.

JOHN CHRYSOSTOM, HOMILY 24 ON ROMANS[1]

Although keeping parrots and curlews, the pagans do not adopt the orphan child. Rather, they expose children who are born at home. Yet, they take up the young of birds. So they prefer irrational creatures to rational ones.

CLEMENT OF ALEXANDRIA, STROMATA[2]

SIX

"FROM THE CRADLE TO THE GRAVE"

Life and Death

LIFE AND DEATH IN THE ANCIENT CHRISTIAN WORLD

Life was cheap in antiquity. Most people lived short, pain-filled lives, scraping out a living from day to day. Abortion was prevalent, dangerous, and nasty. The exposure and abandonment of babies was rampant. To live beyond childhood was a miracle of sorts. Epidemics often rumbled through ancient cities, devouring young and old alike.

In an age when life was so fragile, when the thread between life and death was so thinly woven, how did the ancient church respond to the staggering life-and-death issues surrounding it? What steps did it take to care for the sick, the young, the defenseless, the feeble, the elderly, the dying? What principles concerning the value of life guided the church as it faced immense human suffering and the tragedies of daily existence?

THE QUESTION OF ABORTION

Ancient Jewish and Christian perspectives and practices on abortion are remarkably similar and differ strongly from Roman attitudes and actions on the issue. Josephus, a Jewish historian writing in the first century, comments that the "law, moreover, enjoins us to bring up all our offspring, and forbids women to cause abortion of what is begotten, or to destroy it afterward; and if any woman appears to have done so, she will be a murderer of her child, by destroying a living creature, and diminishing humankind."[3]

Similarly, the Didache, an early second-century church handbook on church life and conduct, warns against aborting unborn life. "You shall not kill; you shall not commit adultery; you shall not sodomize young boys; you shall not steal; you shall not engage in the magical arts; you shall not practice sorcery; *you shall not cause an abortion, nor commit infanticide after the child is born.*"[4]

This is strong language—abortion is homicide—but accurately reflects the ancient church's abhorrence over the killing of innocent life. To take life, any life, was forbidden, an attitude reflected in Christian attitudes toward military service before the conversion of Constantine in AD 312.

Pregnancy and childbirth were perilous and painful affairs in the Roman and Jewish worlds, whether one was a Christian or not. Abortion was available on a broad scale, particularly in the Roman world, and yet uniformly opposed by the Christian community.[5] The rich aborted babies more often than the poor. Indeed, Juvenal comments "how seldom a 'gilded bed' contained a pregnant woman because abortion was so readily available to the rich."[6]

Sadly, as Michael Gorman observes, "the poor aborted too, as did married and unmarried, chaste and prostitute." Many more than simply pregnant women engaged in supporting the abortion industry. "A husband or lover might force a woman to abort. Certain doctors performed nontherapeutic as well as therapeutic abortions. Amateur and paid abortionists and dealers in abortifacient drugs were available."[7]

Should we be surprised that a common reason for aborting a child was the desire to conceal "illicit sexual activity"? Adultery "was generally condemned" in Roman culture "and was punishable under a number of laws, especially since the time of Augustus." Punishments for adultery included "exile and the confiscation of property for women convicted of adultery, and fathers and husbands were sometimes permitted to kill a man caught in the act with a daughter or a wife. Clearly, then, there were compelling reasons that a woman might . . . abort a child conceived out of wedlock."[8]

There were other reasons for procuring an abortion: the fear that illegitimate children might inherit family wealth, an attempt to maintain physical beauty by avoiding the demands and effects of childbirth on the body, a desire to regulate the size of one's family, and perhaps safety considerations.[9] It is possible that a marked decline in the Roman population during the reign of Augustus and later Hadrian is linked to the popularity of abortion.[10] Incest and rape "as a motive for abortion leaves barely a trace in the ancient literary sources."[11]

A variety of medical means were available to procure abortions, including the use of drugs taken orally, "pessaries or substances" introduced directly into the womb, or mechanical procedures conducted by physicians. Tertullian, in his treatise on the human soul, mentions a common procedure for aborting a fetus:

> Among surgeons' tools there is a certain instrument, which is formed with a nicely-adjusted frame for opening the *uterus* first of all, and keeping it open; it is further furnished with an annular blade [*anulocultro*], by means of which the limbs within the womb are dissected with anxious but unfaltering care; its last appendage being a blunted or covered hook, wherewith the entire *foetus* is extracted by a violent delivery.[12]

Why were Jews so deeply opposed to abortion? Ancient Jewish and Christian perspectives concerning abortion and infanticide differ strikingly from the Roman attitude prevalent during the early centuries of the church's existence. As we have already seen, Jews and Christians were not reluctant to call abortion murder.

Jews deeply valued life, an attitude reflected in three specific perspectives. First, it was the duty of all Jews to populate the earth in response to God's command to Adam and Eve to be fruitful; procreation insured the continuance of the Jewish people. Second, it was Israel's responsibility to respect and preserve God's creation and the sanctity of all created life, "a respect extending in various ways to life in all its manifestations and stages." Third, there remained in Israel a consistent and "profound horror" of "blood and bloodshed."[13]

Scholars sometimes distinguish between different Jewish points of view on the question of abortion, represented by the Alexandrian and the Palestinian schools. The Alexandrian school, relying on the Septuagint (Greek) translation of the Old Testament, seems to have drawn a distinction between the unformed and formed fetus. The penalty for destroying an unformed fetus, reflecting the LXX translation of Exodus 21:22-25, was a severe fine. To destroy a formed fetus, though, was to take a fully formed innocent life, a capital crime.

Philo of Alexandria (25 BC–AD 41) directs his readers' attention to the commandment "You shall not kill."

> If a man comes to blows with a pregnant woman and strikes her on the belly and she miscarries, then, if the result of the miscarriage is unshaped and undeveloped, he must be fined both for the outrage and for obstructing the artist Nature in her creative work of bringing into life the fairest of living creatures, a human being. But, if the offspring is already shaped and all the limbs have their proper qualities and places in the system, he must die, for that which answers to this description is a human being, which he has destroyed in the laboratory of Nature who judges that the hour has not yet come for bringing it out into the light, like a statue lying in a studio requiring nothing more than to be conveyed outside and released from confinement.[14]

Philo clearly considers the extent of a fetus's development a key factor in determining the punishment to be meted to the person who has caused the fetus's death. Even when the fetus is "unshaped and undeveloped," to cause its death in the heat of a moment's passion is an "outrage" and obstructs the creation of new life "in the fairest of living creatures, a human being." To cause the death of a fully formed fetus, one whose body is now shaped and limbs developed, is a capital crime. Innocent blood has been shed, and in Philo's thinking a capital crime has been committed.

A common misunderstanding. Athenagoras, an early Christian apologist, employs a common Roman misunderstanding of the Eucharist to comment on the sanctity of human life. Occasional Roman gossip and slander betrays the suspicion that Christians were actually slaughtering and eating human babies at their sacrificial religious meals. After all, weren't they drinking blood and eating bodies?

In his response to this gross misunderstanding of the Eucharist, Athenagoras points to the role of Roman men in both abortion and child exposure:

> Again, we call it murder and say it will be accountable to God if women use instruments to procure abortion: how shall we be called murderers ourselves? The same man cannot regard that which a woman carries in her womb as a living creature, and therefore as an object of value to God, and then go about to slay the creature that has come forth to the light of day. The same man cannot forbid the exposure of children, equating such exposure with child murder, and then slay a child that has found one to bring it up. No, we are always consistent, everywhere the same, obedient to our rule and not masters of it.[15]

Christian teaching across the years on abortion and child exposure remains strikingly consistent. Consider the canons of the Council of Elvira (AD 305), where we find the first canonical regulations concerning abortion. These canons are quite strict, likely reflecting the Christian concern to take a strong stand against common Roman practices. Canons 63 and 68 directly address the issue of infanticide and quite possibly abortion.

> Canon 63: "If a woman becomes pregnant by committing adultery, while her husband is absent, and after the act she destroys [the child], it is proper to keep her from communion until death,

because she has doubled her crime." Note that both adultery and abortion are considered crimes.

Canon 68: "If a catechumen should conceive by an adulterer, and should procure the death of the child, she can be baptized only at the end of her life."[16]

The council is clear in identifying adultery and abortion as crimes worthy of a lifetime ban from communion, and for those not yet baptized, a delay of baptism until the very end of life.

The Council of Ancyra, which met nine years later, took a more lenient approach toward those who had caused or procured abortions, reducing the lifetime ban from communion to a period of ten years. Canon 21 of the council states:

Concerning women who commit fornication, and destroy that which they have conceived, or who are employed in making drugs for abortion, a former decree excluded them [from baptism] until the hour of death, and to this some have assented. Nevertheless, being desirous to use somewhat greater leniency, we have ordained that they fulfill ten years [of penance], according to the prescribed degrees.[17]

Gorman observes that though the Council of Ancyra was more lenient than the Council of Elvira,

the immorality of abortion is not questioned nor its seriousness diminished. Once Christianity introduced a legal system, it, like Judaism, sometimes maintained a distinction between moral and legal evaluations. Legally, abortion was classified somewhere between unpremeditated murder and adultery, each punishable for five to seven years (canons 20 and 23), and willful murder, punishable for life (canon 22).[18]

Basil the Great, writing later in the fourth century, responds to a wide variety of questions posed to him by Amphilochius and writes that a "woman who deliberately destroys a fetus is answerable for murder.

And any fine distinction as to its being completely formed or unformed is not admissible among us. For in this case not only the child which about to be born is vindicated, but also she herself who plotted against herself, since women usually die from such attempts." Basil clearly disagrees with the position of Philo, who distinguished between the formed and unformed fetus.

Basil refers to abortion as a "crime," commenting that "the destruction of the embryo" is a "second murder—at least that is the intent of those who commit these deeds." Though Basil views abortion as homicide, he more leniently does not recommend a lifelong penance for those who have sinned, instead accepting "the term of ten years," a length of time he allows to be adjusted "according to the manner of repentance."[19] In addition, Basil clearly understands the earlier canonical decisions of Elvira and Ancyra to refer to abortion as well as infanticide.[20]

Abortion as contraception. Apparently wealthy Romans had greater access to abortion than most of the Roman population and practiced abortion as a type of contraceptive. Ambrose, who knew the Roman upper class well, writes that "the wealthy, in order that the inheritance may not be divided among several, deny in the very womb their own progeny. By use of parricidal mixtures they snuff out the fruit of their wombs in the genital organs themselves. In this way life is taken away before it is given. . . . Who except man himself has taught us ways of repudiating children?" Ambrose not only considers abortion a grave sin but argues that to abort a child is to violate the status of the unborn child as the "handiwork" of God. "It is written: 'Before I formed you in the womb I knew you, and in the genitals of your mother I sanctified you' (Jer. 1:5). To inhibit your rashness, you are made to notice that the hands of your maker are forming something in the womb into a human being."[21]

Jerome also criticizes the common practice in Roman society of contraception as well as abortion. They "drink potions to ensure sterility and are guilty of murdering a human being not yet conceived. Some, when they learn they are with child through sin, practice abortion by the use of drugs. Frequently they die themselves and are brought before the rulers of the lower world guilty of three crimes: suicide, adultery against Christ, and murder of an unborn child."[22] Gorman perceives that "Jerome introduces a new concept by explicitly calling a woman's own abortion-induced death 'suicide.' His other contribution is to take the biblical connection between physical and spiritual adultery and to associate it with abortion by an unmarried woman."[23] Jerome does distinguish "between the formed and unformed fetus [like Philo and unlike Basil] and argues that a certain stage of development is necessary before there is a person, and, hence, before there can be a murder. This distinction received much more attention and approval in the West than in the East,"[24] as we will see in the thought of Augustine.

The idea that the fetus possesses a soul appears for the first time in the fourth century. The Apostolic Constitutions, or Constitutions of the Holy Apostles, described by Gorman as "indebted in form and content" to the second-century Epistle of Barnabas and the Didache, groups abortion with a number of other sins. "Thou shalt not slay thy child by causing abortion, nor kill that which is begotten. For every thing that is shaped, and has received a soul from God, if it be slain, shall be avenged, as being unjustly destroyed."[25]

The mention of the fetus's soul in this passage is particularly striking, "an idea that was unknown to early second century Christianity and rare in fourth-century Eastern Christianity."

Augustine and Chrysostom. Our discussion of the church fathers' views on abortion comes to a close by taking a look at the views of two great doctors of the church on the topic: Augustine, whom Gorman describes as representing a more "liberal" view, and Chrysostom, who takes a more conservative stance. Both rejected abortion as an evil act, yet differed, as did other ancient Jewish and Christian writers, in their understanding of the status of the unformed fetus in comparison to a fetus that was fully formed.

Augustine clearly distinguishes between the status of the unformed and formed fetus. To abort a formed fetus, Augustine argues, is to commit murder. To abort an unformed fetus, "though immoral and worthy of a fine, was not murder." Augustine also rejects the use of contraceptives and abortifacients, specifically because they deny "the purpose of sex and marriage."

> Sometimes, indeed, this lustful cruelty, or if you please, cruel lust, resorts to such extravagant methods as to use poisonous drugs to secure barrenness; or else, if unsuccessful in this, to destroy the conceived seed by some means previous to birth, preferring that its offspring should rather perish than receive vitality; or if it was advancing to life within the womb, should be slain before it was born.[26]

Though Augustine distinguishes between an unformed and formed fetus, comparing the unformed fetus to a seed that has not germinated, he remains unsatisfied and uncomfortable with his position. In his *Enchiridion* Augustine writes:

> But who, then, would dare to deny—though he would not dare to affirm it either—that in the resurrection day what is lacking in the form of things will be filled out? Thus, the perfection which time would have accomplished will not be lacking. . . . Nature, then, will be cheated of nothing apt and fitting which time's passage would have brought. . . . What is not yet whole will become whole.[27]

I am reminded of Augustine's thoughts in the *City of God* concerning the fate of aborted babies. In *Learning Theology with the Church Fathers* I note that Augustine remains undecided concerning the final state of aborted babies. "I cannot bring myself either to affirm or deny that they will share in the resurrection." "And yet," Augustine continues, "if they are not excluded from the number of the dead, I cannot see how they can be excluded from the resurrection of the dead." "For," Augustine writes, "either it is not all the dead that will rise again, and there will be some souls eternally without bodies, although they had human bodies, even if only in the mother's womb, or else all human souls will receive again the bodies which they had, when those bodies rise again, wherever the bodies they left lived and died."[28]

Augustine appears to acknowledge the occasional necessity for therapeutic abortions but affirms that the aborted child will have a place in God's kingdom. "To deny, for example, that those fetuses ever lived at all which are cut away limb by limb and cast out of the wombs of pregnant women, lest the mothers die also if the fetuses were left there dead, would seem too much." If a fetus has lived, Augustine ultimately decides, it is "God's own work" and will be preserved by God.[29]

We close with a word from John Chrysostom, who explicitly mentions abortion in a sermon on Romans 13:11-14. Chrysostom displays no qualms in his straightforward condemnation of abortion. He perceives that abortion *is frequently linked to a series of correlated sins*, including drunkenness, sexual immorality, and idolatry.

> Why sow where the ground makes it its care to destroy the fruit? Where there are so many efforts at abortion? Where there is murder before the birth? For you do not allow the prostitute to continue as a mere prostitute, but you also make her a murderer. You see how drunkenness leads to sexual temptation, sexual temptation to adultery, adultery to murder; or rather to something worse than murder. For I have no name to give it, since it does not destroy a child who has been born, but prevents its being born. Why then do you abuse the gift of God, and fight with His laws, and follow after what is a curse as if a blessing, and make the chamber of procreation a chamber for murder, and arm for slaughter the woman that was given for childbearing? . . . Hence, too, come idolatries, since many, with a view to become acceptable, devise incantations, and libations, and love-potions, and countless other plans. Yet still after such great unseemliness, after slaughters, after idolatries, fornication seems to many to belong to things indifferent, yes, and to many that have wives, too.[30]

To sum up, the thought of the church fathers on abortion includes the following important points:

+ Some fathers and early church synods drew a distinction between the unformed and fully formed fetus, prescribing a more severe penalty for aborting a fully formed fetus. This distinction between formed and unformed was based on texts such as Exodus 21:22-25 and can also be found in Jewish sources such as Philo.

+ Whether fully formed or not, the early church regarded the fetus as a "living being, the object of God's care." *The early church's high view of the sanctity of human life shaped its specific attitude toward abortion, infanticide, service in the military (before the conversion of Constantine), and attendance at the Roman circus and gladiatorial games.* All these common Roman practices were forbidden because they transgressed the commandment "Do not commit murder." As Gorman comments, "It is this absolute abhorrence of bloodshed in any form which drives them away from looking at practices such as gladiator fights and criminal executions. This view stood in stark contrast to the prevailing Roman lifestyle."[31]

+ The use of abortion as a contraceptive device is strongly condemned by the early church.

+ The early church did not view the fetus as a part of a woman's body that might be discarded or separated from her on the basis of her free, autonomous decision. "The fetus is seen, not as a part of its mother, but as a neighbor. Abortion is rejected as contrary to other-centered neighbor love."[32]

+ The church fathers are not reluctant to classify the willful abortion of a fully formed fetus as homicide, though there is evidence that some fathers recognized the necessity of therapeutic abortions and wrestled with the question of the eternal status of the aborted fetus.

The ancient church's strong condemnation of abortion may well trouble some readers. From the perspective of the fathers, the status of the developing fetus as God's image bearer was the overriding consideration in their ethical analysis of abortion and its consequences. They believed the fetus is a human being. Indeed, the developing baby is a dependent neighbor who is to be nurtured and cared for from the moment of conception by the entire Christian community. If the fetus is our neighbor, and if the heart of God's law is love for God and neighbor, the canon law's strictness and severity concerning abortion makes sense. To take innocent life—whether in war or in failing to protect neighbors who lack the ability to care for themselves, whether in the womb or outside it—is treated with appropriate seriousness by the ancient church.

WHO WILL TAKE THIS CHILD?

As we ponder the heartrending and horrific topic of abortion in the ancient world, I am reminded that abortion was only one aspect of a host of "life" issues facing the ancient church. Consider with me the plight of abandoned and exposed children in the ancient world.[33] First, we must distinguish between abandoned children and exposed children. Angelo Di Berardino observes that the fate of exposed children was unimaginably harsh, but still not as grim as that of the abandoned baby. Exposed babies were left in specific places, with certain precautions also taken by the original birth family; some had a medal placed around the neck, informing passers-by that the baby could be taken in or raised. Abandonment, however, "implied greater disinterest in the newborn's fate."[34]

The term *alumnus* or *alumna*, best known to us as the graduates of an educational institution—I'm a proud graduate of UCLA—meant something entirely different in a Roman context. An *alumnus* was a male baby who had been exposed, for whatever reason, by its parent, and *alumna* an exposed female baby.

The paterfamilias of a Roman family had the legal right to either recognize—or not recognize—the children born to him by his wife. So, if there were too many kids in the family, or if the kids were not of the right sex, deformed, born under a bad omen, and so on, the father possessed the legal right to refuse to recognize the child as a legitimate member of the family. Within hours the baby would be taken outside the family dwelling, perhaps to a recognized site where babies were exposed or abandoned, and left there. These *alumni* or *alumnae* would lie in the open, sometimes taken in by other households, or more often left to die or to be devoured by wild animals.

Girls were abandoned more frequently than boys. And, as Di Berardino comments, the children of slaves were in the greatest danger of all.

> Newborns taken in by others often suffered terrible abuse: they ended up as slaves, prostitutes, or performers in the games. Childless couples did adopt some of the exposed babies, but this practice was more common in the cities that in the countryside. The gravestones of abandoned and exposed babies can occasionally be found in Roman cemeteries, with no proper name engraved; they most often simply read, *"alumnus"* or *"alumna."*[35]

Ancient Christians were strongly opposed to child abandonment and exposure. Justin Martyr comments: "We have learned that it is characteristic of evil persons to abandon their babies at birth; and especially because we see that nearly all of them end up in prostitution—not only girls, but also boys."[36] Daily life in the Roman world was already hard for those who relied on parents and siblings for basic care and hopefully a taste of familial love. For the abandoned and exposed, the future was especially bleak.

What steps did the church take to alleviate this terribly unjust situation? Many ancient Christian writers, as we have seen with Justin Martyr, condemned the mistreatment of children and infants. Writers speaking out include Athenagoras (*Supplica* 35.5), Clement of Alexandria (*Paedagogus* 3.3 and *Stromateis* 2.18.92-93), Tertullian (*Ad Nationes* 1.15, *Apologia* 9), Minucius Felix (*Octavius* 31.4), and Lactantius (*Institutiones Divinae* 6.20). Augustine, perhaps referring to child abandonment and exposure in his home town of Hippo, writes: "Sometimes babies are exposed by merciless parents, to be raised by who knows what kind of person; then they are taken in and brought to baptism by holy virgins" (*Epistle* 98.6).

Roman law before the spread of Christianity generally ignored the problem of child abandonment and exposure. Pliny mentions specific cases where the law addressed "claims of freedom on the part of exposed freeborn children," but it was not until the time of Constantine that consistent steps to ameliorate the effects of abandonment and exposure occurred. These practices continued to occur, but Constantine made funds available for the support of needy children, authorized the sale of newborns, and encouraged the taking in of exposed children.[37]

Di Berardino notes that modern people might well be offended by the sale of children but perceptively comments that the "sanctioning of the sale of babies, to us offensive, nevertheless often saved them from death." At least one foundling—an abandoned child found by another family—grew up to be a famous Christian writer and prophet. Hermas, author of the Shepherd, recalls "the one who fed me, who sold me to a certain Rhode, who lives at Rome."[38] Finally, in 374 child exposure was outlawed by Valentinian.[39] The sale of babies was still allowed, including the sale of only the child's labor for a period of years.[40]

Care for the Sick, the Poor, and the Helpless

In the ancient world, sickness, healing, medicine, and religious belief were inextricably connected. "In antiquity medicine always remained *religious*, and physicians carried out their practice as earthly substitutes and helpers of the divine healers."[41] The Greek healing god Asclepius had the title of *soter*, or "savior," and we have widespread reports of healings at the many temples devoted to Asclepius (over four hundred have been identified in the Mediterranean basin). To worship Asclepius was to expect to be healed by Asclepius, and many apparently were, though Christians such as Justin Martyr attributed these healings to demonic power rather than divine. The point to highlight here is that medical skill, healing skill, and skill in dealing with the gods were talents the ancient mind viewed in common.

How did the church fathers and the early Christian community in general respond to the needs of the sick, the poor, the helpless, the forgotten? The image—and reality—of Christ the Physician was extremely important to the fathers and shaped their ethical imagination and concrete responses to those suffering around them. Origen speaks of Christ as the "only physician of bodies and souls."[42] Irenaeus refers to "Christ the physician as well as of God who, just as a good physician, gives proof of his skill by healing sick humanity."[43] And the fathers are quick to recognize, at times in combating Gnostic teaching, that Christ came to heal both souls and bodies. Clement, for instance, stresses that the *Logos* had come to heal the "entire person: spirit and body."[44]

As Christ the Physician's representative, the church and its leaders acted counterculturally in times of plague and other diseases, often choosing to remain in fever-infested towns and cities to care for the sick while the healthy population fled for their lives. "Christians of every hierarchical order, without fear for their health, took care of the infected sick with an attitude contrary to the norm in pagan practice."[45]

Origen mentions in his apologetic work *Against Celsus* that charisms or spiritual gifts of healing existed in the church in his day, the third century AD.[46] Augustine later mentions much the same thing.[47] In addition to the exercise of charisms of healing, the bishops of the early church took seriously their responsibility of caring for the sick; indeed, we have canons from the Council of Nicaea that require bishops to organize centers (*xenodochium*) that would offer care for the sick and receive the poor and foreigners. In many of these hospitals and *xenodochia*, free medical assistance was offered.[48]

In Cappadocia, where the poor were often marginalized, Basil the Great constructed a "new city" at Caesarea around AD 372, a complex of buildings where "nurses and physicians were, for the most part, ascetics themselves," following the pattern of their bishop.[49] Basil's concerns sum up for us so well the church's deep and lasting concern for the unborn, the abandoned, the helpless, the invisible, the sick, and the marginalized: *to serve our brother or sister is to serve God himself.*[50]

In our next chapter we examine in some detail the church fathers' thoughts on entertainment. Their culture, like ours, loved a good show.

Baths, wine and love-making destroy our bodies, yet love-making, wine and baths make it worth living.

Common Roman graffito[1]

Not inappropriately, one might call the race course and the theater "the seat of plagues." . . . Let spectacles, therefore, and plays that are full of indecent language and abundant gossip, be forbidden. For what base action is there that is not exhibited in the theaters?

Clement of Alexandria, The Instructor[2]

SEVEN

"LET THE RACES BEGIN!"

Entertainment

In this chapter we will examine closely how the church fathers responded to the abundance of entertainments available in the Roman world. Of course, we do so from the perspective of my own Western culture, one saturated with manifold entertainment opportunities. Many North Americans—including Christians—spend hours each week devoting themselves to entertainment of various kinds: film, music, and sports of all kinds top the list of possible options. How might this intense and habitual exposure form us mentally, physically, and spiritually? How does what we listen to and view habitually shape our moral perspectives and responses to the world around us? Can the church fathers help us to more wisely choose among our vast and ever-growing entertainment options? What coaching and cautions might they provide?

The world of the church fathers loved to be entertained. As James Jeffers comments, the Greeks and Romans "took their leisure time seriously."[3] Roman culture in general was sexually overheated and ferociously violent. Both characteristics manifested themselves in popular entertainment, such as the violence of the arena and circus and the erotically charged Roman theater. In addition, almost all Roman entertainment was saturated with Roman religious ideas and practices.

Most Christians possessed little leisure time. When the opportunity to entertain oneself arose, which entertainment options did the church fathers condone, and which did they consider off limits? Why?

We will ponder the thoughts of the church fathers on entertainment because the unity of the fathers' perspective on this particular issue is impressive; they believed the choices Christians make concerning what they choose as entertainment, whether through specific actions of their own or merely viewing the performance of actors or athletes, are freighted with ethical significance for our lives as Christians and indeed for how we think and act in worship and devotion.

Neil Postman writes in *Entertaining Ourselves to Death: Public Discourse in the Age of Show Business*, "I believe I am not mistaken in saying that Christianity is a demanding and serious religion. When it is delivered as easy and amusing, it is another kind of religion altogether."[4] The church fathers would respond with a loud "amen" to Postman's words. They were aware of the deadening effect the wrong kind of entertainment has on the human soul and unhesitatingly argue that some kinds of entertainment are simply wrong.

CYPRIAN COACHES DONATUS

Consider Cyprian's thoughts on entertainment in his brief treatise to his friend Donatus. Cyprian, writing in the late 240s shortly after his conversion to Christ, mentions with horror the cruelty and loss of life in the Roman arena. When "individuals commit homicide," Cyprian writes, "it is a crime; it is called a virtue when it is done in the name of the state." Those who attend the games in the arena are "a multitude sadder than any solitude. A gladiatorial combat is being prepared that blood may delight the lust of cruel eyes." The training that gladiators receive to kill characterizes a culture whose values are upside down. "To be able to kill is a skill, is an employment, is an art. Crime is not only committed but is taught. What can be called more inhuman, what more repulsive? It is a training that one may be able to kill, and that he kills is a glory."[5]

Cyprian considers the Roman theater to be "no less objectionable," a different sort of "contamination." The popular themes of the theater—parricide, incest, and adultery were favorites—contaminate the souls of the actors who portray them and the spectators who watch. If one habitually exposes oneself to these themes, Cyprian believes, it will not be long before one acts them out on the stage of real life. "Adultery is learned as it is seen," Cyprian argues. "How great a collapse of morals, what a stimulus to base deeds, what a nourishing of vices, to be polluted by the gestures of actors. . . . Ask now whether he who looks upon this can be healthy minded or chaste."[6]

ROMAN EXTRAVAGANCE

Among other things, the Romans liked to eat and drink, though the scale of eating and drinking surely depended on what one could afford.

Church fathers such as Clement of Alexandria especially criticized this Roman propensity toward *extravagance and self-indulgence*, two vices the church fathers were deeply concerned Roman entertainment options encouraged.

Clement comments:

> Those who take delight in what they have hoarded up in their store-houses are foolish in their greed. . . . It is farcical and downright ridiculous for men to bring out urinals of silver and chamber-pots of transparent alabaster as if they were introducing their advisors, and for rich women in their silliness to have gold receptacles for excrements made, as though being wealthy they were unable to relieve themselves except in a grandiose style.[7]

The temptation to live in two worlds—the kingdom of this world and the kingdom of God—tugged as consistently on ancient Christians as it does on contemporary believers.

LEISURE ACTIVITIES IN THE ROMAN WORLD

A closer look at Roman perspectives on leisure and entertainment is warranted. While most Romans could make little sense of the Jewish practice of a sabbath day, they regularly took time off from work to celebrate religious festivals, a practice ancient Christians increasingly imitated. "In fact, the holidays observed by the Romans exceed the number of our holidays and weekends combined. The weekend as we know it began to come into existence only in the fourth century, when Constantine the Great made Sunday a holiday."[8]

Again we note the close connection between Greek and Roman entertainment and religious ideas and practices. "On the day of a deity's annual festival, the people decorated and opened the temple, made sacrifices and held parades. The event resembled a modern country fair."[9] Greeks celebrated the Olympic Games in honor of Zeus. The Isthmian Games, located at Corinth, were held "in a grove sacred to the god Poseidon." For the Romans, we have the "Ludi [games] Romani, celebrated in honor of Jupiter"; the Ludi Plebes, "which included drama"; the Ludi Cereales, "in honor of the goddess Ceres"; the "Ludi Megalenses, in honor of the Great Mother; and the Ludi Florales." Not only were these games held in honor of Roman gods, but Roman priests "frequently directed them."[10] This marriage between the games, other forms of Roman entertainment, and the religious life of Rome worried the church fathers, along with the prevalent and pervading violence that marked most Roman spectator sports.

The scale of the Roman games and circus was quite astonishing. Jeffers mentions that the amphitheater in Pompeii had twenty thousand seats and "could have seated the entire city." The Colosseum in Rome, known as the Flavian Amphitheater, "was 158 feet high and seated around fifty thousand people."[11] Games were held frequently in Rome—sixty-five days out of the year—a number that grew to 135 by the second century AD. Indeed, the city of Rome "hosted far more games than the other cities of the Empire because of the wealth of its leaders and the desire to pacify a large and potentially unruly population." As the Roman mime reminded Augustus concerning the games, "It is to your advantage, Caesar, that we keep the public occupied."[12]

Executions of criminals—part of most games—occurred at around noon, perhaps because the crowds did not find them of much interest.

These were jaded spectators with jaded tastes. Occasionally "more imaginative executions were staged. For example, convicted persons might be thrown into the arena to be devoured by hungry, wild beasts. They might be dressed in animal hides or left naked. At times they were dressed as mythological characters and forced to enact a brutal death from literature."

Nero, in AD 64, "executed Christians convicted"—likely on trumped-up charges—"of participating in a conspiracy to burn Rome. He dressed these unfortunates in animal hides and had them torn apart by wild dogs. Others were burned alive as torches."[13] Roman historian Tacitus comments: "Despite their guilt as Christians, and the ruthless punishment it deserved, the victims were pitied. For it was felt that they were being sacrificed to one man's brutality than to the national interest."[14]

THREE CHIEF CONCERNS

The church fathers' comments on entertainment in the Roman world consistently emphasize three chief concerns: first, the intimate link between Roman entertainment and Roman religious life; second, specifically what was being offered as entertainment; and third, the effect of this entertainment on God's image bearers, both the human beings who had been baptized into Christ's body, the church, and those human beings who were not part of the Christian community.

Kyle Harper, in *From Shame to Sin: The Christian Transformation of Sexual Morality in Late Antiquity*, writes that the "material environment of the Greco-Roman city" was "unusually adapted for stimulating the appetites." Harper describes the empire at its height as "the Indian summer of classical nudity, when prosperity carried the culture of public baths and gymnasia further than ever before and when frankly erotic art was ubiquitous in refined and popular media."

Harper mentions the popularity of erotic lamps from the second century AD to the late fourth or early fifth centuries. "The Romans not only had sex with the lamps on—they had sex by the flickering light of lamps that had images of them having sex by lamplight on them!" The Roman slave trade and "its unruly outgrowth, the flesh trade, made pleasure cheap and unceremonious. . . . The inhabitant of the Roman Empire was constantly bombarded with visual allurements, so moderation was a virtue called upon constantly, to perform heroic feats of restraint."[15]

THE ROMAN STAGE

The Romans loved to attend the theater to listen to music and view plays, some classical in nature, others of more common fare. If Christians attended the theater, what were they likely to see or hear?

The Roman mime or actor—the Latin *mimus* or Greek *mimos*—was extremely popular and played a key role on the stage. Most mimes came from the lower classes of Roman society. When we think of a mime in our contemporary context, we imagine a person silently acting out—and often poking fun at—aspects of life familiar to us. Such too was the case with the Roman mime. The modern mime uses body movement and facial expressions rather than words to communicate with the audience. Ancient mimes were quite similar, though they would sometimes speak in monologue or back and forth with a chorus.

Diomedes defined the mime as an actor who employed words and movement to poke fun playfully, irreverently, and often lewdly at the events of the day or common daily struggles, foibles, or temptations all Romans experienced. In some ways, the mime was similar to an ancient Jay Leno or Jimmy Kimmel.[16] This main actor was often joined on stage by fellow performers, who played the role of troupe or chorus; together the mime and chorus presented stories and skits to entertain their audiences, often commenting on the issues, personalities, and gossip of the day.

Certain set pieces or genres such as daily life or themes from Greek and Roman mythology were popular. Actors often portrayed in word and body sexually spicy and suggestive scenes of adultery and other sexual shenanigans, to the great amusement of their audiences. Very little was considered off limits.

Occasionally we find mimes mocking Christian themes and practices such as baptism and martyrdom. As late as the early fifth century

Augustine refers to actors on stage joking about baptism and mockingly mimicking the sacramental liturgy.[17]

Roman pantomime included a number of standard structural elements, including dance, lewd songs and chants, a choir of male and female voices, and accompanying musical instruments. At the beginning of the opening act the plotline would be explained to the audience, and from that point on the cast would improvise on the central theme. The mime sometimes wore the *centuculus*, a cloak with "colored patches, a short tunic, and a tall, pointy cap."[18]

John Chrysostom and the Roman Theater

The response of Christian leaders to the Roman theater was generally quite negative. In a series of Christmas sermons John Chrysostom preached at Antioch in the mid to late 380s, we catch a closer glimpse into the entertainment culture of Antioch. In these sermons John is clearly not pleased with both what is occurring on stage and with his congregation's habit of attending these raucous and sexually charged events. Chrysostom knows that many men in his congregation liked to head off to the theater, some after attending church. Women rarely attended; it was rare for upper-class Roman women to be seen in public.

As we've seen, ancient people, like modern folks, enjoyed a good laugh; actors in the theater were glad to oblige. Chrysostom feared, though, that exposure to the Roman stage was deadening his congregation's sensitivity to the Holy Spirit and to one another. Was what the Roman stage found amusing really funny, a healthy source of amusement, at least when viewed from a Christian perspective? John thought not. "And what is more grievous . . . is the subject of the laughter. For when they that act those absurd things utter any word of blasphemy or filthiness, then many among the more thoughtless laugh and are pleased, applauding in them what they ought to stone them for; and drawing down on their own heads by this amusement the furnace of fire."[19] John worried that the Roman theater, like a parasite, fed off the sinful impulses of human nature; the theater was exploiting the population of Antioch—and its Christian community—to make an easy buck.

In these sermons Chrysostom reminds his flock of Paul's exhortation to the Ephesians to avoid "obscenity, foolish talk or coarse joking"—the bread and butter of the Roman theater. Paul, like Chrysostom, was familiar with the soft, immoral underbelly of Roman society and argues that an appetite for the obscene marks the immoral, impure, or greedy person, one who had no "inheritance in the kingdom of Christ and of God" (Eph 5:4-5). Yet Christians in Antioch were enjoining as entertainment the very things the apostle had earlier warned the Ephesians to flee.

Chrysostom readily acknowledges that the theater offers "art" to its patrons but insists that this art is devilish and exploitative. Consistent theater attendance, John believes, creates dead zones in the spiritual sensitivities of the Christian community; it weakens "Christ's soldiers" and softens "the nerves of their zeal."[20] What first shocks a Christian's sensibilities on the Roman stage gradually deadens them. It's possible for harmful entertainment, Chrysostom believes, to wither the soul.

A sad state of affairs. Who is more to blame for this sad state of affairs, the actors on the stage or the theater patrons, whose ticket purchases make the theater a profitable venture? Chrysostom considers both parties blameworthy. If no tickets were ever purchased, John asks, how long would the theater remain cost effective? "For were there no one to be a spectator in such cases, neither would there be one to act; but when they see you forsaking your workshops, and your crafts, and your income from these, and in short everything, for the sake of continuing there. . . . It is you chiefly who supply the principle and root of such lawlessness."[21]

John was no prude. As we have seen, among the church fathers he had a remarkably healthy understanding of human sexuality. Chrysostom recognizes clearly, though, that human sexual desire is apt to overflow its boundaries, is open to exploitation, and if not protected can wreak havoc on men, women, husbands, wives, families, and societies. For instance, John insists that for women to appear nude in the Roman theater and in public spectacles is to "shame" their nature; it is to expose to public view, exploitation, and lust what was created by God to bring joy and intimacy to husband and wife.

Many Romans would have understood and perhaps appreciated John's point. They recognized the harmful aspects of the theater on Roman society. Roman law, for example, legislated against both actors and actresses. Kyle Harper observes that "actors and actresses suffered from legal discrimination, such as the inability to intermarry with the aristocracy," and notes "a material connection between the theater and the sex industry."[22] Aline Rouselle also emphasizes the ambivalent attitude of Rome toward the theater. Roman citizens enjoyed what the theater had to offer but also wanted to maintain social distance from the entertainers on stage. "The number of people with whom Roman citizens were prevented from entering into a full marriage contract was quite small. They fell into three categories: slaves, people in prostitution, and *those involved in the theatre*."[23]

Consider the water mime, a woman—often from the Roman lower classes—who would swim naked before the stage audience. In Chrysostom's fervent criticism of the theater—in this case, specifically of water mimes—we encounter key elements of the church's opposition to Roman entertainment as a whole.

Key elements of the church's opposition. In his Christmas sermons John had been preaching about the Magi's long pilgrimage to present their gifts to the Christ child. As was often the case in John's sermons, he was improvising as he preached—riffing on the text—and likely preaching without notes. As Chrysostom pondered the length of the Magi's journey, his mind recalled the short distance most people in Antioch traveled to get to church.

John's congregants had received greater benefits from Jesus than the Magi, the Jesus whom Chrysostom describes as "a stranger and naked," lying in a manger. Yet the Antiochian Christian beneficiaries of the Christ child frequently struggled to make their way to church. Some, John scolded, had a hard time making it across the street to attend church unless "they can have mules to draw them."[24] Others in Chrysostom's community were simply too busy or distracted to attend church. Should we be surprised that a chief rival for their attention was the theater? In John's words, "After you see Christ in the manger, you leave him, and head off to see women on the stage."[25]

John was obviously frustrated. "Imagine," he asks his congregation,

> that you are actually in a king's palace. Can you see the king sitting on his throne? Would you still head off to the theater? Yet in a king's palace there would be little for you to gain. Here [in church], though, is a spiritual table gushing fire [possibly a reference to the Eucharist]. Still, you would leave and run off to the theater to see women dishonoring their nature by swimming naked.[26]

Sexual exploitation. Chrysostom is also upset because he was fully aware of the connection we noted earlier between the theater, prostitution, and the exploitation of lower-class women in the Roman sex industry. Stage companies often ran prostitution rings.[27] John argues that to treat sex as a commodity to be bought and sold surely dishonors God and human beings. "These two represent the highest sins," Chrysostom warns, "born each of *a grievous passion*, lust for the body and lust for coin."[28]

Not only women were sexually exploited within the environs of the theater. Boys were prostituted by pimps at theater entrances, a practice Jerome credits Constantine with abolishing, though it appears still common in Chrysostom's time.[29] Sadly, in the fourth century AD, Roman law supported the coercion of women to perform on the stage, though Christian women, through a law promulgated in AD 371, were exempted from this coercion.[30]

Chrysostom draws our attention to the case of Pelagia, a famous, indeed infamous, actress and prostitute in Antioch, who was converted while Chrysostom served as a priest in the same city. John comments that Pelagia "was at one time a prostitute among us, *in fact holding pride of place in the theater*, and her name was famous everywhere, not just in our city but as far as Cilicia and Cappadocia. She emptied many an estate, conquered many an orphan. . . . This prostitute at one time held the brother of the empress under her spell, so great was her tyranny."[31] Still, Chrysostom ardently believes and preaches that no one is beyond the reach of God's grace. Pelagia's conversion proved his point.

Harper comments,

> The conversion of such a celebrity, from the most insalubrious quarters of ancient society, furnished an irresistible opportunity for a crusader like Chrysostom to make a point about the quality of divine mercy. The woman—a stage actress and quite possibly a courtesan, *for the two professions shaded into one another in law, ideology, and reality*—had attained a reputation stretching across the eastern Mediterranean. We need not doubt the ability of an exquisitely beautiful woman, in a world where respectability meant seclusion, to capture the public mind.[32]

Pelagia's conversion and subsequent behavior, in Chrysostom's words, "exhibited a diligence proportionate to the grace (given her)," and so "she ended her life, having washed off all through grace, and after her baptism having shown great self-restraint. For not even a mere sight of herself did she allow to those who were once her lovers."

No one was beyond the reach of God's grace. No one. As Harper puts it, "God, in the dispensation of forgiveness, was not a respecter of persons, and nothing symbolized the limitless potential of grace like the moral rehabilitation of a prostitute."[33] Or, in Chrysostom's words, "Let no one then who lives in vice despair." Likewise, "let no one who lives in virtue slumber."[34]

The ancient church's opposition to attendance at the theater, then, was connected to a number of related issues: the lewdness, obscenity, and sensuality that often were the thematic core of Roman theatrical productions; the intimate link between the theater and the wider Roman sex industry; and the sexual exploitation of women and boys in the theater and its immediate environs.

What of the Great Roman Playwrights and Poets?

We have said little about Christian reactions to the drama offered by great Roman playwrights such as Plautus. Jerome's ambivalent response to classical art forms demonstrates the struggle many educated Christians experienced as they attempted to reconcile their Christian faith with their love for classical drama, poetry, and rhetoric, rather than the common street fare we have discussed so far.

In a famous letter Jerome wrote to Eustochium, the daughter of his close friend and patron Paula, his love-hate relationship with secular writers such as Cicero and Virgil is quite evident. On the one hand, Jerome tells Eustochium that many years ago he had left family and friends "to be a soldier of Christ" in Jerusalem. On the other hand, he also admits,

> I could not do without the library which I had collected for myself at Rome by great care and effort. And so, poor wretch that I was, I used to fast and then read Cicero. After frequent night vigils, after shedding tears with the remembrance of past sins brought forth from my inmost heart, *I would take in my hands a volume of Plautus.* When I came to myself and began to read a prophet again, I rebelled at the uncouth style and—because of my blinded eyes I could not look upon the light—I thought this fault not of my eyes but of the sun [my emphasis].[35]

Clearly Jerome loved Plautus, and equally clearly he felt guilty for doing so. In the midst of the struggle to justify and reconcile his love for Roman playwrights and literature and his love for Christ, Jerome fell ill and in his feverish state dreamed that he was standing before the judgment seat of Christ. Christ asked him his status. Jerome replied that he was a Christian. "And He who sat upon the judgment seat said: 'You lie. You are a Ciceronian, not a Christian. *Where your treasure is, there is your heart also.*' I was struck dumb on the spot."[36] Jerome begged for and received mercy, provided that he never read again "books of pagan literature."

Was Jerome able to keep his promise? Allusions to pagan authors fill his writing, perhaps creeping uninvited to the surface of a mind soaked in their thought. We might well argue that Jerome's writing is that much richer because of his conscious or unconscious willingness to interact with—indeed, love—the best writers and literature his culture had to offer him. His grounding in classical texts and the linguistic skills developed over the years aided him in his many translation projects, including his well-known translation of the Hebrew Scriptures and the Greek New Testament into Latin, later to be known as the Vulgate. Nevertheless, it is unlikely that Jerome's ambivalence over his deep-seated affection for playwrights such as Plautus ever left him.

The Roman Circus and Arena

The Roman circus was filled with sights and sounds, blood and dust, pleasure and pain, titillation and toxicity. Keith Hopkins, in his book *A World Full of Gods: The Strange Triumph of Christianity*, re-creates a typical scene in one of the most popular Roman entertainments, the arena or amphitheater. As Hopkins paints the scene for us, two gladiators have fought gallantly, entertaining a packed stadium at Pompeii, with the rookie among the two finally defeated by his experienced rival, a local hero named Crescens the Netman. Nemesis, the goddess of fortune, has let the younger gladiator down, and now there is a price that must be paid.[37]

As Hopkins describes the scene from a first-person perspective, he weaves in details that bring the arena to life. In the front row of the amphitheater we spot the mayor of Pompeii, a politician who has funded the games to the hefty sum of 150,000 sesterces; the mayor will determine the fate of the young gladiator. "All eyes switched from victim to plump, balding mayor, visibly sweating in his seat of honor in the front row. He had paid for the entire show, a small fortune. . . . But the expense went with the job. Now it was his day of glory, his to decide who survived, who died."[38] The mayor's young son sat next to him, his eyes filled with tears, for just the previous evening he had eaten with the now-doomed young gladiator. "Military service, killing Jews or Britons, will soon toughen him up," his father, Marcus Popidius, thought, "and with a grandiose gesture so that everyone in the amphitheater could see, he gave the signal for execution."

Who was watching as the defeated young gladiator died in the dust of the arena? Rich Roman patrons and public officials occupied the best seats in the house. After all, it was they who paid for these events, expecting public recognition and loyalty as a result of their generosity. The vast

majority of the crowd, occupying less expensive seats, were men, trades-
men and guild members thankful for a break from their daily routine and
the chance to view their favorite gladiator or charioteer. Were women
also present in the stands? Perhaps a few, separated from the men and
seated "separately in the worst seats at the top of the amphitheater."

From a Roman perspective, humans were not the only ones pleased
with the games; Roman goddesses and gods were also present, fully expecting their due recognition. As we've already seen, Nemesis, the
goddess of fortune, had decided in favor of the city's favorite gladiator,
Crescens. Pluto, god of the underworld, was also present in the form of
an attendant, wearing a mask of Pluto's face; this attendant handed
Crescens the "specially sharpened dagger of execution," with which he
"gently slit" the throat of his inexperienced young adversary. As the
young gladiator's life ended, a "water organ ground out a funeral march,
while attendants masked as Charon, the ferryman to Hades, loaded the
corpse onto a stretcher and took it out by the Gate of Death."[39]

The previous day Pompeii had been buzzing with anticipation for the
games. Posters decorated street walls; "tomorrow there would be 'what
the whole world wants': games in honor of the emperor Vespasian, a
wild-beast show in the morning, gladiators fighting after lunch, and an
extra temptation, gift tokens scattered to the crowd."[40]

Gladiators and charioteers were the Super Bowl stars of the ancient
world; Hopkins calls them "the local film stars," with nicknames such as
Lord of the Dolls, Crowd's Roar, Hector, and Hercules. Mothers could
purchase a baby's milk bottle "stamped with the design of a gladiator
fighting, and local ships had dozens of gladiator oil lamps for sale, as
well as bronze bells attached to gladiators posing."[41]

The day before the games, a procession from the city forum, derided
by Christians as the *pompa diaboli* or "parade of the devil," wove through
the city streets. Leading the way was the "town band," followed by Roman lictors carrying the symbols of Roman authority, rods and "cud-
gels." Next came the mayor, "town councilors, priests of Augustus, and
district officers."[42]

Roman religion was ubiquitous. "Statuettes and busts of the twelve great Gods, carried by horse and cart, or by porters in what looked like sedan chairs, garlanded and perfumed with incense, so that you could both see and smell them coming."[43]

There would also have been wild animals in the procession: zebras, wild boar, bears.[44] Then came the superstars, gladiators with well-oiled skin and "wrapped like generals in purple cloaks." A huge supper was celebrated, "the magistrates and their chosen guests feasting at long trestle tables, the Gods nearby on banquettes."

The people lucky to attend the games eagerly awaited gifts of sweetened wine and cake (*crustum et mulsum*). With one voice they would toast the donor of the games (*Principi munerarium feliciter*).

The next day the games were held. More gifts, souvenirs of a sort, would be thrown to the crowd. They were called *missilia*, "small bone tokens, each dated and with a number, scattered disciminately . . . into the crowd."[45] These were fancy favors, marked with numerals indicating what the lucky spectator had won: "I for wine, II for incense, III for a sausage, and so on." The animal combats and killing of beasts took place in the morning. Wild dogs might be set on a bull. Archers might use a bear for target practice. Next came the execution of public criminals around noon. And then entered the gladiators.[46]

VIOLENCE AS ENTERTAINMENT

Any ambivalence the church fathers felt over pagan literature and drama is entirely absent from their response to the violence of the Roman arena, circus, and hippodrome. The church with one voice condemned any entertainment in which human beings were killed for amusement. To watch a man killed for entertainment was tantamount to killing him yourself.

Theophilus of Antioch, writing to Autolycus in the second century AD, stresses that Christians do not live "indifferently," avoid illicit sexual intercourse, and "are forbidden so much as to witness shows of gladiators, lest we become partakers and abettors of murders."[47] Athenagoras, also writing in the second century, mentions "the contests of gladiators and wild beasts" and deems "that to see a man put to death is much the same as killing him."[48] Clement of Alexandria argues that the expensive public spectacles sponsored by most Roman cities are not only unwise expenditures but are "cruel," "fatal," and surely not "sport,"[49] while admitting that athletic exhibitions and gymnastic exercises might be admirable if practiced with moderation.[50] Augustine, writing close to 250 years later, makes much the same point as these earlier writers, classifying gladiators as public sinners.[51]

Recall that Roman entertainment such as the arena and circus was inseparable from Roman religious ideas and practice. Consider the *pompa diaboli*, the parade of the devil, described so vividly by Hopkins, with its multitude of Roman gods seated on portable thrones. In the church's baptismal rite catechumens were required to renounce publicly "the devil, his pomp, and his angels (*renuntio diabolo et pompae et angelis suis*)."[52] Memories of the *pompa diaboli* might well be part of this liturgical confession.

We, like our ancient Christian relatives, must carefully and prayerfully ask how we should respond to the entertainment possibilities offered to us early in the twenty-first century. Outright rejection? Enthusiastic embrace? Are there books or films that should be considered off limits? What should one listen to? What should one avoid for the sake of spiritual health and obedience to Jesus? Which films harm us? And which expand our capacity to love? Can one be a well-educated, deeply loving Christian while simultaneously living in a Christian ghetto, unfamiliar with entertainment trends that often truthfully reflect on noteworthy social, historical, literary, and political issues and concerns? How are our entertainments shaping us? Sensitizing us or jading us, nourishing us or poisoning us? Are they increasing our ability to love or creating dead zones in our souls?

Is a film's rating or level of violence the only criteria we should employ in choosing whether to watch it or not? Consider, for example, *Schindler's List*. It is an extremely violent and occasionally sexually explicit film, with an R rating. Yet is it possible to make a truthful film about the Holocaust that is rated PG? I wanted my children—when they had reached an appropriate age—to watch *Schindler's List.* Why? I believed that it would expand their ability to love and their sensitivity to evil. Likewise, I would be disappointed if my kids developed an appetite for watching Freddy Krueger happily eviscerating the neighborhood in Wes Craven's *A Nightmare on Elm Street.* Spielberg's film enables us to love more deeply, and it hones our moral sensibilities; Craven's work too easily creates dead zones in a soul no longer sensitive to human suffering.

How might the church fathers' views—both positive and negative—help us deepen our perspective and response to modern entertainment options?

Just as Jerome rejected Cicero and Plautus, while simultaneously drawn to them, so he would have been attracted to the beauty and wisdom of Shakespeare *while feeling guilty for doing so.* This is unfortunate. Great art is a gift from God and reflects the creative abilities God has lovingly placed in his image bearers.

The fathers forbid engaging in entertainment created for the sake of sexual arousal alone. They are wise for doing so. Yet the Bible is far from a prudish book. Sexual life—its beauty, blessings, and dangers—is portrayed throughout the pages of Scripture openly and honestly. Is an artist's portrayal of sexual relationships—whether in film or in print—expanding our ability to love God and neighbor or diminishing it?

Likewise, the patristic rejection of violence as entertainment is praiseworthy. Yet there are aspects of life—human warfare and its sad results—that cannot be portrayed truthfully apart from the portrayal of graphic violence. What has resulted from a failure to truthfully portray the horrors of war?

Finally, the fathers rightly understand that skewed, sinful appetites should not be fed and reflect Paul—and Jesus—in doing so. "Put to death," Paul writes, "whatever comes from your earthly nature: sexual immorality, impurity, lust, evil desires, and greed, which is idolatry" (Col 3:5).

Our exploration of the ethics of the church fathers is near to an end. In our last chapter we will explore the key question that underlies every chapter in this book: How can we learn to live a good life with God?

It is well said, then, that it is by doing just acts that the just man is produced, and by doing temperate acts the temperate man; without these no one would have even a prospect of becoming good.

ARISTOTLE, NICOMACHEAN ETHICS[1]

The barbarians are not waiting beyond the borders; they have already been governing us for quite some time. And it is our lack of consciousness of this that constitutes part of our predicament. We are waiting not for a Godot, but for another—doubtless very different—St. Benedict.

ALASDAIR C. MACINTYRE, AFTER VIRTUE

EIGHT

LEARNING TO LIVE
A GOOD LIFE WITH GOD

The Well-Ordered Heart

In this final chapter of *Living Wisely with the Church Fathers* I explore a very specific question. If we invited a group of church fathers over for dinner—which three would you choose?—and asked during the course of the evening, "How can God's image bearer learn to live a good life with God?" how might they respond?

In all likelihood, the fathers' response to our question would include a careful analysis of the "what" of a good life. That is, what specifically and habitually characterizes a good life, a life lived well before Father, Son, and Holy Spirit?

Without doubt, the fathers would reply that love for God and love for neighbor are the primary markers of a good life. Indeed, from the church fathers' perspective, if one genuinely loves God—as all Christians claim to do—love for neighbor surely will blossom. Love for God and love for neighbor are wedded in the fathers' thinking.

If love for neighbor fails to appear in a Christian image bearer's life, the church fathers would consider the claim to love God as hollow and false. For instance, Maximus the Confessor writes: "The actualization and proof of perfect love for God is a genuine and willing attitude of goodwill towards one's neighbor. 'For he who does not love his brother whom he has seen,' says St John, 'cannot love God whom he has not seen' (1 John 4:20)."[2]

Once the church fathers explain the "what" of a good life—love for God and love for neighbor—we need to ask them a second question: How can I learn to love? How can I *learn* to be less greedy, to be less in love with money and more in love with how money might help those in need around me? How can I *learn* to love my enemy, rather than harming him in return for the harm he does to me? How can I *learn* to love those who are persecuting me, those who would readily take my life because of my faith in Jesus, and believe they are offering service to God by doing so? (cf. Jn 16:2).

In fact, Tertullian insists that the ability to love enemies and persecutors is the unique mark of the Christian. "Our religion commands us to love even our enemies, and to pray for those who persecute us. . . . For everyone loves those who love them. It is unique to Christians to love those who hate them."[3] So, we ask Tertullian and other ancient Christian writers, how can we *learn* to love in such a distinctively Christian fashion?

In the final analysis, the church fathers' views on every ethical issue I addressed in this book are related to the fundamental issue of love. Who are we loving? What are we loving? Are our various loves—with their associated dispositions, inclinations, desires, and behaviors—grounded in our love for God, nourished by our love for God, or are they indicators that we have drifted far from home, from our lodestar, from the shining, loving light beaming at the core of all reality?

If we have indeed swerved off course, how can we get back on track and cultivate a life that looks like Jesus living his life through our minds and bodies? This is the heart of the matter: How can I learn to live my life in such a way that Jesus naturally appears in it? How can I learn to live powerfully, lovingly, and habitually in the wonder of Christ's kingdom? Our last chapter will attempt to answer this question from the viewpoint and practice of the church fathers.

MODERN QUERIES AND CONNECTIONS

I continue to be amazed at how the church fathers communicate so well to modern Christians, often raising our awareness and refocusing our attention. Mark Noll, for example, writes movingly of how his mind has changed across the years and the role classical Christian faith has played in his theological, spiritual, and historical formation. "As the years have passed, the basic dogmas of the Nicene Creed have become more important; they now seem truer than in the hour I first believed."[4]

From Noll's earliest days as a believer, he "knew that Christianity was deep and that it was beautiful." Yet as the years passed, he came "to believe the depth was unfathomable and the beauty supernal beyond telling. . . . The deeper and wider ramifications of Nicene Christianity are difficult for me to disentangle because it has been through experiencing their unfathomable depths that the surpassing breadth of classical Christian faith has grown as well."[5]

Others have had the same experience as they encountered ancient Christian perspectives. Tom Oden writes of his dramatic conversion and the role Nemesius played in it:

> Then while reading Nemesius something clicked. I realized that I must listen intently, actively, without reservation. Listen in such a way that my whole life depended upon hearing. Listen in such a way that I could see telescopically beyond my modern myopia, to break through the walls of my modern prison, and actually hear voices from the past with different assumptions about the world and time and human culture.[6]

Roberta Bondi recalls her time of graduate study at Oxford University.

> I was a graduate student at the time, and though I was struggling with Christianity, I had not found a form of it that could draw both my heart and my head to God. I did not know why this was so, but I knew that it was. One day, sitting in the library, I began to read a collection of sermons written by a sixth-century representative of

this tradition, Philoxenus of Mabbug, and I started to see glimpses of what it might mean to be a Christian, to love God and other human beings, to pray. Over the intervening years I have met as many others of this tradition as I could, and I have found in them a real fleshing out of what Christian love is: God's for all of us, ours for each other, God's world, and God. Their warmth, insights, helpfulness have been a continuous source of life for me, the greatest gift I have ever received.[7]

Perhaps you have experienced the same thing. Maybe it is just this experience of the ancient church's insights and practices that attracted you to this book. We have seen that the church fathers are not perfect; none of God's image bearers are. They surely have their blind spots and shortcomings. Yet, as I have argued throughout the four volumes of this series, these ancient Christians frequently see clearly where our modern and postmodern eyesight is often blurred.

THE DEFINING CHARACTERISTIC

Behind the specific conclusions the church fathers reached on the various ethical issues we have explored together is a fundamental assumption they all share: Jesus and the apostles spoke with one voice concerning the centrality of love, and that single voice was strong, clear, and consistent.

Recall the occasion when an expert in the law tested Jesus. "Teacher," the expert asks, "What must I do to inherit eternal life?" Jesus responds by asking the inquirer what the Torah teaches, the Torah that both Jesus and this teacher loved. The expert correctly answers, quoting Deuteronomy 6:5 and Leviticus 19:18. "'Love the Lord your God with all your heart, and with all your soul, and with all your strength, and with all your mind; and your neighbor as yourself" (Lk 10:25-27).

The conversation might well have ended at this point—Jesus fully agrees with Moses' teaching—but the expert isn't satisfied; there are some people he wishes to exclude from the circle of his neighborhood. "And who is my neighbor?" the expert asks. Jesus answers his question by telling the story of the Good Samaritan. Jesus wants to widen the perspective of the expert and of Israel as a whole as to the meaning of the command "You shall love your neighbor as yourself." Samaritans, the traditional enemies of the Jews, were to be loved as neighbors (Lk 10:30-37), a shocking teaching from a Jewish outlook. The Good Samaritan serves as a pristine example of how a good neighbor loves.

THE CIRCLE OF LOVE EXPANDS

Jesus' expansion of the circle of love is continued by Paul; not only are Jews and Samaritans to be loved, but all God's image bearers—all the Gentile nations—are now to be treated as neighbors. In writing to the churches in Galatia—largely Gentile communities—Paul teaches that in Christ previous boundary markers have been removed: "For in Christ Jesus neither circumcision nor uncircumcision counts for anything; *the only thing that counts is faith working through love*" (Gal 5:6 NIV). No longer does circumcision serve as a religious and cultural boundary marker for those in relationship with Jesus. "In Christ," Paul teaches, all image bearers receive and give love, love from God and for God, love for the neighbor and from the neighbor. Concrete, consistent, impartial love is the fundamental mark of a genuine, healthy Christian community.

John Chrysostom understood the dynamic of love well. In a sermon on the epistle to the Hebrews, John writes: "We have no need of labors or of drops of sweat if we love one another." Love "*is a pathway leading of itself toward virtue.* For on the highway, if one finds the beginning, he is guided by it and has no need of one to take him by the hand. So is it also in regard to love. Only lay hold on the beginning, and at once you are guided and directed by it."[8] The highway of love leads to a good, virtuous life.

Chrysostom pictures love as a trustworthy guide for the Christian pilgrim, if the traveler at the beginning of his journey with Christ "lays hold of love." Ah, there's the rub. As John would readily acknowledge, laying hold of love is far from an easy task. We must *learn* to love. Hence Chrysostom's sermons are filled with advice and exhortation on how to deepen one's love for God and neighbor.

TO LIVE A GOOD LIFE, SPECIFIC TRAINING
IS NECESSARY

The mark of the Christian is love. Just as Roman soldiers were tattooed as a sign of their status and responsibility as Roman legionnaires, so Christians by faith bear the brand of the crucified and risen Christ and are expected to act accordingly through the power of the Spirit.

Did the tattoo a Roman soldier gladly received as he entered the legions immediately, automatically transfer the ability to fight well as a soldier? Obviously not. Every Roman soldier had to *learn through strenuous effort* how to thrust well with a sword and at what specific target, how to maintain ranks during battle, how to survive in rugged terrain and on short rations, how to sleep in the cold or in the heat day after day. To perform well in battle he had to first enter into rigorous, demanding, constant training. He had to learn how to wield a sword, how to carry a shield, how to throw a spear, how to maintain strict discipline in the midst of battle. Tough training lay ahead before the meaning of the tattoo and the skill set and behavior of the soldier matched.

A similar dynamic, the church fathers believed, is true for the Christian. For all ancient Christians, baptism was the entryway into the church and a relationship with Christ. Through baptism Christians were marked as Christ's own. The baptized were joined to Christ's body and became part of his family; they were his renewed, restored, regenerated, re-created image bearers.

Did the mark of baptism and the accompanying seal of chrismation, though, guarantee that the behavior of Christian image bearers would automatically change, that love for God, one's neighbor, or one's enemies would immediately, effortlessly appear? The church fathers knew better. To live a good life, the church fathers contended, involves strenuous effort fueled by grace. For the fathers, learning to love is far from a passive affair.

The fathers understood that *vigorous training is not divorced from God's grace but empowered by God's grace.* All believed that Christians had been reborn in baptism; now by God's grace and the power of the

Holy Spirit, these infants in Christ would have to grow up. First, the new babies in the church's nursery had to be fed milk; after all, they were babies. There were many basics Christ's infants had to learn and practice. Finally, though, the Christian child had to be weaned from milk; he had to become steady on his feet, learn to walk, begin to eat solid food, and learn more thoroughly who God is and what God required of him (1 Cor 3:1-4). Most importantly, all God's image bearers had to learn to love well—and to live well—in all the circumstances and challenges of life in the midst of the present evil age.

A NEW WORLD

When people in the world of the church fathers believed in Christ, they by faith entered a community whose values radically differed from their surrounding Roman culture. Imagine how different the lay of the land looked to a Roman soldier converted to Christ in the second century AD. The cultural, historical, political, and religious narrative framing his life up to his conversion had profoundly shaped him; for years he had learned to perceive and interpret the world through the eyes of a Roman soldier. Crucial, largely unquestioned principles for living well as a Roman had been habitually drilled into his mind and body until they became second nature: Caesar was king. Caesar was divine. Caesar demanded absolute political, religious—and in the case of a Roman soldier—military loyalty and sacrifice. Honor rather than love was the guiding, fundamental principle for all ethical decisions.

Our Roman soldier had imbibed Rome's religious values as a child imbibes his mother's milk. He had learned that the Roman gods ruled the world and must constantly be placated. The gods expected his respect and loyalty.

Did he love the gods? Perhaps. Surely he was loyal to them. But their unpredictability likely frightened him. One day the gods seemed to meet his needs, as long as he had made the proper sacrifice and manifested the correct devotion. Yet he had observed, often from firsthand experience, that even when the suitable sacrifice had been offered, life could still splinter at a moment's notice. Our soldier likely thought to himself, *Everything possible must be done to keep the gods happy—and at a distance.*

Recall that Roman power ruled nearly the entire known world: Africa, Egypt, Israel, Phoenicia, Syria, and Europe. The Roman Eagle, a sharpened sword blade, a polished shield, Roman troops in lockstep descending relentlessly on their enemy—these had been reality for our Roman convert. If one Roman soldier died, there was always another to replace him. Honor was everything, shame abhorred. Obedience was absolute. Enemies were to be conquered, not loved.

These deeply ingrained values permeated the Roman mind: strength, courage, loyalty, power, and honor were admired and embedded as character traits. Humility, weakness, vulnerability, and cowardice were despised. Romans feared and abhorred shame, not sin. To act shamefully was to violate the deepest Roman ideals, while to sin was to simply transgress the temple rituals of a particular god or goddess. No Roman would have embraced or likely comprehended the idea of a "personal relationship with the gods." The gods were unpredictable, occasionally kind, often cruel. One never knew what they were going to do. As a Roman convert entered Christ's kingdom, he or she would be called to adopt and imitate dramatically new values and models for living, as is also true for the modern Christian living early in the twenty-first century.

DEVELOPING A WELL-ORDERED HEART

Converts to Christ—whether in the ancient or modern world—face more than significant cultural and religious shifts in values and perspectives as they enter Christ's kingdom. Any human being who comes to Christ in faith must face what the church fathers describe as a *disordered heart*, one characterized by a host of *disordered loves*.

A modern writer, John Ortberg, directs our attention to the importance of a "well-ordered heart" if we are to respond habitually to Jesus' call to love wholeheartedly God and our neighbor, an insight Ortberg derives directly from Augustine.[9] Ortberg asks the right question, one that would have made sense to the church fathers. "What does it mean to have a well-ordered heart?" He then turns to Augustine's thoughts in the *City of God* to answer this question.

Ortberg concisely summarizes Augustine's thinking: to have a well-ordered heart "is to love the right thing to the right degree in the right way with the right kind of love."[10] Of course, the opposite is also true. A disordered heart loves the wrong things to a wrong degree in a wrong way with a wrong love. Just think for a moment of the things we have loved that have gravely harmed us because they were inherently unworthy of our love. God never meant for them to be loved. In all likelihood, they were not only things that were intrinsically unlovable—a love of violence, for instance—but the fact that we loved them demonstrated how deeply disordered our hearts were and are. All sin, Augustine believed, is related to the issue of a disordered heart.

Happily, the opposite is also true. As Ortberg puts it, "When the heart is well-ordered, we are not only increasingly free from sin, but also increasingly free from the desire to sin."[11] Rather than sin attracting us, we increasingly find it repulsive, unattractive, and unappealing. "Why would we want to do that?" we ask ourselves, a question that naturally arises from a well-ordered heart. Or, in Augustine's words, "a rightly directed will is love in a good sense and a perverted will is love in a bad sense."[12] Augustine specifically mentions the will rather than the heart but would affirm that the condition of the core of our being, the "heart," manifests itself in the choices we make as we exercise our will. Disordered heart, disordered will, disordered choices. Ordered heart, ordered will, ordered choices, with the flourishing of love the wondrous, grace-empowered result.

Joy and Obedience

Augustine teaches that a person who habitually leads "a right life" attains joy, while an image bearer who purposely and habitually leads an evil life, a person who loves "in a bad sense," experiences profound unhappiness.[13] What characterizes a right life, a good life, a grace-filled life, a loving life? Obedience to God. For, as Augustine puts it, obedience is "the mother and guardian of all the other virtues in a rational creature, seeing that the rational creation has been so made that it is to man's advantage to be in subjection to God, and it is calamitous for him to live according to his own will, and not to obey the will of his Creator."[14] Augustine has packed a lot into this sentence. Let's break it down.

Obedience, *living in accord with reality as God has designed it*, births, nurtures, and preserves all virtues. If I am to love, to treat others kindly and gently, to live a sexually sane life, to keep my promises, to give generously of my time and money—all key virtues—I must live in the power of the Holy Spirit in line with how God has wired *reality*. If I disobediently choose to live against the grain of the universe as created by God, I should expect to suffer, to be deeply unhappy, to experience life as unsettling, confusing, and constantly frustrating. I will be relentlessly spitting into the wind. Life will not make sense. The tonal quality of my life will be frequent and relentless pain on a very deep level. As Augustine teaches, "it is calamitous" to live according to the desires of a disordered heart.

Why Do We Choose to Live This Way?

Why in the world would we choose to live in such a profoundly unhappy way? Augustine believed that humans disobey God because we have willingly turned away from God and placed ourselves at the center of our world, a position we were never created to occupy. We have turned in on ourselves away from God, attempting to exist apart from our Creator, or with God at the periphery of our lives, the very one who has given us our existence and knows how life works when lived well. What could be crazier than this? What could be more upside down than this?

Augustine argues that a human being in his disordered state "has turned towards himself" and is "*less real* than when he had adhered to him who exists in a supreme degree." A sinful human has willingly chosen to "abandon God and to exist in oneself, that is to please oneself." When we place our self at the center, we become less substantial, less real; indeed, we are approaching "nothingness." "That is why the proud are given another name in Holy Scripture; they are called 'self-pleasers.'

(2 Peter 2:10)."[15] In seeking to please the self apart from God—the primary *characteristic* of a disordered heart—we end up losing the very self we were hoping to find and fulfill.

Disobedience to God becomes its own punishment. Why? Disobedience—the fruit of a disordered heart—in its pursuit of a self-centered, unreal life, *inevitably generates human misery on a grand scale*, individually and communally. It cannot help but do so. "The retribution for disobedience is simply disobedience itself."[16] To disobey—to regard oneself as one's own "light"—is to step into thick, impenetrable darkness. Indeed, Augustine regards the proud, autonomous self as "the original evil: man regards himself as his own light, and turns away from that light which would make man himself a light if he would set his heart on it."[17]

In response to our crooked, inward turn away from God, God allows us to experience its results: human wretchedness. The disordered heart says to itself: "If I live this way, my way, I'll experience all I've ever wanted." "Yes," the Lord responds, "you will experience what you desire, but the desires of your disordered heart will bring you great sadness and misery, rather than joy." Or, in Augustine's words, "He was handed over to himself, and because he did not obey God he could not obey himself. Hence came the more obvious misery where man does not live as he wishes to live."[18]

WE ALL SUFFER FROM A DISORDERED HEART

While the church fathers all agree that the goal of a good life is love, each struggled in his own way with learning to love, renouncing sin, responding to God's grace, and the like. The fathers, like us, came from a variety of family backgrounds and life experiences; their personalities were often strikingly different. Yet all realized the heart of a good life was the call to love God and neighbor. Some moved more deeply into love than others. Some fathers' struggles were more apparent than others. They were cracked image bearers, just like you and me, yet were also convinced that the ravages of sin could be substantially reduced in an image bearer's life. *Transformation was possible.*

Think of John Chrysostom. John took the call to love very seriously. Whether preaching to his congregation in Antioch or later to his congregants in Constantinople, whether in caring for the poor or disciplining a wayward priest, John knew that genuine life with God should be characterized by concrete, habitual, self-giving, self-sacrificial love.

And yet I recall a dear rabbi friend commenting to me as he spotted a book of Chrysostom's sermons on my desk during a visit, "Oh. Chrysostom. My favorite anti-Semite." I don't think the rabbi's comments were entirely fair, but the good rabbi did make a point. Fourth-century relationships between the largely Gentile Christian church and the Jewish community were harsh, heated, and occasionally hateful. Chrysostom's rhetoric against Jewish religious and cultural perspectives is unrelentingly aggressive and often dismissive. At times, Chrysostom's rhetorical flourishes and illustrations cross over the line of the excusable rhetorical device to the inexcusable. And, to be fair, the Jewish community knew how to respond in kind.

I think it would be inaccurate, though, to identify Chrysostom's anti-Jewish rhetoric with, say, the horrendous anti-Semitic racial ideology unleashed by the Nazis in Europe in the 1930s. This would be an anachronistic misstep. The ancient Christian and Jewish communities were arguing about religious texts, practices, experiences, and history: the meaning of the Bible, the validity of continued Torah practice, whether Jesus was the promised Messiah or not, who was ultimately responsible for his trial and execution, and so on. These remain extremely important issues and points of disagreement between modern Christians and Jews. Yet both Christian and Jew would point to the Holocaust as a horrific instance of political, cultural, and moral madness.

It is true, though, that seeds were planted by Chrysostom and other Christian leaders across the years—Martin Luther comes to mind—that were to bear bitter fruit in the lives of Jews and Christians. Animosity between church and synagogue, one of the great tragedies of the past two thousand years, still occasionally raises its head. It saddens me to acknowledge and admit this.

Chrysostom could be acerbic, tough on other people and tough on himself. John was occasionally shortsighted and ill-tempered, yet do these personal shortcomings mean ipso facto he has nothing to offer us, nothing to teach us about love? Might not John's own struggle to love people outside his religious and cultural boundaries, for reasons he was convinced were legitimate, help us to analyze, understand, and confess our own moral shortcomings today? Who is the "other" for us, the person or group beyond the scope of our concern, our care, our prayers, our love?

If only perfectly loving image bearers may legitimately speak of the importance of love, the church would be a very silent place, muzzled by its own shortcomings from proclaiming the message Jesus longs for us to speak and *live*. The church fathers' attempt to speak and model a life of love and goodness is not a perfect one; other than Christ himself, we don't find perfect examples of the good life in human history. Yet the church fathers took the attempt to live a life of love with great seriousness and determination. Through their insights, lives, and struggles, we can learn to live better lives as God's image bearers.

THE PROBLEM OF THE PASSIONS

The church fathers' insistence on the heart's disordered nature is related to their concern with the problem of the passions, a topic we have addressed at some length in this book.[19]

Maximus the Confessor taught that the passions are especially related to the soul and if not channeled properly can dominate the soul and lead it away from God. Some church fathers viewed the passions as entirely negative, while others such as Isaac the Syrian viewed them as created by God but distorted by sin. Hence, Isaac would say, the passions need to be educated or transformed, rather than completely eradicated.[20]

THE GOAL OF A HEALTHY SPIRITUAL LIFE

The goal of a healthy spiritual life, then, would be "dispassion" or *apatheia*, a Greek word related etymologically to the English words *apathy* and *apathetic*. While the connotations of *apathy* and *apathetic* in English are entirely negative—apathetic people don't care about things they should care about—the meaning of the Greek word *apatheia* is quite different. Image bearers who are passionless are not attached to or centered on unimportant things. They are people who are free, free to love God and to love their neighbor. They are not indifferent to human suffering—that would be modern apathy—but deeply sensitive to it. Often in the church fathers, this healthy and wise *apatheia* is linked to genuine, safe, selfless love. *Apatheia* in this sense "is among the gifts of God," as we saw in our case study of Clement of Alexandria.[21]

Maximus understands well the struggles God's image bearers inevitably encounter as they learn by the power of the Spirit to overcome deeply habituated patterns of sinful thoughts and behaviors. He realizes it is not easy to change. He knows that if we are to love habitually, more will be required than simply desiring to love. To love well requires training—a workout program of sorts—that Maximus teaches that all Christ's disciples must begin and strenuously engage.

WHERE TO BEGIN?

Where to begin? Let's examine one phrase of Maximus that reveals the heart of his teaching on learning to live a good life. Maximus explains that to live a good life with God requires moral *training*: "He who has just begun to follow a holy way of life, and has received instruction about how to act righteously, devotes himself wholly to *the practice of the virtues* in all obedience and faith, nourishing himself, as if on meat, on their manifest aspects, that is to say, on *moral training*."[22]

Consider the verbs Maximus employs as he urges us to a "holy way of life": *follow, nourishing, received, act,* and *devotes.* Or the nouns: *way, life, instruction, practice, virtues, obedience,* and *faith.* Let's now add the adverbs: *just* begun, act *righteously,* devotes himself *wholly.* Finally, the adjectives: a *holy* way, *all* obedience and faith, *manifest* aspects, *moral* living.

For Maximus, a holy way of life—living a good life with God—is a pattern of living that one *receives* from others; it is a way of life we *devote* ourselves to; it is a form of life we *train ourselves* in; it is something we *practice.* Through a willingness to receive instruction, to exert ourselves, to devote ourselves, to practice something wholeheartedly, transformation occurs. If this way of life—with all its accompanying practices—were the whole story, though, most pagan Greeks would nod their heads in agreement. In fact, ancient Greeks described a similar program for life transformation as *paideia*, disciplined training in learning to live well.

The thinking and practice of church fathers such as Maximus and Chrysostom on learning to live well significantly differ from Greek *paideia*. *For the fathers, everything in living a good life begins with the grace of God made known to us in Christ.* This is the absolute starting point for all the church fathers when it comes to spiritual transformation. By way of contrast, Greek *paideia* is not grace-filled, Spirit empowered life, the life offered by God through Christ to all God's image bearers. For the Christian, transformation is possible only through the grace of God and the empowerment of the Spirit, an idea one never finds in Plato, Aristotle, or other Greek or Roman thinkers.

Union with Christ Leads
to the Way of the Cross

Christians who live well, Chrysostom believes, are firmly planted in the love, grace, and goodness of God. And where has God's love been most clearly manifested? In the cross. Chrysostom delights in the way the cross of Christ has turned the values of the Roman world upside down. Out of apparent defeat, disgrace, weakness, suffering, and death emerges unimaginable victory. For John, life lived well before God, then, surely should reflect this distinct, loving, sacrificial, cruciform pattern.

For Chrysostom, all the key themes of living well before God are extruded from the cruciform pattern modeled by Jesus. If what appears to be the greatest tragedy in the history of the world *is actually* the most blessed event, Christians can view the circumstances, challenges, and ethical choices of their own lives in a dramatically new way. The ethical decisions we make on a daily basis must be predicated, Chrysostom argues, on Jesus' cross as "the foremost good," "a proof of God's great providence, goodness and love." For the broader Roman world, a cross represented shame, horrendous pain, abandonment, disloyalty, punishment. For the Christian community, in Chrysostom's time and today, the cross—in light of Christ's resurrection—provides the cruciform pattern Jesus calls us to imitate as we seek through the power of the Spirit to live a good life with God.

Chrysostom also believed that how we live in the midst of this present evil age should be shaped by God's *ultimate goal for human history*. The *present* must be viewed and lived in light of the *end*. God's character, promises, and providence are the guarantee "that in every circumstance all things that come to us from him have a favorable outcome—provided that our activities don't get in the way."[23] The key, then, is learning to act well, regardless of the circumstances we find ourselves in.

CALLED TO BE LIKE GOD

Christ's apprentices will surely be training, but with what goal in mind and by what power? First, regarding the goal: the church fathers believed that the goal of human life is to be like God, to live as though Jesus himself were living his life through our bodies, our minds, our souls.

Let's explore this idea more deeply. Origen writes, "Every spiritual being is, by nature, a temple of God, created to receive into itself the glory of God."[24] Over a hundred years later Basil of Caesarea writes similarly, "The human being is an animal who has received the vocation to become God."[25]

Origen and Basil are arguing that human beings are wired for God. We were created for God. Adam and Eve's great turn inward has blinded us and prevents us from fulfilling God's destiny for us. As God's image bearers, we bear characteristics in common that other members of God's created order do not possess or reflect. Gregory of Nyssa comments that "the sky is not an image of God, nor is the moon, nor the sun, nor the beauty of the stars, nor anything of what can be seen in creation." Only human beings "have been made the image of the Reality that transcends all understanding, the likeness of imperishable beauty, the imprint of true divinity, the recipient of beatitude, the seal of the true light. When you turn to him you become that which he is himself."[26] God, then, has created human creatures to be like God, to reflect his glory in the world, to love God and to love our neighbor. As God's image bearers, we have a unique opportunity and call, one closely related to what Olivier Clément describes as our "capacity for transcendence."[27]

As a point of comparison, consider my dog Poncho. Poncho is loved by God; Poncho is one of God's beloved creatures. But, as far as I can tell, Poncho spends none of his day thinking about God. His mind is occupied with the deer, foxes, cats, birds, and squirrels that live in our neighborhood, with his morning and evening meals, with the expectation of a long evening run and perhaps a happy encounter with one of his female friends. These basic interests and needs form the boundary of Poncho's world. After all, Poncho is a dog and perfectly happy as such.

When we see human beings living like Poncho, *solely* occupied with such basic interests, concerns, and delights, we sense that something is missing, that a life is being squandered, that humans are made for more than this. The church fathers would say, "Of course you are. You bear on your soul and body the image of God."

Human beings, as Clément observes, are intelligent, loving, thinking beings, reflecting God's wisdom, intelligence, and love. We are concerned about meaning, the rhyme and reason of things, why life is worth living and how it should be lived. As Gregory of Nyssa puts it,

> The fact of being created in the image of God means that humanity right from the moment of creation was endowed with a royal character.... The godhead is wisdom and *logos* [reason, meaning]; in yourself too you see intelligence and thought, images of the original intelligence and thought.... God is love and the source of love: the divine Creator has drawn this feature on our faces too.[28]

Irenaeus describes an "order," "rhythm," and "movement" related to God's creation of human beings in God's "image and likeness." "The Father makes the decisions and gives the commands, the Son carries them out and adapts them, the Spirit provides nourishment and growth, and humanity progresses little by little."[29] Progresses little by little into what? Into looking more and more like God, like God in human flesh, *like Jesus.* We can never become God in essence. All the fathers are clear on this. But we can become more and more like God in our attitudes and actions; we can all grow in love, for God and for neighbor. How so? By being conformed ever more fully to the image of the incarnate Son, Jesus Christ, for "he is the image of the invisible God, the firstborn of all creation" (Col 1:15). Jesus' life, his words and actions, provide us with the fundamental pattern and model for living for all God's image bearers.

Not only is Jesus the pattern and the model; he is *the life of God* given to us through the Spirit. In Athanasius's words: "The Word made himself 'bearer of the flesh' in order that human beings might become bearers of the Spirit."[30] Or, to quote Irenaeus, "How could the human race go to God if God had not come to us? How should we free ourselves from our birth into death if we had not been born again according to faith by a new birth generously given by God, thanks to that which came about from the Virgin's womb?"[31]

Transformation occurs through our union with the living, resurrected Christ; we are transformed through faith in Christ and through *learning* how to live our lives through the power of the Spirit. It is possible, the church fathers insist, to live my life in my body as though Jesus himself were living it. We are not disembodied spirits; we are embodied selves made in the image of God, the incarnate Son. In our embodied self Christ's life manifests itself through the Spirit. "It is not in a part of [human] nature that the image is found, but nature in its totality is the image of God."[32] "Spirits without bodies will never be spiritual men and women. It is our entire being, that is to say, the soul and flesh combined, which by receiving the Spirit of God constitutes the spiritual man."[33]

Think of the various ethical issues we have considered together in this book. How can I learn to deal with issues of wealth and poverty in a manner that reflects my union with the Word made flesh? How can I change in such a way that love for other image bearers automatically emerges as I spend my money, in a movement from greediness and hoarding to sharing and giving? If Jesus is living his life through my soul, mind, and body—and he does so to the extent I allow him through the Spirit—what choices might he desire me to make concerning wealth and poverty, resistance to evil, service in the military, abortion, care for the neglected, the invisible, the nobodies, entertainment options, and so on, as he lives through me?

We come now to a crucial question. What should our *askesis*—our workout program—be for learning to live a good life with God? How did Jesus himself stay in good spiritual shape? The church fathers were extremely interested in these questions, for they understood well that love for God and for neighbor did not arise in a vacuum. Rather, the fathers teach, the ability to live a life of love for God and neighbor is developed through the grace-filled, Spirit-empowered practice of specific spiritual disciplines. We will close this chapter—and this book—by taking a look at the discipline as described by Athanasius in his biography of Antony the Great.

"Working Out" on a Regular Basis

I distinctly remember the time when my dear friend and mentor Tom Oden said to me, "Chris, a spiritual life without *askesis* is impossible." When Tom said this to me, he had already invested years soaking his mind and heart in Scripture and in the teachings and key practices of the church fathers; he had formed deeply ingrained spiritual habits of mind and body under the wise coaching of these ancient guides.

I was in my early forties at the time Tom mentioned the necessity of *askesis* to me. My previous twenty years as a Christian had been lived in a largely evangelical environment. The practice of an ascetic lifestyle, I had heard and sometimes read, was the misguided attempt by ill-informed monks to earn their way to heaven, or so was the impression I received on the rare occasions when the term would come up in conversation or reading. Now unexpectedly, early in my doctoral studies with Tom Oden, he was telling me that it was impossible to stay healthy spiritually without engaging in some kind of *askesis*!

THE HOW QUESTION

Thus far in this chapter we have analyzed in some detail the church fathers' thoughts on learning to lead a good life. We have seen that a disordered heart inevitably leads to disordered, sinful actions. And we have pondered the grace God has shown to us in the incarnation, ministry, crucifixion, resurrection, and ascension of Jesus. We have learned that in union with Christ genuine transformation is possible in the midst of this present evil age.

So now we come to the how question. How does a healthy, wise, disciplined *askesis* help us to develop a good life in Christ? A quick look at the word *askesis* will prove helpful. *Askesis* is best translated "exercise regimen."[34] I will be freely using "workout program" in place of the Greek word *askesis* and the English word *asceticism* in this section. All Greek athletes engaged in a specific exercise regimen or workout program, much like athletes today; *askesis* "was really a sports term before it became a monastic one."[35]

The key point is this: if an athlete is to perform well in her sport, she has to work out on a regular basis. Think, for example, of the workout program or *askesis* of professional football players during summer training camp for the upcoming fall season. Training camp is just that—constant drills to train mind and body to respond habitually to the challenges of playing professional football.

Some training exercises are immediately related to football itself: receivers run the same routes over and over again. Quarterbacks repeatedly run the same play with their running backs and offensive line. Coaches repetitively go over defensive schemes for hours with linebackers, defensive linemen, and defensive backs. Other exercises such as wind sprints or mental exercises such as memorizing the playbook are also essential. And, of course, any football player will be spending lots of time in the weight room. Weight work, though essential, is not directly connected to specific football skills. Instead, it develops the muscle strength that will facilitate a player's ability to play football well. Weak football players lose to strong football players, even when their specific football skills are equal.

Few football players enjoy training camp; it is tedious, stressful, and exhausting. Yet these athletes know that the hard work done in training is indispensable if they are to be *free* to play their sport well. The freedom to play well does not arise in a vacuum. It comes from the faithful, disciplined practice of training camp, consistent practice in which essential mental and bodily habits are formed.

The athlete's ability to respond immediately and skillfully during the heat of the game is largely derived through the disciplined workout program he has practiced so faithfully. *Freedom and discipline, spontaneity and habit formation, fulfillment and exertion are intimately linked.* In all likelihood, the church fathers might not have been terribly interested in North American professional football, but they would have surely understood and affirmed the absolute necessity of training, discipline, and habit formation if God's image bearer is to thrive in living a good life before God.

GOD'S ATHLETES

We should not be surprised, then, that the church fathers described healthy, maturing believers as God's athletes. William Harmless turns our attention to the great desert monk Antony to illustrate the dynamics of *askesis* in the life of a specific image bearer, one of the greatest athletes of God. Harmless specifically focuses on the daily rule of life or workout program that Antony practiced in his particular learning space, the desert.[36]

Harmless observes that the "routine Antony adopted was as physically demanding as any athlete's." Harmless's point is an extremely important one to grasp if we are to learn from the fathers how to live a good life. Spiritual formation, a process always connected to some kind of *askesis* or training program, is a mental, physical, and spiritual matter. The church fathers understood that God's image bearers are physical creatures created by God as *embodied* selves. The desert spirituality demonstrated in the life of Antony is clearly a physical, embodied spirituality. The spiritual disciplines of the fathers were often directly related to disciplining the body, not only to train the body's impulses to act in a holy, loving fashion but also to harness the resources of the body—the body's inherent power—as a power source for the graceful work of the Holy Spirit.

Consider the specific practices that formed the heart of Antony's training program. First, Harmless notes, Antony spent the day doing manual labor (such as weaving baskets) to support himself. Second, he practiced "watchfulness," spending whole nights without sleeping, in vigilant prayer. And when he did sleep, his bed was a rush mat, or even the bare ground. Third, he maintained an austere diet: bread, salt, water, no meat, no wine. "He ate at most once a day, and sometimes fasted so that he ate only every other day or even less often." Antony practiced other disciplines as well: the "weighing of thoughts . . . a technique of introspection that enabled him to attend to, without being seduced by, the flood of feelings and memories that might divert him from his single-minded purpose"; unceasing prayer, based on Paul's teaching in 1 Thessalonians 5:17; and a deep immersion in the Scriptures themselves. Antony, largely through hearing Scripture read, memorized vast sections of the Bible.[37]

Antony's rule of life or workout program, specific exercises he practiced daily to nourish his life with God and his love for God and neighbor, provides examples to twenty-first-century image bearers of a training program that can be adapted to a modern setting for learning to live a good life before God. Such a program would likely include the following elements:

- a specific learning space (in Antony's case, the desert);
- meaningful work (in Antony's case, manual labor);
- a vigilant, consistent prayer life;
- regularized sleep patterns;
- a simple, disciplined diet;
- regular times of fasting;
- attentiveness to emotions, thoughts, and memories; and

◆ a deep immersion in the Bible, with an emphasis on the memorization of Scripture.

The spiritual disciplines Antony practiced—his specific *askesis*—don't have to be exactly the same disciplines we might make part of our own training program. They do provide, though, a clear example of what ancient Christians viewed as key practices for learning to live a good life with God, a life with love of God and neighbor at its goal. The church fathers understood and taught that spiritual formation is not a passive affair. Instead, it requires strenuous effort, much like the exertion an athlete engages in to acquire the freedom to perform well in her particular sport.

Legalism?

The church fathers' emphasis on *askesis*—a training program—if life is to be lived well may initially strike some readers as simply a misguided step into legalism. Aren't they trying to earn their salvation? After all, salvation is by grace, not by works. Any sane Christian knows that. The fathers would readily agree, at least regarding the issue of legalism. They might well reply, though, "Who is trying to earn anything from God? Paul himself, the great apostle of grace, also engaged in a training program." And the fathers would be right.

Paul specifically employs an athletic metaphor in 1 Corinthians 9:24-27 to describe how he stayed in spiritually good shape. He describes how hard Greek athletes worked out to gain the skills and stamina to win in their sport. Paul then says that *we do the same thing* to win an imperishable crown. Indeed, Paul's letters and Jesus' teaching are replete with specific examples of practices both engaged in on a regular basis. A single example from Jesus' life will have to suffice.

In Luke 5:15, Luke describes how busy Jesus is. People are constantly bringing the sick and demon possessed to Jesus to be healed. Luke wants us to see that Jesus is engaged in the most important work in human history. Jesus' healings are signs that God's kingdom is breaking into the midst of this present evil age, that the anointed one of Israel has finally come, that redemption is at hand. And yet Luke, who seems to like to juxtapose opposite emphases to catch our attention, writes in Luke 5:16 that Jesus "would withdraw to deserted places and pray." Silence, solitude, and prayer, then, from Luke's perspective, were a key part of Jesus' *askesis*, his workout program. If Jesus was to do the work his Father had called him to do, Luke teaches, Jesus had to have consistent times apart from the very people he had come to save, times of prayer and renewal so that he could do what his Father was asking him to do. If such was the case with Jesus, *how much more for us in our much more troubled condition?*[38]

So, as I draw this book on the ethics of the church fathers to a close, I can hear the fathers saying to all of us, "Learn to live a good life with God. How? Through faith in your Lord and Savior. Trust in him for your salvation. Heed his teaching and example. Grow in him through immersing your mind in the Scriptures. Feed on him in the Eucharist. Engage in the same spiritual disciplines that he himself practiced: study, simplicity, silence, solitude, service, and worship. Allow Jesus to live his life through your mind, your soul, your body. Become like him. Be ever-increasingly formed into his image through the power of the Spirit. And the grace-filled result will be a life lived well with God in the midst of this present evil age. Life will make sense. And the world will be a better place because you have been here."

NOTES

INTRODUCTION

[1]Gregory of Nyssa, *The Life of Moses* (New York: Paulist Press, 1978), 32.

[2]Christopher A. Hall, *Reading Scripture with the Church Fathers* (Downers Grove, IL: IVP Academic, 1998), 8.

[3]Cf. Athanasius, *On the Incarnation* 6.6–8.4, trans. in *We Believe in the Crucified and Risen Lord*, ed. Mark J. Edwards, ACD 3 (Downers Grove, IL: IVP Academic, 2009), 70.

[4]Augustine, *Tractates on the Gospel of John* 17.7-9, trans. in *We Believe in the Crucified and Risen Lord*, 57.

[5]I first learned the importance of learning spaces from reading Parker Palmer's *To Know as We Are Known: Education as a Spiritual Journey* (San Francisco: HarperOne, 1993), see 40-46, 69-73. Palmer speaks of the importance of the learning space of the desert for the ancient desert fathers and mothers. "So the desert teachers disciplined themselves to stand their ground, to stay within the boundaries of the learning space so that truth might seek them out" (73).

[6]Aristotle, *The Ethics of Aristotle: The Nicomachean Ethics*, trans. J. A. K. Thomson (Baltimore: Penguin Books, 1953), book 1, chap. 5, 30.

[7]Gregory of Nyssa, *On Virginity* 23, trans. in *Romans*, ed. Gerald Bray, ACCS New Testament 6 (Downers Grove, IL: InterVarsity Press, 1998), 306.

[8]Ambrosiaster, *Commentary on Paul's Epistles*, trans. in Bray, *Romans*, 306.

[9]Chrysostom, *Homilies on Romans* 20, trans. in Bray, *Romans*, 306.

[10]Origen, *Commentary on the Epistle to the Romans*, in Bray, *Romans*, 308.

[11]Ibid.

[12]Ibid.

[13]Readers interested in exploring these issues more thoroughly should consult Edwin Hatch, *The Influence of Greek Ideas and Usages upon the Christian Church*, ed. A. M. Fairbairn, 5th ed. (Peabody, MA: Hendrickson, 1995); Charles Norris Cochrane, *Christianity and Classical Culture: A Study of Thought and Action from Augustus to Augustine* (Oxford: Oxford University Press, 1957); Jaroslav Pelikan, *Christianity and Classical Culture: The Metamorphosis of Natural Theology in the Christian Encounter with Hellenism* (New Haven, CT: Yale University Press, 1993); and Robert Wilken, *The Spirit of Early Christian Thought: Seeking the Face of God* (New Haven, CT: Yale University Press, 2003).

[14]Aristotle, *Ethics of Aristotle*, book 3, chap. 1, p. 80.

[15]Ibid., book 2, chap. 1, 55.

[16]Ibid., book 2, chap. 1, 56.

[17]Ibid.

[18]Plutarch, *Life of Pericles* 1-4, trans. in Wilken, *Spirit of Early Christian Thought*, 263, emphasis added.

[19]I am here following the discussion in Wilken, *Spirit of Early Christian Thought*, 263-70.

[20]Gregory the Wonderworker, *Panegyric* 6.75, 78, trans. in Wilken, *Spirit of Early Christian Thought*, 267.

[21]I am here drawing on material from Christopher A. Hall, *Worshiping with the Church Fathers* (Downers Grove, IL: IVP Academic, 2009), 93-94, 147-49.

[22]Roberta Bondi, *To Love as God Loves* (Philadelphia: Fortress, 1987), 57.

[23]Ibid., 58.

[24]Ibid., 57.

[25]John Ortberg, *The Life You've Always Wanted* (Grand Rapids: Zondervan, 1997), 180.

[26]Olivier Clément, *The Roots of Christian Mysticism: Texts from the Patristic Era with Commentary* (Hyde Park, NY: New City Press, 1993), 167.

[27]John Cassian, *The Conferences*, trans. and ed. Boniface Ramsey (New York: Newman, 1997), 2.3, p. 330.

[28]Gregory of Nyssa, *The Lord's Prayer*, trans. Hilda C. Graef, ACW 18 (New York: Paulist Press, 1954), 26.

[29]Chrysostom, *On Providence*, introduction, 2, trans. in Hall, *Worshiping with the Church Fathers*, 25.

[30]Chrysostom, *On Providence*, introduction, 4, trans. in Hall, *Worshiping with the Church Fathers*, 25.

[31]Chrysostom, *Homilies on the Acts of the Apostles and the Epistles to the Romans,* in *NPNF¹* 9:99, Homily 15, cf. PG 60.126C-D. I have slightly modified the translation.

[32]Chrysostom writes: "If I had not already made my discourse exceedingly long and exceeded the proper measure, I would have much to say about death from a Christian perspective and would have shown especially in this the wisdom and providence of God. I would have said much concerning corruption, putrefaction, worms, and ashes. Since most people mourn and lament bitterly that our bodies will be reduced to ashes, dust, and worms, I would have shown God's unspeakable providence and care from the very reality of death itself." Chrysostom, *On Providence* 7.34, my translation.

[33]Ibid., 7.36.

[34]Ibid., 7.37.

[35]Ibid., 10.20.

[36]Ibid., 10.21, emphasis added.

[37]Ibid., 10.24, emphasis added.

[38]Ibid., 10.30.

[39]Ibid., 10.31, emphasis added.

[40]Ibid., 10.33, emphasis added.

[41]Ibid., 10.23, emphasis added.

[42]Ibid., 10.40.

[43]Palladius, *Letter to Lausus* 2, quoted in Wilken, *Spirit of Early Christian Thought,* 265.

[44]I first encountered this question as the title of a book by Francis Schaeffer. See Francis Schaeffer, *How Should We Then Live?* (Wheaton, IL: Crossway Books, 1983).

1 "They Looked like Flaming Angels": Martyrdom

[1]In *ANF* 4:177, quoted in David W. Bercot, ed., *A Dictionary of Early Christian Beliefs* (Peabody, MA: Hendrickson, 1998), 430.

[2]In *ANF* 1:254, quoted in Bercot, *Dictionary of Early Christian Beliefs,* 427.

[3]The quotation comes from Eric Metaxas's foreword to Paul Marshall, Lela Gilbert, and Nina Shea, *Persecuted: The Global Assault on Christians* (Nashville: Thomas Nelson, 2013), ix.

[4]Ibid.

[5]Ibid., x.

[6]Andrew F. Walls, introduction to *The Missionary Movement in Christian History: Studies in the Transmission of Faith* (Maryknoll, NY: Orbis, 1996), xiii,

quoted in Mark A. Noll, *From Every Tribe and Nation: A Historian's Discovery of the Global Christian Story* (Grand Rapids: Baker Academic, 2014), 91.

[7]Origen, *Against Celsus*, in *ANF* 4:470, quoted in Bercot, *Dictionary of Early Christian Beliefs*, 430, emphasis added.

[8]Bert Ghezzi, *Voices of the Saints* (New York: Image Books/Doubleday, 2000), 183.

[9]*The Martyrdom of Polycarp*, in *The Apostolic Fathers: Greek Texts and English Translations*, 3rd ed., ed. and trans. Michael W. Holmes (Grand Rapids: Baker Academic, 2007), 309.

[10]Boniface Ramsey, *Beginning to Read the Fathers* (Mahwah, NJ: Paulist Press, 1985), 128. I first noticed the significance of the Polycarp excerpt in my reading of Ramsey and have found his analysis to be helpful and enlightening.

[11]Ibid., 130.

[12]Ibid., 122.

[13]Cf. Robert Wilken, *The Christians as the Romans Saw Them* (New Haven, CT: Yale University Press, 1984), 10.

[14]Trajan, *Epistle* 10.34, cited in Wilken, *Christians as the Romans Saw Them*, 12-13.

[15]Wilken, *Christians as the Romans Saw Them*, 13.

[16]Pliny, *Epistle* 96, cited in Wilken, *Christians as the Romans Saw Them*, 16.

[17]Cited in Wilken, *Christians as the Romans Saw Them*, 22.

[18]Ibid., 23.

[19]Ibid.

[20]Ibid.

[21]Laurie Guy, *Introducing Early Christianity: A Topical Survey of Its Life, Beliefs, and Practices* (Downers Grove, IL: InterVarsity Press, 2004), 74.

[22]Tertullian, *Apology* 40.2, cited in Guy, *Introducing Early Christianity*, 74.

[23]Tacitus, *Annals* 15.44.2-8, cited in Guy, *Introducing Early Christianity*, 62-63.

[24]Bryan M. Litfin, *Early Christian Martyr Stories: An Evangelical Introduction with New Translations* (Grand Rapids: Baker Academic, 2014), 10. Litfin footnotes the words of Cicero, who, though not referring to Christianity, represents well the Roman aversion to foreign religious beliefs. "I thought I should be rendering a great service both to myself and to my countrymen if I could tear up this superstition by the roots. But I want it distinctly understood that the destruction of superstition does not mean the destruction of religion. For I consider it the part of wisdom to preserve the institutions of our forefathers by retaining their sacred rites and ceremonies" (*On Divination* 2.72.148, quoted in Litfin, *Early Christian Martyr Stories*, 10).

[25]Lactantius, *On the Death of the Persecutors* 10-15; Lactantius's treatise is included in Litfin, *Early Christian Martyr Stories*, 139-45.

[26]Litfin, *Early Christian Martyr Stories*, 140.

[27]Lactantius mentions Romula, the mother of the Caesar Galerius, one of Diocletian's right-hand men. Romula "was a highly superstitious woman and a worshiper of the mountain gods. When she was [*text missing*], she used to hold religious banquets almost every day and offer the sacrificial meat to the villagers of her district. But while she was feasting with the pagans, the Christians abstained and continued with their fasts and prayers. Thus, she conceived hatred for them in her heart. And by constantly complaining . . . she provoked her son, who was no less superstitious than she, to get rid of these men." Ibid., 140-41.

[28]Eusebius Pamphili, *Ecclesiastical History* 6-10, trans. Roy J. Deferrari, Fathers of the Church 29 (Washington, DC: Catholic University of America Press, 1955), 6.39, 66.

[29]Henri Crouzel, *The Life and Thought of the First Great Theologian* (San Francisco: Harper & Row, 1989), 35.

[30]Origen, *Prayer, Exhortation to Martyrdom*, trans. and annotated by John J. O'Meara, ACW 19 (New York: Newman, 1954), 2, p. 142.

[31]Ibid., 3, pp. 142-43.

[32]Ibid., 4, p. 143. Cf. Phil 4:7. I have slightly modified the translation.

[33]Ibid., 4, p. 144.

[34]Ibid., 5, p. 145.

[35]Ibid., 6, p. 147.

[36]Ibid., 8-10, pp. 148-50.

[37]Ibid., 19, p. 160.

[38]Ibid., 11, p. 151.

[39]Ibid.

[40]Ibid., 12, p. 153.

[41]For readers interested in learning more about Origen's spiritual hermeneutic, consult Christopher A. Hall, *Reading Scripture with the Church Fathers* (Downers Grove, IL: IVP Academic, 1998), 141-55.

[42]Origen, *Prayer, Exhortation to Martyrdom* 13, trans. O'Meara, pp. 153-54.

[43]Ibid., 14, p. 155; cf. Mk 10:30.

[44]Ibid., 14, pp. 155-56.

[45]Ibid., 15, p. 156.

[46]Ibid., 18, p. 158.

[47]Ibid., 20, p. 160.

[48]Ibid., 22, p. 162.

[49]Cf. 2 Maccabees 6–8.

[50]Ibid., 22, pp. 162-63. Cf. 2 Maccabees 6:18-31.

[51]Ibid., 23, p. 163. Cf. 2 Maccabees 7.

[52]Ibid., 24, p. 165.

[53]Ibid.

[54]Ibid., 23, p. 164.

[55]Ibid., 23, p. 164; cf. 2 Maccabees 7:6.

[56]Ibid., 25, p. 166.

[57]Ibid., 27, p. 167.

[58]Ibid.; cf. Phil 4:13; 1 Tim 1:12.

[59]Ibid., 25, p. 165; cf. 2 Maccabees 7:10, 15-17.

[60]Ibid., 28, p. 168.

[61]Ibid., 28, pp. 168-69; cf. Mt 20:22; 26:39; Mk 10:38. O'Meara observes that "Origen is repeating the then accepted view that martyrs were not judged by God, but rather sat in judgment with Him." Ibid., 30, p. 171.

[62]Ibid., 30, p. 171.

[63]Ibid., 30, p. 172.

[64]Ibid., 32, p. 173.

[65]Ibid.

[66]Ibid. I have slightly modified the translation.

[67]Ibid., 34, pp. 174-75; cf. Mt 10:5, 17-23; Lk 12:11-12; 21:14-19; Mk 13:9-13.

[68]Ibid., 34, pp. 176-77.

[69]Ibid., 35, p. 178.

[70]Ibid., 35, p. 178; cf. Dan 3:6; Mt 13:42, 50.

[71]Athanasius, *On the Incarnation*, trans. and ed. A Religious of C.S.M.V. (Crestwood, NY: St. Vladimir's Seminary Press, 1982), 57.

[72]Ibid., 57-58.

[73]Ibid., 58.

[74]Ibid., 59.

[75]Ibid., 60.

[76]Susan Bergman, *Martyrs: Contemporary Writers on Modern Lives of Faith* (San Francisco: HarperSanFrancisco, 1996), 3.

[77]David Platt, *Radical: Taking Back Your Faith from the American Dream* (Colorado Springs: Multnomah Books, 2010), 13.

[78]Dallas Willard, *The Divine Conspiracy: Rediscovering Our Hidden Life in God* (San Francisco: HarperSanFrancisco, 1998), 214.

2 "A Solid Drop of Gold": Wealth and Poverty

[1] Quoted in Everett Ferguson, *Inheriting Wisdom: Readings for Today from Ancient Christian Writers* (Peabody, MA: Hendrickson, 2004), 34.

[2] Quoted in ibid., 36-37.

[3] John Chrysostom, *On Wealth and Poverty*, trans. and introduced by Catharine P. Roth (Crestwood, NY: St. Vladimir's Seminary Press, 1984), 36.

[4] J. Patout Burns Jr. and Robin M. Jenson, *Christianity in North Africa: The Development of Its Practices and Beliefs* (Grand Rapids: Eerdmans, 2014), 575.

[5] Steven J. Friesen notes that "the vast majority of people lived in rural areas or in small towns, with only about 10 to 15 percent of the population in big cities of ten thousand people or more. . . . Most of the population worked in agriculture (80-90 percent) and . . . large-scale commercial or manufacturing activity was rare." Steven J. Friesen, "Injustice or God's Will? Early Christian Explanations of Poverty," in *Wealth and Poverty in Early Church and Society*, ed. Susan R. Holman (Grand Rapids: Baker Academic, 2008), 19.

[6] Helen Rhee comments that "a vast majority of the Roman world (75-90 percent in range,—both urban and rural contexts combined), lived near or on subsistence level, struggling for survival and sustenance." Helen Rhee, *Loving the Poor, Saving the Rich: Wealth, Poverty, and Early Christian Formation* (Grand Rapids: Baker Academic, 2012), 11.

[7] Ibid., 21.

[8] Peter Brown, *Through the Eye of a Needle: Wealth, the Fall of Rome, and the Making of Christianity in the West, 350–550 AD* (Princeton, NJ: Princeton University Press, 2012), 235.

[9] Suetonius, *Vitellius* 13.2, trans. R. Graves, cited in Michael Grant, *The Twelve Caesars* (New York: Charles Scriber's Sons, 1975), 199, and in Christopher A. Hall, *Reading Scripture with the Church Fathers* (Downers Grove, IL: InterVarsity Press, 1998), 33.

[10] Brown, *Through the Eye of a Needle*, 15-17.

[11] Ibid., 17.

[12] Ibid., 219.

[13] Ibid., 28.

[14] Ibid., 317-18.

[15] Ibid., 103.

[16] Augustine, *Ennarrationes in Psalmos* 147.7, quoted in Brown, *Through the Eye of a Needle*, 354.

[17] For a helpful introduction to the sermons, cf. Catharine P. Roth's introduction in Chrysostom, *On Wealth and Poverty*, 7-18.

[18]St. John Chrysostom, *On Wealth and Poverty*, sermon 1, 20.

[19]Rhee comments on the invisibility of the poor in Roman society: "The recipients of public benefactions—which evidently were not designed to relieve poverty—were identified as the members of particular civic communities, including the privileged elite, and the recipients' needs were not considered favorable factors in distribution. The poor received gifts only indirectly. When they were included in the distribution, it was not because they were poor but because they were simply part of and participated in the civic community; the poor were never singled out for any special treatment, let alone for any public distributions (e.g., alimentary). In this sense, the poor were 'ubiquitous but more or less invisible.'" Rhee, *Loving the Poor, Saving the Rich*, 19.

[20]Jerome, *On Lazarus and Dives*, quoted in Thomas C. Oden, *The Good Works Reader* (Grand Rapids: Eerdmans, 2007), 54.

[21]Cyprian, *Works and Almsgiving* 15, quoted in Oden, *Good Works Reader*, 54; emphasis added.

[22]Ibid., 22-23.

[23]Chrysostom, *Homilies on the Gospel of Matthew* 77.6, cited in Peter C. Phan, *Social Thought*, Message of the Fathers of the Church 20 (Wilmington, DE: Michael Glazier, 1984), 146.

[24]Lactantius, *The Divine Institutes* 6.10, cited in Phan, *Social Thought*, 96.

[25]Basil the Great, "Homily Delivered in Times of Famine and Drought" 2, emphasis added, cited in Phan, *Social Thought*, 119.

[26]Gregory of Nyssa, *Love of the Poor*, emphasis added, cited in Phan, *Social Thought*, 133.

[27]Chrysostom, *On Wealth and Poverty*, sermon 1, 23.

[28]Jason Byassee, *An Introduction to the Desert Fathers* (Eugene, OR: Cascade Books, 2007), 71.

[29]Clement of Alexandria, *Stromata*, ANF 1:506, book 6, chap. 14.

[30]The rich fool of Luke 12:16-20 is considered by many fathers the classic example of the fool's response to blessing from God. Cyril of Alexandria poses the right question: "What does the rich man do, surrounded by a great supply of many blessings beyond all numbering? He does not raise his eyes to God. He does not count it worth his while to gain for his soul those treasures that are above in heaven. He does not cherish love for the poor. He does not even desire the value it gains. He does not sympathize with suffering. It neither gives him pain nor awakens his pity. Still more irrationally, he settles himself into a comfortable pattern of life, and pretends he owns his life." Cyril of Alexandria, *Commentary on Luke* 89, on Luke 12:16-20, quoted in Oden, *Good Works Reader*, 41.

[31]Clement of Alexandria, *Paedagogus* 3.6.35, quoted in Rhee, *Loving the Poor, Saving the Rich*, 83.

[32]Chrysostom, *On Wealth and Poverty*, 29.

[33]Ibid.

[34]Ibid., 30.

[35]Ibid.

[36]Ibid.

[37]Ibid., 31.

[38]Ibid.

[39]Ibid., 31-32.

[40]Ibid., 34.

[41]Ibid., 35.

[42]Ibid.

[43]Ibid., 36.

[44]Ibid., 36-37.

[45]Ibid., sermon 2, 43, emphasis added.

[46]Ibid., 39.

[47]Ibid., 40.

[48]Chrysostom, *Homilies on the Epistles of Paul to the Corinthians* 2.17.1, on 2 Corinthians 8:9, quoted in Oden, *Good Works Reader*, 36.

[49]Chromatius, *Tractate on Matthew* 17.2.1-2, on Matthew 5:3, quoted in Oden, *Good Works Reader*, 32.

[50]Ambrose, *Exposition of the Gospel of Luke* 5:53-54, quoted in Oden, *Good Works Reader*, 31.

[51]Clement of Alexandria, *Who Is the Rich Man That Shall Be Saved?*, in *ANF* 2:594.

[52]Cf. Rhee, *Loving the Poor, Saving the Rich*, 79.

[53]Chrysostom, *On Wealth and Poverty*, sermon 2, 40.

[54]Ambrose, *On Naboth* 4, emphasis added, cited in Phan, *Social Thought*, 169.

[55]Chrysostom, *On Wealth and Poverty*, sermon 2, 46.

[56]Ibid., 47.

[57]Ibid.

[58]Ibid.

[59]Ibid., 48.

[60]Ibid.

[61]Ibid.

[62]Ibid., 49.

[63]Didache 1.5, cited in Phan, *Social Thought*, 45.

[64]Shepherd of Hermas, Second Mandate 2.4, cited in Phan, *Social Thought*, 52.

[65]Didache 4.5, cited in Phan, *Social Thought*, 45.

[66]Shepherd of Hermas, First Similitude, 1.6-9, cited in Phan, *Social Thought*, 52-53.

[67]Ambrose, *Letters* 2.11, cited in Phan, *Social Thought*, 181.

[68]Clement of Alexandria, *Who Is the Rich Man That Is Saved?* 11, cited in Phan, *Social Thought*, 72.

[69]Clement of Alexandria, *Who Is the Rich Man That Is Saved?* 12, cited in Phan, *Social Thought*, 73.

[70]Clement of Alexandria, *Who Is the Rich Man That Is Saved?* 13, cited in Phan, *Social Thought*, 73.

[71]Clement of Alexandria, *Who Is the Rich Man That Is Saved?* 14, cited in Phan, *Social Thought*, 74. Clement describes well how difficult it is for the sick in soul to handle money safely. "Imagine. . . . the man who has money in his soul, who carries in his heart not the Spirit of God but gold or land; who is constantly accumulating his possessions and always on the lookout for more; whose eyes are fixed downward; who is trapped in the snares of the world; who is earth and to earth will return. How can such a man set his desires or thoughts on the kingdom of heaven, who carries about with him not a heart, but an estate or a mine?" Clement of Alexandria, *Who Is the Rich Man That Is Saved?* 17; cited in Phan, *Social Thought*, 76.

[72]Basil the Great, Homily on "I Will Pull Down My Barns" 2, cited in Phan, *Social Thought*, 114.

[73]Tertullian, *On Patience* 7.2, cited in Phan, *Social Thought*, 84.

[74]Cyprian, *On Works and Almsgiving* 25, cited in Phan, *Social Thought*, 91. I have slightly modified the translation.

[75]Gregory of Nyssa, *Love of the Poor*, cited in Phan, *Social Thought*, 132.

[76]Chrysostom, *Homilies on the First Letter to Timothy* 13.3, cited in Phan, *Social Thought*, 160.

[77]Ambrose, *On Naboth* 2, cited in Phan, *Social Thought*, 168.

[78]Basil the Great, Homily on "I Will Pull Down My Barns" 7, cited in Phan, *Social Thought*, 117.

[79]Chrysostom, *Homilies on the First Letter to Timothy* 11.2, cited in Phan, *Social Thought*, 157.

[80]Ibid.

[81]Ibid.

[82]Basil the Great, Homily on "I Will Pull Down My Barns" 7, cited in Phan, *Social Thought*, 117.

[83]Basil the Great, *The Short Rules*, question 92, cited in Phan, *Social Thought*, 121.

[84]Augustine, *Letter* 12, cited in Phan, *Social Thought*, 206-7.

[85]Chrysostom, *Homilies on the Acts of the Apostles* 20.4, cited in Phan, *Social Thought*, 149.

[86]Chrysostom, *Homilies on the Gospel of John* 65.3, cited in Phan, *Social Thought*, 148.

[87]Augustine, *On Free Choice of the Will* 1.7, 15, emphasis added, cited in Phan, *Social Thought*, 202-3.

[88]Augustine, *On Free Choice of the Will*, cited in Phan, *Social Thought*, 203.

[89]Chrysostom, *Homilies on the First Letter to the Corinthians* 11.5, cited in Phan, *Social Thought*, 152-53.

[90]Gregory of Nazianzus, *On the Love for the Poor* (XIV) 15, cited in Phan, *Social Thought*, 124.

[91]Gregory of Nazianzus, *On the Love for the Poor* (XIV) 15, cited in Phan, *Social Thought*, 124. Oden comments: "The pattern in the Christian life for clothing the naked is Jesus' own clothing of our nakedness of sin and guilt." Oden, *Good Works Reader*, 126.

[92]Origen, *Commentary on Matthew* 72, cited in Oden, *Good Works Reader*, 137.

[93]Ibid., 39, cited in Phan, *Social Thought*, 126-27.

[94]Chrysostom, *Homilies on the Gospel of Matthew* 12.5, cited in Phan, *Social Thought*, 141.

[95]Phan, *Social Thought*, 131.

[96]Ibid., 131-32.

[97]Ibid., 136.

[98]Ibid., 136.

3 "The Misery of These Evils": War and Military Service

[1]A new translation by Henry Bettenson with an introduction by John O'Meara (New York: Penguin Books, 1984), book 19, chap. 7, 861.

[2]Quoted in George Kalantzis, *Caesar and the Lamb: Early Christian Attitudes on War and Military Service* (Eugene, OR: Cascade Books: 2012), 119. Along with Kalantzis's book, I have also found the following books to be helpful for research and for key insights in writing this chapter: Ronald J. Sider, *The Early Church on Killing: A Comprehensive Sourcebook on War, Abortion, and Capital Punishment* (Grand Rapids: Baker Academic, 2012); John Helgeland, Robert J. Daly, and J. Patout Burns, *Christians and the Military: The Early*

Experience (Philadelphia: Fortress, 1985); Louis J. Swift, *The Early Fathers on War and Military Service*, Message of the Fathers of the Church 20 (Wilmington, DE: Michael Glazier, 1983); Peter J. Leithart, *Defending Constantine: The Twilight of an Empire and the Dawn of Christendom* (Downers Grove, IL: IVP Academic, 2010); Robert L. Wilken, *The Christians as the Romans Saw Them* (New Haven, CT: Yale University Press, 1984); C. John Cadoux, *The Early Christian Attitude to War* (New York: Seabury, 1982).

[3]James Waller, *Becoming Evil: How Ordinary People Commit Genocide and Mass Killing* (Oxford: Oxford University Press, 2002), x, emphasis original.

[4]Ibid.

[5]*Clement* 37.1-4, in *The Apostolic Fathers: Greek Texts and English Translations*, 3rd ed., ed. and trans. Michael W. Holmes (Grand Rapids: Baker Academic, 2007), 95. George Kalantzis argues, "Within the context of the Corinthian situation . . . *1 Clement 37:1-5* cannot be interpreted as endorsing either war or military service, but, on the contrary, it needs to be placed alongside the language of Eph. 6:10-17." Kalantzis, *Caesar and the Lamb*, 78.

[6]Swift, *Early Fathers*, 34.

[7]Justin Martyr, *First Apology* 39, ANF 1:175-76, cited in Sider, *Early Church on Killing*, 25. Justin's life indeed came to an end as he confessed Christ as a martyr. He and six of his friends were interrogated before the prefect of Rome around 165/66, ordered to sacrifice to the gods, refused to do so, and were subsequently beaten with rods and beheaded. Cf. Kalantzis, *Caesar and the Lamb*, 81. Kalantzis also notes that Tatian, a well-known pupil of Justin, refused to serve in the military and "attributed wars to the inspiration of demons." Ibid., 82.

[8]Cf. Swift, *Early Fathers*, 35.

[9]Justin Martyr, *1 Apology* 16:3-4, quoted in Kalantzis, *Caesar and the Lamb*, 82-83.

[10]Athenagoras, *Plea for the Christians* 37.2-3, cited in Swift, *Early Fathers*, 35.

[11]Athenagoras, *Plea for the Christians* 37.2-3, in ANF 2:134, cited in Sider, *Early Church on Killing*, 31.

[12]Athenagoras, *Plea for the Christians* 37.2-3, in ANF 2:147, cited in Sider, *Early Church on Killing*, 31-32.

[13]Lactantius, writing over one hundred years later, demonstrates the same revulsion at making sport and entertainment of violence and murder in a passage worth quoting at length: "We must avoid them [i.e., the shows] because they are a strong enticement to vice, and they have an immense capacity for corrupting souls. Rather than contributing something to a happy life they are,

in fact, exceedingly harmful. For anybody who finds it pleasurable to watch a man being slain (however justly the person was condemned) has violated his own conscience as much as if he had been a spectator and participant in a clandestine murder. The actual term used by the pagans for these events in which human blood is spilled is 'games.' *They are so alienated from their own humanity that they believe they are playing when they take human lives.* In fact, however, the perpetrators are more harmful than all those people whose blood is a source of delight to them. I ask, then, whether anyone can be just and reverent if he not only permits men who are facing imminent death and are pleading for mercy to be slain but also flogs his victims and brings death through cruel and inhuman punishments whenever he finds himself unsated by the wounds already inflicted or by the blood already spilled." Lactantius, *Divine Institutes* 6.20.9-12, cited in Swift, *Early Fathers*, 62, emphasis added.

[14]Athenagoras, *Plea on Behalf of the Christians* 4, quoted in Kalantzis, *Caesar and the Lamb*, 89-90.

[15]Quoted in Origen's *Against Celsus* 8.68, cited in Swift, *Early Fathers*, 36-37.

[16]Swift, *Early Fathers*, 37.

[17]Tertullian, *Apology* 5.6, in *ANF* 3:22, cited in Sider, *Early Church on Killing*, 138-39.

[18]Tertullian, *Apology* 6.22.

[19]Eusebius, *Ecclesiastical History* 5.5.1-6, cited in Sider, *Early Church on Killing*, 139-40.

[20]Swift, *Early Fathers*, 38. Tertullian, whom Swift describes as "the first articulate spokesman for pacifism in the Christian Church," openly acknowledges the presence of Christians in the Roman army. "We, no less than you, sail the sea, serve in the army, farm the land, buy and sell." *Apology* 42.2-3, cited in Swift, *Early Fathers*, 39.

[21]Sider, *Early Church on Killing*, 137. Kalantzis notes that in the latter part of the second and the beginning of the third century, "the Severan reforms resulted in the unprecedented militarization of the Empire and many new inducements were offered to citizens, even those of the most remote provinces, to join the armies of Rome. This new reality meant that Tertullian faced in his own lifetime a situation unimaginable just a few decades earlier, namely that not only was Christianity making inroads into the camp, but now a military career was seen as an attractive option for some baptized Christians." Kalantzis, *Caesar and the Lamb*, 104.

[22]Tertullian, *Apology* 37, emphasis added, cited in Sider, *Early Church on Killing*, 45.

[23]Tertullian, *On Idolatry* 19.1-3, cited in Swift, *Early Fathers*, 41-42, and in Sider, *Early Church on Killing*, 50-51. Cf. Mt 26:52-55.

[24]Tertullian, *On Idolatry* 17.2.3, cited in Swift, *Early Fathers*, 40-41. ·

[25]Tertullian, *On Idolatry* 11.1-7, cited in Swift, *Early Fathers*, 44-45.

[26]Tertullian, *On Idolatry* 11.1-7, cited in Swift, *Early Fathers*, 45.

[27]*Apostolic Tradition*, canon 16, cited in Swift, *Early Fathers*, 47.

[28]Swift, *Early Fathers*, 47.

[29]Cyprian, *To Donatus* 6, cited in Sider, *Early Church on Killing*, 85, emphasis added.

[30]Cyprian, *To Donatus* 7, cited in Sider, *Early Church on Killing*, 85.

[31]Cyprian, *On the Good of Patience* 14, in *ANF* 5:488, cited in Sider, *Early Church on Killing*, 87, emphasis added.

[32]Cyprian, *To Demetrian* 20, in *ANF* 5:463, cited by Sider, *Early Church on Killing*, 86. Modern historians disagree as to the meaning of Cyprian's comment to Demetrian. Louis Swift believes Cyprian is "praying for the success of the imperial armies in warding off enemies," while Ron Sider writes that Cyprian is praying "for the warding off of enemies of [Rome]. But that is not the same thing as praying" for the success of the Roman armies. Sider, *Early Church on Killing*, 66; Swift, *Early Fathers*, 48-49. Kalantzis argues that Cyprian's use of military metaphors and illustrations "cannot be taken as endorsing Christian participation in military service any more than Paul's exhortation for Christians to put on the full armor of God (Eph. 6:10-18) can be interpreted as an apostolic call to enlistment. The same holds true for Cyprian's letter *To Demetrianus* 20. . . . Again, it would be quite a stretch of the evidence to argue that commonplace sentiments like these may be taken as endorsing Christian participation in the imperial armies." Kalantzis, *Caesar and the Lamb*, 132.

[33]Kalantzis, *Caesar and the Lamb*, 79.

[34]Clement of Alexandria, *Exhortation to the Greeks* 11, in *ANF* 2:204, cited in Sider, *Early Church on Killing*, 35.

[35]Swift, *Early Fathers*, 51.

[36]Clement of Alexandria, *Exhortation to the Greeks* 10.100.2, emphasis added, cited in Swift, *Early Fathers*, 52.

[37]Kalantzis thinks it likely that Clement is "instructing soldiers who converted to Christianity to obey their new 'Commander who gives just commands' rather than the military hierarchy of the legions." He thinks it is highly unlikely that Clement envisions a situation in which a Christian soldier would respond to his Roman commander's commands order by order, only obeying those commands that seemed to be in line with the teaching of Christ. "Con-

scientious objection was not an option for the Roman army." Kalantzis, *Caesar and the Lamb*, 93. To disobey an order in all likelihood would result in summary execution.

[38] Origen, *Against Celsus* 8.73, cited in Swift, *Early Fathers*, 55. Origen continues: "What is more, by overcoming with our prayers all the demons who incite wars, who violate oaths and who disturb the peace we help emperors more than those who are supposedly doing the fighting. . . . We do not go out on the campaign with him [i.e., the emperor] even if he insists, but we do battle on his behalf by raising a special army of piety through our petitions to God." Origen, *Against Celsus* 8.73, cited in Swift, *Early Fathers*, 55.

[39] Origen, *Against Celsus* 3.8, cited in Swift, *Early Fathers*, 57.

[40] Origen, *Against Celsus*, in *ANF* 4:621, cited in Sider, *Early Church on Killing*, 76.

[41] G. E. Caspary, *Politics and Exegesis: Origen and the Two Swords* (Berkeley: University of California Press, 1979), quoted in Swift, *Early Fathers*, 56.

[42] Origen, *Against Celsus* 5.33, cited in Swift, *Early Fathers*, 57.

[43] Origen, *Against Celsus* 7.19, cited in Sider, *Early Church on Killing*, 75.

[44] Origen, *Against Celsus* 7.22, cited in Sider, *Early Church on Killing*, 75.

[45] Swift comments: "The numerical growth of Christians in the army during the second half of the third century is attested by the fact that Diocletian made them the first object of his persecution in 303 AD." Swift, *Early Fathers*, 69.

[46] Lactantius, *Divine Institutes* 6.20.15-17, cited in Swift, *Early Fathers*, 62-63, emphasis added.

[47] Swift, *Early Fathers*, 81.

[48] Eusebius of Caesarea, *In Praise of Constantine* 16.3-7, cited in Swift, *Early Fathers*, 84. Kalantzis notes the presence of "confessors" at the Council of Nicaea, people who bore the scars of their faithfulness to Christ during persecution. "These confessors were a constant reminder of the collision of these two worlds: one that had come to an end, and another now inaugurated: Christ's millennial kingdom was at hand—or so Eusebius and those around him thought." Kalantzis, *Caesar and the Lamb*, 197.

[49] Swift, *Early Fathers*, 87-88.

[50] Eusebius of Caesarea, *In Praise of Constantine* 4.56.3, cited in Swift, *Early Fathers*, 88.

[51] Eusebius of Caesarea, *Demonstration of the Gospel* 1.8, cited in Swift, *Early Fathers*, 88-89.

[52] Eusebius of Caesarea, *Demonstration of the Gospel* 1.8, cited in Swift, *Early Fathers*, 89.

[53]Swift, *Early Fathers*, 91.

[54]Council of Nicaea, canon 12, cited in Swift, *Early Fathers*, 91.

[55]*Canons of Hippolytus*, canon 14, cited in Swift, *Early Fathers*, 93. Swift comments that these canons are "a late fourth or early fifth century compilation of disciplinary and liturgical rules from earlier periods." Swift, *Early Fathers*, 93.

[56]Basil, *Letter* 188.13, cited in Swift, *Early Fathers*, 94.

[57]The McGuckin quote is found in Kalantzis, *Caesar and the Lamb*, 201.

[58]Swift, *Early Fathers*, 111.

[59]Ibid.

[60]Augustine, *Letter* 153.6.16, cited in Swift, *Early Fathers*, 112.

[61]Augustine, *City of God*, trans. Bettenson, 19.5, p. 858.

[62]Augustine, *City of God* 12.28.1, cited in Carol Harrison, *Augustine: Christian Truth and Fractured Humanity* (Oxford: Oxford University Press, 2000), 158.

[63]Augustine, *City of God*, trans. Bettenson, 19.5, p. 858, emphasis added.

[64]Ibid., 19.5, p. 859.

[65]Augustine, *City of God* 19.17, quoted in Benedict Groeschel, *Augustine: Major Writings* (New York: Crossroad Publishing, 1995), 147.

[66]Augustine, *Letter* 138.2.14, cited in Swift, *Early Fathers*, 122.

[67]Augustine, *City of God*, trans. Bettenson, 19.6, p. 860, emphasis added.

[68]Ibid., 19.7, pp. 861-62.

[69]Ibid., 15.4, p. 599.

[70]Ibid., 15.4, p. 600.

[71]Ibid.

[72]Ibid., 19.10, pp. 864-65.

[73]Swift, *Early Fathers*, 112.

[74]Augustine, *City of God*, trans. Bettenson, 5.25, p. 221.

[75]Ibid., 3.10, p. 98.

[76]Ibid., 5.24, p. 220.

[77]Ibid., 2.25, p. 81.

[78]Ibid., 1.21, p. 32.

[79]Augustine, *Letter* 229.2, cited in Swift, *Early Fathers*, 115.

[80]Augustine, *City of God*, trans. Bettenson, 1.21, p. 32.

[81]Augustine, *Letter* 189.4, cited in Swift, *Early Fathers*, 126-27.

[82]Augustine, *Letter* 189.4, cited in Swift, *Early Fathers*, 127.

[83]Swift's insight, *Early Fathers*, 127.

[84]Augustine, *Against Faustus* 22.74, cited in Swift, *Early Fathers*, 127.

[85]Augustine, *Against Faustus* 22.75, cited in Swift, *Early Fathers*, 129.

[86]Augustine, *Letter* 138.13, cited in Swift, *Early Fathers*, 126.

[87] Augustine, *Against Faustus* 22.74, cited in Swift, *Early Fathers*, 120, emphasis added.

[88] Swift's words, *Early Fathers*.

[89] Augustine, *Questions on the Heptateuch* 4.44, cited in Swift, *Early Fathers*, 135.

[90] Augustine, *City of God* 4.6, cited in Swift, *Early Fathers*, 134.

[91] Augustine, *Questions on the Heptateuch* 6.10, cited in Swift, *Early Fathers*, 138.

[92] Augustine, *Letter* 189.6, cited in Swift, *Early Fathers*, 139.

[93] Augustine, *Against Faustus* 22.74, cited in Swift, *Early Fathers*, 120.

[94] Swift, *Early Fathers*, 120.

[95] Ibid., 121.

[96] Ibid.

[97] Paulinus of Nola, *Letter* 25.3, cited in Swift, *Early Fathers*, 153.

4 "The Closest of Relationships": Sex and the Dynamics of Desire

[1] Trans. Catharine P. Roth and David Anderson, introduction by Catharine P. Roth (Crestview, NY: St. Vladimir's Seminary Press, 1986), 43-44. I have slightly modified the translation.

[2] Trans. John Ferguson (Washington, DC: Catholic University of America Press, 1991), book 3.7.58.1-2, p. 292.

[3] Cited in Everett Ferguson, *Inheriting Wisdom: Readings for Today from Ancient Christian Writers* (Peabody, MA: Hendrickson, 2004), 7, emphasis added.

[4] Quoted in Peter Brown, *The Body and Society: Men, Women, and Sexual Renunciation in Early Christianity* (New York: Columbia University Press, 1988), 205.

[5] Eve Tushnet, *Gay and Catholic: Accepting My Sexuality, Finding Community, Living My Faith* (Notre Dame, IN: Ave Maria Press), 113.

[6] Ibid.

[7] Cyril of Alexandria, *Commentary on Luke*, Homily 105, quoted in *Luke*, ed. Arthur A. Just Jr., ACCS (Downers Grove, IL: InterVarsity Press, 2003), 240.

[8] Chrysostom, *On Marriage and Family Life*, trans. Roth and Anderson, 43-44. I have slightly modified the translation.

[9] Tertullian, *On the Apparel of Women* 1.1, *ANF* 4:14, quoted in David C. Ford, *Women and Men in the Early Church: The Full Views of St. John Chrysostom* (South Canaan, PA: St. Tikhon's Seminary Press, 1996), 13.

[10]Elizabeth Carnelley comments, "Concepts such as sexism and feminism, widely understood now, are alien to the first three centuries. It is anachronistic to expect Tertullian to be feminist, and when he is not, to call him a misogynist. In fact, he did not hate, or fear, women. Rather, Tertullian's writings must be understood in the context of the prejudices and concerns of his time." Elizabeth Carnelley, "Tertullian and Feminism," *Theology* 92 (January 1989): 31, cited in Ford, *Women and Men in the Early Church*, 15.

[11]Elizabeth Clark, *Women in the Early Church*, Message of the Fathers of the Church 13 (Wilmington, DE: Michael Glazier, 1983), 47, cited in David C. Ford, *Women and Men in the Early Church: The Full Views of St. John Chrysostom* (South Canaan, PA: St. Tikhon's Seminary Press, 1996), 29.

[12]Clement of Alexandria, *Stromateis*, trans. John Ferguson (Washington, DC: Catholic University of America Press, 1991), 3.7.58.1-2; 3.7.59.1-2, p. 292.

[13]Clement of Alexandria, *Stromateis*, trans. Ferguson, 3.4.1-3, p. 258, emphasis added.

[14]Kyle Harper, *From Shame to Sin: The Christian Transformation of Sexual Morality in Late Antiquity* (Cambridge, MA: Harvard University Press, 2013), 53.

[15]Dallas Willard, "Beyond Pornography: Spiritual Formation Studied in a Particular Case," *Journal of Spiritual Formation & Soul Care* 9, no. 1 (2016): 6.

[16]Ibid.

[17]Lawrence S. Cunningham, *The Seven Deadly Sins: A Visitor's Guide* (Notre Dame, IN: Ave Maria Press, 2012), 30.

[18]Henry Fairlie, *The Seven Deadly Sins Today* (Notre Dame, IN: University of Notre Dame Press, 1979), 178, quoted in Cunningham, *Seven Deadly Sins*, 30.

[19]Clement of Alexandria, *Stromateis*, trans. Ferguson, 258.

[20]Ibid., 3.5.43.1, p. 282, emphasis added.

[21]Ibid., 3.5.44.4, p. 283, emphasis added.

[22]Roberta Bondi, *To Love as God Loves* (Philadelphia: Fortress, 1987), 58.

[23]Ibid., 57, emphasis added.

[24]The illustration is from John Ortberg, *The Life You've Always Wanted: Spiritual Disciplines for Ordinary People* (Grand Rapids: Zondervan, 2002), 180.

[25]Olivier Clément, *The Roots of Christian Mysticism* (New York: New City Press, 1993), 167.

[26]Peter Brown, *The Body and Society: Men, Women, and Sexual Renunciation in Early Christianity* (New York: Columbia University Press, 1988), 129-30.

[27]Clement of Alexandria, *Stromateis*, trans. Ferguson, 3.4.1-3, p. 258.

[28]Ibid., 3.5.44, p. 283, emphasis added.

[29]Ibid., 3.7.57.1-2, p. 291, emphasis added; I have slightly modified the translation.

[30]Socrates, *Ecclesiastical History* 1.11, quoted in Brown, *Body and Society*, 256.

[31]Ford, *Women and Men in the Early Church*, 17n19. Ford notes, "The Eastern Church to this day does prohibit celibate priests to then marry—since marriage is usually a sign of stability and maturity, and to avoid the unseemliness of a priest courting one of his parishioners. Also, by about the seventh century, married priests could not become bishops unless they were widowed (or had separated from their wives by mutual consent) and had entered monastic life. This development did not reflect an incipient disparagement of marriage, but the recognition that bishops' celibacy would give them greater freedom of movement in ministering to their dioceses, the growing belief that all bishops should come from the monastic ranks in order to better ensure their soundness of doctrine, and the desire to prevent bishoprics from becoming hereditary." Ibid., 17.

[32]Christopher A. Hall, *Worshiping with the Church Fathers* (Downers Grove, IL: InterVarsity Press, 2009), 57.

[33]Irenaeus, *Against Heresies* 5.2, ANF 1, cited in Steven A. McKinion, *Life and Practice in the Early Church* (New York: New York University Press, 2001), 106. I have slightly modified the translation.

[34]For all ancient Christians, to be unmarried was to refrain from sexual activity; only in *very recent* times have sexual activity and procreation outside the boundaries of marriage become acceptable practices, largely in the Western world.

[35]Gregory of Nyssa, *De virginitate* 8; cited in Boniface Ramsey, *Beginning to Read the Fathers* (New York: Paulist Press, 1985), 137.

[36]Ramsey, *Beginning to Read the Fathers*, 135. As Peter Brown perceives, for Augustine the martyr was a much greater Christian than the virgin. "For Augustine, martyrdom always represented the highest peak of human heroism. To have triumphed over the bitter fear of death was a far greater sign of God's grace than to have triumphed over the sexual urge. . . . The workings of God's grace were deeply hidden; the fashionable fascination with virginity paled before the ancient and terrible grace of martyrdom: 'For a virgin of the church may not yet be able to be a Thecla, while she [the married woman] may have been called by God to be a Saint Crispina.'" Brown, *Body and Society*, 397-98.

[37]Ambrose, *Concerning Virgins*, in NPNF[2], book 1, chap. 2, 364.

[38]Methodius of Olympus, *Symposium* 7.3, cited in Ramsey, *Beginning to Read the Fathers*, 136.

[39]Ramsey, *Beginning to Read the Fathers*, 136.

[40] Augustine, *Of Holy Virginity*, in *NPNF¹* 3:433, para. 42. I have slightly modified the translation.

[41] Ibid. I have tried to smooth out the *NPNF* translation.

[42] Ibid., para. 47, p. 435.

[43] Ambrose, *Concerning Virgins*, book 2, chap. 2, para. 7, p. 374.

[44] Augustine, *Of Holy Virginity*, para. 4, p. 418.

[45] Ambrose, *Concerning Virgins*, book 2, chap. 2, para. 9, p. 375.

[46] Augustine, *Of Holy Virginity*, para. 3, p. 418.

[47] Ambrose, *Concerning Virgins*, book 2, chap. 2, para. 13, p. 375.

[48] Ibid., para. 4, p. 418.

[49] Ibid., para. 5, p. 418.

[50] Ibid., para. 6, p. 419.

[51] Clement of Alexandria, *Paedagogus* 1.6, PG 8.300-301, cited in Luigi Gambero, *Mary and the Fathers of the Church: The Blessed Virgin Mary in Patristic Thought* (San Francisco: Ignatius Press, 1999), 71.

[52] Ambrose, *Concerning Virgins*, book 2, chap. 2, para. 33, p. 429.

[53] Ibid., para. 35, p. 429. I have slightly modified the *NPNF* translation. Cf. Mt 11:29.

[54] Ibid., para. 37, p. 430.

[55] Ibid., para. 47, p. 435.

[56] Justin Martyr, *Dialogue with Trypho* 100, PG 6.709-12, cited in Gambero, *Mary and the Fathers of the Church*, 47.

[57] Irenaeus, *Adversus haereses* 5.19, PG 7.1175-76, cited in Gambero, *Mary and the Fathers of the Church*, 54. In a beautiful passage Ephrem the Syrian writes: "Mary gave birth without having relations with a man. As in the beginning Eve was born from Adam without a carnal relationship, so it happened for Joseph and Mary, his wife. Eve brought to the world the murdering Cain; Mary brought forth the Lifegiver. One brought into the world him who spilled the blood of his brother (cf. Gen 4:1-16); the other, him whose blood was poured out for the sake of his brothers. One brought into the world him who fled, trembling because of the curse of the earth; the other brought forth him who, having taken the curse upon himself, nailed it to the Cross (cf. Col 2:14)." Ephrem the Syrian, *Diatessaron* 2.2, SC 121, 66; cited in Gambero, *Mary and the Fathers of the Church*, 117.

[58] Origen, *Fragments on Matthew* 281, *Die griechischen christlichen Schriftsteller* 41/1, 126, cited in Gambero, *Mary and the Fathers of the Church*, 76.

[59] Cyril of Jerusalem, *Catecheses* 12.34, PG 33.768A-769A, cited in Gambero, *Mary and the Fathers of the Church*, 138.

[60]Cf. A. W. Richard Sipe, *Living the Celibate Life: A Search for Models and Meaning* (Liguori, MO: Liguori/Triumph, 2004).

5 "One Hope, One Desire, One Way of Life": Life as Male and Female, and the Goodness and Beauty of Marriage

[1]Cited in Elizabeth Clark, *Women in the Early Church*, Message of the Fathers of the Church 13 (Wilmington, DE: Michael Glazier, 1983), 164.

[2]Peter Brown, *The Body and Society: Men, Women, and Sexual Renunciation in Early Christianity* (New York: Columbia University Press, 1988), 130.

[3]Gregory of Nazianzus, *Carmina I, Sectio II, Moralia* I, lines 262-75, cited in Everett Ferguson, *Inheriting Wisdom: Readings for Today from Ancient Christian Writers* (Peabody, MA: Hendrickson, 2004), 5.

[4]Augustine, *De Genesi ad litteram* 9.5.9, cited in Boniface Ramsey, *Beginning to Read the Fathers* (Mahwah, NJ: Paulist Press, 1985), 140.

[5]Gregory of Nazianzus, *Oration* 18:7-8, cited in Ferguson, *Inheriting Wisdom*, 6.

[6]Tertullian, *To His Wife* 2.8, cited in Ferguson, *Inheriting Wisdom*, 6.

[7]Christopher A. Hall, *Reading Scripture with the Church Fathers* (Downers Grove, IL: InterVarsity Press, 1998), 43-49. I am drawing freely on this earlier material in the present chapter.

[8]Cited in ibid., 45-46; also in Christopher A. Hall, "Letters from a Lonely Exile," *Christian History* 13, no. 4 (1994): 44.

[9]*Life of Olympias*, SC bis. 408, cited in. Clark, *Women in the Early Church*, 204, and in Hall, *Reading Scripture with the Church Fathers*, 46.

[10]Jaroslav Pelikan, *Christianity and Classical Culture: The Metamorphosis of Natural Theology in the Christian Encounter with Hellenism* (New Haven, CT: Yale University Press, 1993), 8.

[11]Ibid.

[12]Gregory of Nyssa, *Life of St. Macrina*, SC 178.136, para. 3, cited in Clark, *Women in the Early Church*, 238.

[13]Gregory of Nyssa, *Life of St. Macrina*, para. 6, cited in Clark, *Women in the Early Church*, 241.

[14]Gregory of Nyssa, *Life of St. Macrina*, para. 17, cited in Clark, *Women in the Early Church*, 242-43.

[15]Basil, *Epistle* 223.3, cited in Pelikan, *Christianity and Classical Culture*, 303.

[16]I have borrowed the phrase "models and mentors" from Clark, *Women in the Early Church*, 204.

[17]Jerome, *Epistle* 127, CSEL 56.146, cited in Clark, *Women in the Early Church*, 207-8.

[18]Jerome, *Epistle* 108, CSEL 55.308, cited in Clark, *Women in the Early Church*, 209.

[19]Jerome, *Epistle* 108, CSEL 55.308, cited in Clark, *Women in the Early Church*, 211-12.

[20]Jerome, *Epistle* 108, CSEL 55.308, cited in Clark, *Women in the Early Church*, 211-12.

[21]Palladius, *The Lausiac History of Palladius*, ed. C. Butler (1898; repr., Hildesheim, Germany: Georg Olm, 1967), cited in Clark, *Women in the Early Church*, 164-65.

[22]John Chrysostom, *On Virginity* 21.1, cited in Ford, *Women and Men in the Early Church*, 76. Catharine Roth observes the same emphasis on celibacy and the monastic life in John's earlier writings. "He wrote to advise his friend Theodore (later bishop of Mopsuestia) not to abandon the monastic life. Other works of St John combat the attackers of monasticism and defend the preference for virginity. His early life as the son of a widow and as a young monk perhaps failed to give him the opportunity of fully appreciating the potential for grace in married life." Catharine Roth, introduction to St. John Chrysostom, *On Marriage and Family Life*, trans. Catharine P. Roth and David Anderson (Crestwood, NY: St. Vladimir's Seminary Press, 1986), 8.

[23]Chrysostom, *Homily 49 on Acts*, in *NPNF[1]* 9:262; cited in Ford, *Women and Men in the Early Church*, 65.

[24]Ford, *Women and Men in the Early Church*, 60.

[25]Chrysostom, *On Marriage and Family Life*, trans. Roth and Anderson.

[26]Ibid., 25.

[27]Ibid., 26, emphasis added.

[28]Ibid., 27.

[29]Ibid., 43-44. Lactantius, a North African church father writing roughly one hundred years before Chrysostom, also defends sexual pleasure as a good created by God. "If someone cannot restrain these impulses, he should control them within the prescribed limit of a legitimate marriage. In this way he will attain what he eagerly desires and yet not fall into sin. . . . Certainly pleasure is a consequence of honorable works; if they seek it properly, they are permitted to enjoy right and legitimate pleasure." Lactantius, *The Divine Institutes*, in *ANF* 7:189-90; cited in Ford, *Women and Men in the Early Church*, 26.

[30]Chrysostom, *Homily 12 on Colossians*, in *NPNF[1]* 13:319; cited in Ford, *Women and Men in the Early Church*, 57.

[31]Ford, *Women and Men in the Early Church*, 28.

[32]Ibid.

[33]Ibid.

[34]John Chrysostom, *Homilies on Colossians* 12.5-6, on Col 4:18, cited in Ferguson, *Inheriting Wisdom*, 8-9.

[35]Roth, introduction to Chrysostom, *On Marriage and Family Life*, trans. Roth and Anderson, 20.

[36]Chrysostom, *On Marriage and Family Life*, trans. Roth and Anderson, 85.

[37]John Chrysostom, *Homilies on Ephesians* 20.1.6, on Eph. 5:22ff., cited in Ferguson, *Inheriting Wisdom*, 10.

[38]Chrysostom, *On Marriage and Family Life*, trans. Roth and Anderson, Homily 20 on Ephesians 5:22, 50.

[39]Ibid., 51.

[40]Ibid.

[41]Ibid., 55.

[42]Ibid., 55-56.

[43]Ibid., 56.

[44]Ibid., 57.

[45]Wesley Hill, *Washed and Waiting: Reflections on Christian Faithfulness and Homosexuality* (Grand Rapids: Zondervan, 2010).

[46]Clement, *Letter to the Romans*, in ANF 1:34; quoted in *A Dictionary of Early Christian Beliefs*, ed. David W. Bercot (Peabody, MA: Hendrickson, 1998), 347.

[47]Tertullian, *Against the Valentinians*, in ANF 3:509; quoted in Bercot, *Dictionary of Early Christian Beliefs*, 347.

[48]Hill, *Washed and Waiting*, 52-53.

[49]Ibid., 51.

[50]Ibid., 53; see Congregation for the Doctrine of the Faith, *Letter to the Bishops of the Catholic Church on the Pastoral Care of Homosexual Persons* (October 1986), paragraph 7, www.vatican.va/roman_curia/congregations/cfaith/documents/rc_con_cfaith_doc_19861001_homosexual-persons_en.html.

[51]Chrysostom, *On Providence* 97.

[52]Hill, *Washed and Waiting*, 145; see Thomas Hopko, *Christian Faith and Same-Sex Attraction: Eastern Orthodox Reflections* (Ben Lomond, CA: Conciliar, 2006), 48.

[53]Hill, *Washed and Waiting*, 108.

[54]Ibid., 103.

6 "From the Cradle to the Grave": Life and Death

[1]Quoted in Michael J. Gorman, *Abortion in the Early Church* (Downers Grove, IL: InterVarsity Press, 1982), 72-73. I have found Gorman's book to be invaluable and draw on it throughout my discussion of abortion.

[2]*ANF* 2:368, book 2, chap. 18, quoted in David W. Bercot, ed., *A Dictionary of Early Christian Beliefs* (Peabody, MA: Hendrickson, 1998), 2.

[3]Flavius Josephus, *Against Apion*, trans. William Whiston (Peabody, MA: Hendrickson, 1987), 2.202, p. 806.

[4]*Didache* 1.2, quoted in Everett Ferguson, *Inheriting Wisdom: Readings for Today from Ancient Christian Writers* (Peabody, MA: Hendrickson, 2004), 289, emphasis added.

[5]Bruce Metzger comments, "It is really remarkable how uniform and how pronounced was the early Christian opposition to abortion," foreword to Gorman, *Abortion and the Early Church*, 9.

[6]Gorman, *Abortion and the Early Church*, 14-15.

[7]Ibid. Patrick Gray also notes that "abortion and infanticide are fairly common by the imperial period," though it should be noted that by the late "fourth century . . . Roman laws equate abortion and infanticide with homicide." Patrick Gray, "Abortion, Infanticide, and the Social Rhetoric of the *Apocalypse of Peter*," *Journal of Early Christian Studies* 9, no. 3 (Fall 2001): 319.

[8]Gray, "Abortion, Infanticide," 319-20.

[9]Gray comments that safety levels for pregnancy were about the same for fetuses that were aborted and children that were exposed after birth, a topic we will consider later in this chapter. "It is not certain whether disposing of an unwanted child by exposing it would have been safer for the mother than aborting it, since the former entailed all the risks involved in carrying the child to term." Ibid., 327.

[10]Gorman, *Abortion and the Early Church*, 15.

[11]Gray, "Abortion, Infanticide," 328.

[12]Tertullian, *De anima* 25, cited in Gorman, *Abortion and the Early Church*, 17.

[13]All three perspectives are listed in Gorman, *Abortion and the Early Church*, 34.

[14]Philo, *Special Laws* 3.108-9, quoted in Gorman, *Abortion and the Early Church*, 36.

[15]Athenagoras, *Embassy for the Christians*, trans. and annotated by Joseph Hugh Crehan, SJ, ACW 23 (New York: Newman Press, n.d.), 35.76; this also appears in *Plea for the Christians* 35, quoted in Ferguson, *Inheriting Wisdom*, 290.

[16]Both canons are cited in Gorman, *Abortion and the Early Church*, 64.

[17]*The Seven Ecumenical Councils*, Council of Ancyra, canon 21, in NPNF² 14:73.

[18]Gorman, *Abortion and the Early Church*, 66-67.

[19]Saint Basil, *The Letters*, with an English trans. by Roy J. DeFerrari, Loeb Classical Library 3 (Cambridge, MA: Harvard University Press, 1930), Letter 188, pp. 21, 23.

[20]Gorman, *Abortion and the Early Church*, 64.

[21]Ambrose, *Hexameron* 5.18.58, cited in Gorman, *Abortion and the Early Church*, 68. Gorman does not provide a detailed reference for the quotation.

[22]Jerome, *Letter* 22.13 (to Eustochium), cited in Gorman, *Abortion and the Early Church*, 68.

[23]Gorman, *Abortion and the Early Church*, 68-69.

[24]Ibid., 69.

[25]*Apostolic Constitutions* 7.3, cited in Gorman, *Abortion and the Early Church*, 69.

[26]Augustine, *On Marriage and Concupiscence* 1.1-17, cited in Gorman, *Abortion and the Early Church*, 71.

[27]Augustine, *Enchiridion* 23.86, cited in Gorman, *Abortion and the Early Church*, 72.

[28]Augustine, *City of God* 22.13, cited in Christopher A. Hall, *Learning Theology with the Church Fathers* (Downers Grove, IL: InterVarsity Press, 2002), 265.

[29]Augustine, *On Marriage and Concupiscence* 1.1, cited in Gorman, *Abortion and the Early Church*, 72-73.

[30]Chrysostom, *Homily 24 on Romans*; I have slightly modified the translation given by Gorman, *Abortion and the Early Church*, 72-73.

[31]Gorman, *Abortion and the Early Church*, 54. Tertullian writes: "In our case, murder being once for all forbidden, we may not destroy even the fetus in the womb, while as yet the human being derives blood from other parts of the body for its sustenance. To hinder a birth is merely a speedier man-killing; nor does it matter whether you take away a life that is born, or destroy one that is coming to the birth. *That is a human being who is going to be one*; you have the fruit already in the seed" (emphasis added). Tertullian, *Apology* 9.6, quoted in Gorman, *Abortion and the Early Church*, 55.

[32]Gorman's comment on the *Epistle of Barnabas* 19.5. Cf. Gorman, *Abortion and the Early Church*, 49.

[33]I have found the article "Abandoned and Exposed Children" by Angelo Di Berardino in the *EAC* to be of particular help in mapping out the contours of this sad yet daily reality in Roman antiquity. *EAC* 1:3.

[34]Ibid.

[35]Ibid.

[36]Justin Martyr, *1 Apology* 27.1.

[37]CTh 11.27.1-2, 5.10.1, 5.9.1, all cited in Di Berardino, "Abandoned and Exposed Children," in *EAC* 1:3.

[38]*Shepherd of Hermas*, Vision 1.1, cited in Di Berardino, "Abandoned and Exposed Children," in *EAC* 1:3.

[39]CTh 8.51.2, cited in Di Berardino, "Abandoned and Exposed Children," in *EAC* 1:3.

[40]Augustine, *Epistle* 10, cited in Di Berardino, "Abandoned and Exposed Children," in *EAC* 1:3.

[41]V. Lombino, "Christ the Physician," in *EAC* 3:187.

[42]Origen, *Homily on Leviticus* 7.1, cited in Lombino, "Christ the Physician," in *EAC* 3:186.

[43]Irenaeus, *Adversus Haereses* 3.5.2, 4.20.7, cited in Lombino, "Christ the Physician," in *EAC* 3:186.

[44]Clement of Alexandria, *Paedagogus* 1.6.1-4; *Stromateis* 3.17.104.4, cited in Lombino, "Christ the Physician," in *EAC* 3:188.

[45]Lombino, "Christ the Physician," in *EAC* 3:186; cf. Cyprian, *De Mortalitate*; cf. also the Letter of Dionysius of Alexandria in Eusebius, *Historia Ecclesiastica* 7.22.7.

[46]Origen, *Contra Celsus* 1.46.

[47]Augustine, *Retractions* 1.13.7.

[48]Council of Nicaea, Collectio Araba Canon 75; Lombino, "Christ the Physician," in *EAC* 3:191.

[49]Gregory of Nazianzus, *Orationes* 43.55; 43.66; Basil, *Epistle* 94, cited in Lombino, "Christ the Physician," in *EAC* 3:191.

[50]Basil, *Regula Breviarum* 160, cited in Lombino, "Christ the Physician," in *EAC* 3:191.

7 "LET THE RACES BEGIN!": ENTERTAINMENT

[1]Quoted in James S. Jeffers, *The Greco-Roman World of the New Testament Era: Exploring the Background of Early Christianity* (Downers Grove, IL: IVP Academic, 1999), 29.

[2]*ANF* 2:289-90, chap. 9, quoted in David W. Bercot, ed., *A Dictionary of Early Christian Beliefs* (Peabody, MA: Hendrickson, 1998), 231.

[3]Jeffers, *Greco-Roman World of the New Testament Era*, 29.

[4]Neil Postman, *Entertaining Ourselves to Death: Public Discourse in the Age of Show Business* (New York: Penguin Books, 1986), 121. Postman is well aware that tyrants throughout human history have often used entertainment as a means of pacifying discontented populations and to defuse the clear thinking and courageous acts required in resistance to evil. "Tyrants of all varieties have always known about the value of providing the masses with amusements as a means of pacifying discontent." Ibid., 141. The Roman emperors did this very thing.

[5]Cyprian, *To Donatus*, trans. Roy J. Deferrari (Washington, DC: Catholic University of America Press, 1958), 12-13. Gladiators "fight with beasts not because they are convicts but because they are mad. Fathers look upon their own sons; a brother is in the arena and his sister nearby, and, although the more elaborate preparation of the exhibition increases the price of the spectacle, o shame! The mother also pays this price that she may be present at her own sorrows. And at such impious and terrible spectacles they do not realize that with their own eyes they are parricides." Ibid., 13. Cf. Franz Lidz, "Blood Sport: A 2,000-Year-Old Gladiator School Brings the Men Who Fought in Roman Empire Arenas Back to Life," *Smithsonian*, July/August 2016, 36-45.

[6]Cyprian, *To Donatus*, trans. Deferrari, 13-14.

[7]Clement of Alexandria, *The Tutor* 2.3.38, in SC 108:82.

[8]Jeffers, *Greco-Roman World of the New Testament Era*, 30-31.

[9]Ibid., 31.

[10]Ibid., 32.

[11]Ibid.

[12]Ibid., 34.

[13]Ibid., 33.

[14]Tacitus, *Annals* 15.14, quoted in Jeffers, *Greco-Roman World of the New Testament Era*, 33.

[15]Kyle Harper, *From Shame to Sin: The Christian Transformation of Sexual Morality in Late Antiquity* (Cambridge, MA: Harvard University Press, 2013), 53.

[16]I am drawing on the helpful article "Entertainment," by O. Pasquato, in *EAC*, 1:803-6.

[17]Augustine, *On Baptism: Against the Donatists*, in NPNF[1] chap. 53, 512-13.

[18]Pasquato, "Entertainment," in *EAC* 1:803.

[19]John Chrysostom, *The Gospel of St. Matthew*, trans. Rev. Sir George Prevost (Grand Rapids: Eerdmans, 1986), Homily 6, 10.42.

[20]Ibid.

[21]Ibid.

[22]Harper, *From Shame to Sin*, 48.

[23]Aline Rouselle, *Porneia: On Desire and the Body in Antiquity* (Oxford: Blackwell, 1993), 78-79, emphasis added.

[24]John Chrysostom, *The Gospel of St. Matthew*, in *NPNF*[1], Homily 7, 6.48.

[25]Ibid., 804. I have modified the somewhat stilted *NPNF* translation.

[26]We should note that Roman society was an honor-based society; John is purposely and publicly shaming the men in his congregation.

[27]Ibid., 186.

[28]Quoted in Harper, *From Shame to Sin*, 191.

[29]Jerome, *Commentary on Isaiah* 1.2.5-6, cited in Harper, *From Shame to Sin*, 283.

[30]Harper, *From Shame to Sin*, 289.

[31]John Chrysostom, Homily 67 on Matthew, quoted in Harper, *From Shame to Sin*, 291.

[32]Harper, *From Shame to Sin*, 192, emphasis added.

[33]Ibid., 191.

[34]Chrysostom, *The Gospel of St. Matthew*, Homily 67, in *NPNF*[1] 3:412.

[35]Jerome, *The Letters of St. Jerome*, trans. Charles Christopher Mierow, ACW 33 (New York: Newman Press, 1963), 1:165.

[36]Ibid., 1:166.

[37]Keith Hopkins, *A World Full of Gods: The Strange Triumph of Christianity* (New York: The Free Press, 1999), 38.

[38]Ibid.

[39]Ibid., 39.

[40]Ibid., 38.

[41]Ibid.

[42]Ibid., 40.

[43]Ibid., 40-41.

[44]Ibid., 41.

[45]Ibid., 42.

[46]Ibid.

[47]Theophilus of Antioch, *Theophilus to Autolycus*, in *ANF* 2, book 3.15, 115.

[48]Athenagoras, *A Plea for the Christians*, in *ANF* 2, chap. 35, 147.

[49]Clement of Alexandria, *The Instructor*, in *ANF* 2, book 3, chap. 11, 290.

[50]Ibid., book 3, chap. 11.

[51]Augustine, *De Fide et operibus* 18.33.

[52]P. Marone, "Pompa Diaboli," in *EAC* 3:250.

8 Learning to Live a Good Life with God: The Well-Ordered Heart

[1]Quoted in Dallas Willard, *Renewing the Christian Mind: Essays, Interviews, and Talks*, ed. Gary Black Jr. (New York: HarperOne, 2016), 115.

[2]St. Maximos the Confessor, *Various Texts on Theology, the Divine Economy, and Virtue and Vice: First Century*, in *The Philokalia*, vol. 2, trans. from the Greek and ed. G. E. H. Palmer, Philip Sherrard, and Kallistos Ware (London: Faber and Faber, 1990), 36.172.

[3]Tertullian, *To Scapula* 1, in *ANF* 3:105, quoted in David W. Bercot, ed., *A Dictionary of Early Christian Beliefs* (Peabody, MA: Hendrickson, 1998), 409.

[4]Mark A. Noll, *From Every Tribe and Nation: A Historian's Discovery of the Global Christian Story* (Grand Rapids: Baker Academic, 2014), 50.

[5]Ibid.

[6]Thomas C. Oden, *The Word of Life* (San Francisco: Harper & Row, 1989), 219.

[7]Roberta C. Bondi, *To Love as God Loves: Conversations with the Early Church* (Philadelphia: Fortress, 1987), 7.

[8]John Chrysostom, *On the Epistle to the Hebrews* 19.4, quoted in *Hebrews*, ACCS New Testament 10, ed. Erik M. Heen and Philip D. W. Krey (Downers Grove, IL: InterVarsity Press, 2005), 162.

[9]John Ortberg, *The Life You Always Wanted* (Grand Rapids: Zondervan, 2002), 198.

[10]Ibid.

[11]Ibid., 199.

[12]Augustine, *City of God*, a new translation by Henry Bettenson with an introduction by John O'Meara (New York: Penguin Books, 1984), book 14, chap. 7, 557.

[13]Ibid., book 14, chap. 9, 566.

[14]Ibid., book 14, chap. 13, 571.

[15]Ibid., book 14, chap. 13, 573.

[16]Ibid., book 14, chap. 15, 575.

[17]Ibid., book 14, chap. 13, 573.

[18]Ibid., book 14, chap. 24, 589.

[19]Cf. Christopher A. Hall, *Worshiping with the Church Fathers* (Downers Grove, IL: InterVarsity Press, 2009), 93-94, 147-49.

[20]Palmer, Sherrard, and Ware, *Philokalia*, glossary, 385-86.

[21]Ibid., 381.

[22]St. Maximos the Confessor, "Second Century of Various Texts," in ibid., century 14, p. 191, emphasis added.

[23]Chrysostom, *On Providence* 27.

[24]Origen, *Commentary on St. Matthew's Gospel* 16.23, quoted in Olivier Clément, *The Roots of Christian Mysticism: Texts from the Patristic Era with Commentary* (Hyde Park, NY: New City Press, 2004), 76.

[25]Basil of Caesarea, quoted by Gregory of Nazianzus in his funeral oration for Basil, quoted in Clément, *Roots of Christian Mysticism*, 76.

[26]Gregory of Nyssa, *Second Homily on the Song of Songs*, PG 44.765, quoted in Clément, *Roots of Christian Mysticism*, 79.

[27]Clément, *Roots of Christian Mysticism*, 79.

[28]Gregory of Nyssa, *On the Creation of Man*, PG 44.136-37, quoted in Clément, *Roots of Christian Mysticism*, 80.

[29]Irenaeus, *Against Heresies* 4.38.3; quoted in Clément, *Roots of Christian Mysticism*, 76.

[30]Athanasius, *On the Incarnation and Against the Arians* 8, quoted in Clément, *Roots of Christian Mysticism*, 56.

[31]Irenaeus, *Against Heresies* 4.33.4, quoted in Clément, *Roots of Christian Mysticism*, 37.

[32]Gregory of Nyssa, *On the Creation of Man*, PG 44.185, quoted in Clément, *Roots of Christian Mysticism*, 83.

[33]Irenaeus, *Against Heresies* 5.8.2, quoted in Clément, *Roots of Christian Mysticism*, 83.

[34]I have found William Harmless's discussion of *askesis* in William Harmless, SJ, *Desert Christians: An Introduction to the Literature of Early Monasticism* (New York: Oxford University Press, 2004), to be extremely helpful and am drawing on his insights.

[35]Ibid., 61.

[36]I have learned the phrase "learning space" from Parker Palmer. See Palmer's book *To Know as We Are Known: Education as a Spiritual Journey* (San Francisco: HarperOne, 1993), 69-71.

[37]Harmless, *Desert Christians*, 61-62.

[38]One of Dallas Willard's favorite expressions. Cf. Dallas Willard, *The Spirit of the Disciplines* (San Francisco: Harper & Row, 1988), 29.

NAME AND SUBJECT INDEX

SCRIPTURE INDEX

Finding the Textbook You Need

The IVP Academic Textbook Selector
is an online tool for instantly finding the IVP books
suitable for over 250 courses across 24 disciplines.

---

ivpacademic.com
